In the conventional analysis of human behaviour, power and ethics are frequently considered contrary principles, in that power enforces, while ethics elicits a free response. But, as James Mackey forcefully shows, a more adventurous philosophical study of human morality escapes the sense of contraries, and sets us instead on a quest for the kind of power that liberates human creativity. It then becomes possible to establish the framework for a critical assessment of the kind of power that ought to be operative in the major structures of human society, civil or ecclesiastical, state governments and church hierarchies. Mackey analyses the religious question which then quite naturally emerges, as to whether this Eros-type power so manifest in human society originates from beyond the more empirical structures of churches, states, and 'nature'; and the effort to detect the specifically Christian characterisation of an allegedly ultimate power working in us for final well-being finds its natural context.

POWER AND CHRISTIAN ETHICS

NEW STUDIES IN CHRISTIAN ETHICS

General editor: Robin Gill

Editorial board: Stephen R. L. Clark, Anthony O. Dyson,
Stanley Hauerwas and Robin W. Lovin

In recent years the study of Christian ethics has become an integral part of mainstream theological studies. The reasons for this are not hard to detect. It has become a more widely held view that Christian ethics is actually central to Christian theology as a whole. Theologians increasingly have had to ask what contemporary relevance their discipline has in a context where religious belief is on the wane, and whether Christian ethics (that is, an ethics based on the Gospel of Jesus Christ) has anything to say in a multi-faceted and complex secular society. There is now no shortage of books on most substantive moral issues, written from a wide variety of theological positions. However, what is lacking are books within Christian ethics which are taken at all seriously by those engaged in the wider secular debate. Too few are methodologically substantial; too few have an informed knowledge of parallel discussions in philosophy or the social sciences. This series attempts to remedy the situation. The aims of New Studies in Christian Ethics will therefore be twofold. First, to engage centrally with the secular moral debate at the highest possible intellectual level; second, to demonstrate that Christian ethics can make a distinctive contribution to this debate – either in moral substance, or in terms of underlying moral justifications. It is hoped that the series as a whole will make a substantial contribution to the discipline.

BOOKS IN THE SERIES

Rights and Christian ethics by Kieran Cronin

Biblical interpretation and Christian ethics by Ian McDonald

Power and Christian ethics by James Mackey

Sex, gender and Christian ethics by Lisa Sowle Cahill

The moral act and Christian ethics by Jean Porter

The environment and Christian ethics by Michael S. Northcott

Plurality and Christian ethics by Ian S. Markham

POWER AND CHRISTIAN ETHICS

JAMES P MACKEY

Thomas Chalmers Professor of Theology,
University of Edinburgh

CAMBRIDGE
UNIVERSITY PRESS

Published by the Press Syndicate of the University of Cambridge
The Pitt Building, Trumpington Street, Cambridge, CB2 1RP
40 West 20th Street, New York, NY 10011–4211, USA
10 Stamford Road, Oakleigh, Melbourne 3166, Australia

© Cambridge University Press, 1994

First published in 1994

Printed in Great Britain at the University Press, Cambridge

A catalogue record for this book is available from the British Library

Library of Congress cataloguing in publication data

Mackey, James Patrick.
Power and Christian ethics/by James. P. Mackey.
p. cm. – (New studies in Christian ethics)
Includes bibliographical references and index.
ISBN 0 521 41595 0 (hardback)
1. Christian ethics. 2. Power (Christian theology) I. Title. II. Series.
BJ1275.M34 1994
241–dc20 93–8053 CIP

ISBN 0 521 41595 0

CE

Contents

General editor's preface

This is the third monograph to appear in the *New Studies in Christian Ethics* series. It fits very well the interdisciplinary nature of the series, and is written by one of the most significant theologians in Britain today.

The theme of power has been a sub-text of Professor James Mackey's writings for more than a decade. It is present in the early chapters of his major study *The Christian Experience of God as Trinity*. It is more prominent in his *Modern Theology* and indeed in his innovative and most recent work in Celtic theology. He is a philosopher by training and background, but through the influence of writers such as Alasdair MacIntyre he has also read deeply in the social sciences. His range of scholarship is broad, but he always brings to his writings insights that are clearly his own. Sharp observations – sometimes eirenic, but more often polemical – appear on almost every page of his writings.

For James Mackey power is to be located on a spectrum between force and authority. On moral grounds power exercised as authority is usually to be preferred to power exercised as force, since the latter tends to eliminate the possibility of genuinely moral behaviour. At most, power exercised as force should be used to protect the perimeters of the area within which moral agents are to act. Once individuals are coerced (through secular or ecclesial means) they are no longer free to act as moral agents. Yet ironically both states and churches have long histories of attempting to coerce individuals in areas which might otherwise be fertile ground for moral creativity.

Implicit within this understanding of power in society are a number of presuppositions about the nature of morality and about Christianity. James Mackey expertly unpacks these presuppositions, arguing that morality is a creative way of interacting with the world, rather than a constrained way of following rules. In addition, the accretion of power exercised as force – not just the propensity of the Catholic Church, but also of many Reformed Churches – he sees as quite alien to the world of the New Testament. The use of force and fear he maintains to be incompatible with the true nature of Christianity.

This is a challenging and uncomfortable book for secularists and religious believers alike. If Professor Mackey argues for the moral significance of religious communities in present-day society, he is also fully aware of their historical frailties. He remains a committed, but critical, Catholic.

In short, this is a powerful book. Its theme is power and it is also written by one who has obvious moral and intellectual authority/power.

ROBIN GILL

CHAPTER I

The anatomy of power

Power and ethics must at first sight seem strange bedfellows even in a book title. Power corrupts; ethics is designed to improve. Power constrains, enforces, overcomes; ethics liberates, at least in so far as it requires, and as it would therefore promote, the freedom of all those it attracts to its high ground. A book on power and ethics would be expected, then, to cover the wars between these opposing parties, and to plot if possible the victory of the latter over the former.

Not quite so.

The most obvious impression made by the first sight of these terms in tandem can yield, on a little further reflection, to prospects of more positive relationships. It is not altogether unusual to come upon the expressions in literature, or the experience in oneself, of images of desirable goodness for which the power to realise them seems somehow lacking. Then talk of a power for good becomes entirely natural, and, since goodness is that which ethics describes and, indeed, prescribes, power and ethics look more like allies when before this they had looked like natural enemies.

The nature of ethics is a later concern, the nature of power more immediate; and it must already be obvious from the few preceding remarks that the broadest possible understanding must be sought, resisting the temptation to confine attention to stereotypes and to common impressions, however widespread these may appear to be, even in the higher literature on the subject.

Introducing a book which is most frequently recommended these days to those who inquire after the nature of power,

Steven Lukes advises against the determination to define it.[1]
The book itself is a collection of representative and authoritative views on the nature of power, and Lukes' introduction a
preliminary survey and assessment which finds shortcomings
at every new advance. 'Each does say something true and relevant', Lukes admits, and he summarises the accumulating
truth as follows:

The effects of power seem clearly to bear some relation to intention
and will: someone whose actions regularly subvert his intentions and
wants can scarcely be called powerful. The outcome of resistance is
certainly relevant where comparisons of power are at issue. Affecting
behaviour is certainly a centrally important form of power ...[2] The
cooperative and communicative aspects of empowerment certainly
require attention, as do the ways in which power maintains social
systems and advances conflicting collective interests within them.

'Perhaps', he then adds, 'a generally satisfying definition can
be devised by fitting these various insights together into a
single picture?'[3] This generally satisfying definition might be
construed as follows: 'Power is that which achieves the realisation of one's intentions and will, affecting to that end one's
own behaviour and that of others, and overcoming resistance
in both cases. It is frequently a function of social systems by
which it is communicated and propagated to the
advancement of collective interests.' But Lukes doubts that
such cumulative definitions can ever be successful. Instead he
himself sets out in pursuit of more descriptive accounts of what
he calls the outcomes of power and the locus of power. The
former he describes as that which serves the interests of the
powerful, and there follows a lengthy analysis of interests; the
latter, the locus of power, is not often easily located in single
responsible individuals and may have to be found by seeking
groups who benefit from collective practices or systems, or
those who change the course of events. Yet, after all of this
Lukes remains sceptical of definition. To the question, what is
power? or its equivalents, he would wish to say only this: 'in
our ordinary unreflective judgments and comparisons of
power, we normally know what we mean and have little difficulty in understanding one another, yet every attempt at a

single general answer to the question has failed and seems likely to fail'.[4]

That, however, will not do. There is something unpalatable about concluding that we normally know what we mean by power, yet seem likely to fail in any general answer to the question of its nature. There is even something untoward about such a negative conclusion when it follows such a fine summary analysis of so many of the aspects and manifestations of power.

The word 'power' looks in so many ways like the word 'myth'. Its first impressions are vague and diffuse, but decidedly pejorative. It is something that is probably bad, and for that very reason, it is tempting. Yet, like myth, it seems to name something that will not go away, something endemic in the human condition; and on a little reflection it begins to appear that we have little option but to rehabilitate in our philosophies the thing so named, and to work towards a more neutral and comprehensive meaning of the term than those which are normally current in unreflecting discourse. Lukes may well be right if what he means to suggest is that we cannot produce at the outset a generally satisfying single definition of power, since power is clearly not a simple thing, no more than myth is a simple thing. That may be why myth is often used to describe power in practice, as in myths of kingship, or of social contracts. But initial definitions need not be designed to tell all about their objects, and write *finis* to the subject in that sense. They may be designed simply to help identify the object through all its manifold transformations until it disappears into the depths of the sources of present existence or into the unpredictable future. And that minimum we may require in the case of power in any book about it: something sufficient to establish the basic family resemblance wherever the phenomenon appears, whenever the word is used.

Lukes was concerned mainly, as were the others in the volume he edited, and most writers on the subject, with the social, or at least the interpersonal, manifestations of power. But power, as many of its myths suggest, may come from the trans-human sphere, and, as many an anguished confession testifies, it has intra-individual reference. We seem to be in the grip of powers within us, as often as we find ourselves under their external sway. An initial identifying analysis of it, then, should be open to questions about its cosmic source and its private presence. And, as has already been hinted, it must be capable of traversing the moral, the immoral, and perhaps the amoral spheres of behaviour.

A. P. D'Entrèves' *The Notion of the State*,[5] one of the clearest and most comprehensive accounts of the theory and practice of political government in the West, contains, in fact, an analysis of power which might, with adjustments, be put to much broader use. D'Entrèves is concerned with the development of the state, not with the notion of power for its own sake; in effect, power is just one of the notions which he uses in order to plot this development in theory and practice. Freely admitting the similarity of his analysis to that of Max Weber, D'Entrèves describes political government in terms of force, power, and authority, treating these as elements in the make-up of the state, and appearing to discover that none of these can appear without some hint of the presence of at least one of the others. It is this tripartite distinction of essentially interrelated elements that suggests the initial definition we need.

Force, then, for D'Entrèves is the factor that is dominant in the state or kingdom ruled by the Machiavellian prince, and force is detected and measured by the sheer efficacy with which the state is secured against external threat and internal disruption; it is often detected also by such negative indicators as the absence of a rule of law and of the influence of moral value to which the prince's choice of action might be subjected. Power, next, is recognised as the dominant factor of government where the rule of law holds sway, for then the use of what might otherwise be called force without more ado, is applied and regulated by a system of law to which all can appeal, both government and governed, and by which all are constrained. Authority, finally, names that factor by which a system of law, any system of law, is itself legitimised or validated, if only because it indicates the common goals that motivate a social group which takes the law to be obligatory upon itself. Authority refers in the first instance to the operative influence of certain values – order, freedom, or something as diffuse and evocative as 'the common good' – in the activity of those who rule and are ruled, values which legitimise or validate, in short, which justify before the court of reason, the expedient of recourse to a constraining system of law. Power refers to the operative influence of a system of law in the activities of rulers and ruled; force, in the absence of these two, to the operative influence of might indifferent to right.

These three factors – force, power, and authority – are required for any adequate account of the theory and practice of government, of states or comparable social entities, and, however some analysts might wish to confine analysis to one of these, and to exclude all reference to the others, in the name perhaps of empiricism or 'realism', it is difficult to find an example of human society in which one is operative to the total exclusion of the others. But that conviction cuts both ways. If it would be deemed cynical to suggest that a human society could be secured by naked force, it could equally well be deemed naive to think that a social group could for long cohere in free-wheel pursuit of general moral values.

The conviction of the need for some presence and interrelation of these three factors in any adequate account of a governed, or an ordered, society, is balanced in D'Entrèves' book by fulsome appreciation of the essential contribution made to political wisdom by the most adamant exponents of each factor in turn, even when they appeared to see their favoured factor dominate to the point of exclusion of others. So, the 'political realists' who wish to tear away all verbal illusions and simply to look at the facts (hence their claim to realism), who concentrate on the force factor and see the state (if their more recent representatives use that term at all) as nothing more than a system of force-relations between individuals, have this at least to their credit, that they realise the 'fictive' nature of such societies as are now commonly called states. In other words they realise the extent to which the state is a human artifact – as Hobbes put it, the state is 'an artificial man'. This need not be taken to endorse the more naive of social contract theories of the origin of human society, or to deny Aristotle's insight that humans are *by nature* animals who live in a *polis* or its many equivalents. Political realists need not be taken to deny that there is *something* anterior to the free-floating decision of individuals to co-operate socially; or that social groupings, even if they be but extended families, can be said to form individuals as much as individuals can be said to form structured societies. But these force theories of the state can claim to their credit a sturdy resistance to mystifying ideas of corporate personality, personified abstractions of their nature subversive of all individual autonomy.

Similarly, those who analyse political society predomin-antly, if not exclusively, in terms of power, those who believe that law is the very nature and extent of government, whether the law be promulgated by 'the One, or the Few, or the Many', can count amongst their achievements the end of subordi-nations of secular governments to religious pretenders, even if they cannot always claim to their merit the facilitating of those pluralist societies which too rigid a view of the sovereignty of law seemed at times to prevent. Finally, those few brave souls who might still wish to introduce moral values to modern political thought, who would see society predominantly, though they would scarcely dare to see it exclusively, as the locus and pursuit of such values, those believers in authority above power and force, might reasonably see in their prefer-ence for value over fact the only effective antidote to that modern poison which, in the name of the freedom of the masses to govern themselves, results only too often in the totalitarian-ism of majority rule.

Nevertheless it is the impressions of mutual need that these three factors seem naturally to reveal, each for some com-plementary presence of the others, and not the impressions conveyed by partisan accounts of their individual achieve-ments, that must provide the impetus towards the more general definition of the term 'power' that might prove most useful for the purposes of this book. Instead of confining power to that factor in the construing of human societies which consists in the existence and exercise of legal systems, as D'Entrèves does, suppose one were to consider power as a phenomenon that effects things, that brings about states of affairs, but tends to oscillate between the extremes of force and authority, both of these being understood more or less as D'Entrèves defined them. Some of the reasons for this change would better appear later, when for instance it is shown that law and values are alternative forms of human morality, so that they can scarcely be held so distinct as to define alternatively power and authority – although there will always be a sense in which some very generally perceived values will resist codification, if only because they must be held in a position from which they must justify codes of any kind in the most comprehensive of human societies. In a similar vein in another later context the possibility of any clear distinction between state law and morality must be challenged. And, as far as the idea of power is concerned, de Jouvenel is shortly to be called to witness that power seems inherently inclined, in the human condition at least, to emerge as raw force, and that it then constantly needs the control and conscious corrective of operative moral values in order that it should cease to be destructive of the freedom and dignity of human beings.

The suggestion is that an initial definition of power, for general purposes of identification, could derive from a slight rearrangement of D'Entrèves' three elements: power is a phenomenon which brings about states of affairs and which can be located on a continuum between the extremes of force and authority. It is possible for it to appear as pure force or pure authority, although it is more normally in our experience located somewhere on the continuum between these extremes, and its precise location on this continuum can be plotted by the relative presence or absence of the properly moral factor. It remains to be determined later what a properly moral factor is, but, since it is impossible to do everything thoroughly at the same time, take it that where a rational will in pursuit of a value (or an anti-value), perceived by that will itself to be such, is operative, the moral factor is present. Where that factor is altogether absent, power takes the form of force; where that factor is exclusively operative in bringing about a state of affairs, power takes the form of authority.

It would take but a little reflection to realise that the alternatives are seldom, if ever, found in pure form. The play of power at what are called in popular game-show parlance the vegetable and mineral levels, and even at the animal level if humanity is excluded, might seem at first sight to provide a broad panoply of the instances of power as force. But what if the resources of the physical, the vegetable, and the animal realms are being manipulated by human beings for their own goals? If these in turn are in pursuit of values or anti-values, must we not then detect some presence of power as authority rather than the pure presence of force. Flooding takes thousands of lives. A natural disaster? A phenomenon of raw force? But, if the greed of developers stripped surrounding lands of trees which could retain soil, and the soil water, is the ensuing disaster really an example of pure force? As the God of Genesis said, having decided to make male and female in its image: 'let them have dominion over the fish of the sea, and over the birds of the air, and over the cattle, and over all the earth, and over every creeping thing that creeps upon the earth' (Genesis 1, 26). To the extent that that dominion is exercised, to the extent that it is exercised in pursuit of moral ends, good or bad, the resulting states of affairs might better be attributed to power in the mixed form of force and authority.

Mention of the ordering and arranging God of Genesis may well tempt one to carry that last thought a good deal further. For this God is surely a moral being, inspired in all actions only by the highest of moral values, and, when the idea of this God creating out of nothing develops from the Genesis image of ordering all things in providential fashion, it becomes quite difficult for Jews and Christians to see in the emergence of any state of affairs in this world an instance of power in terms of pure force. For them, every single state of affairs that exists and is active upon us is held in being and in activity by this divine rational will, a will motivated by moral values such as faithfulness, loving kindness, justice, or others which the subsequent books of the Bible may suggest. That is presumably why believers adversely affected by disease or other 'natural forces' which do harm to people, ask the question, 'why me?' Just as some of the same believers, seeing some others relieved of disease or of the worse effects of 'natural disasters' ask the question, 'why them?'

Christian theologians who can see how quickly this topic opens up before them the daunting vistas of theodicy, the task of justifying God's ways to man, can sometimes move just as quickly to distance God as much as possible from the empirical states of affairs which immediately harm individuals, and just as unexpectedly sometimes heal them. God's all-power, some will say, is not a manipulative, interfering, tinkering power *vis-à-vis* intra-mundane causes, but the original bringing-into-existence power, and subsequently a power of 'letting be'.[6] Such solutions seem more verbal than real. God can also let be the killer tiger whose 'fearsome symmetry' on this account of the matter God has somehow forged; and letting be is not in all cases the way in which love as a moral value rather than indifference as at times at least an anti-value, might be expected to manifest itself. It is not necessary, and it would not be wise, to enter here into the treacherous marshlands of theodicy. Suffice it to say that all the efforts to produce a theodicy, from the most ingenious to the most evasive, bear their own testimony to the fact that it is extremely difficult for any believer in a creator God to point to any state of affairs in the resulting creation as an instance of power as pure force. The whole must seem a play of moral power, and that means power in the form of authority, rather than power in the form of pure force. Reference to a creator God makes this point relevant well beyond the religions of Judaism and Christianity. Indeed the greatest *tour de force* in Western literature in the effort to show that the last detail in what might otherwise be seen as the effects of the force of impersonal fate is in reality the effect of the minute care of personal providence, Boethius' *The Consolation of Philosophy*, has persistently puzzled commentators who search for some distinctively Christian elements within it.[7]

But that, it might be said, is to look at states of affairs brought about, from the point of view of their sources or creative origins, their authors. Would they all seem like exercises of authority still if looked at from the viewpoint of those they affect? For rational agents can be affected by states of affairs as much as they can be the authors of these. There is a social, as well as a cosmic, dimension to the play of power.

Rational agents act upon each other as often as they act in consort. Both sorts of activity are characteristic, and perhaps together constitutive, of human societies. When they act in consort and produce the intended effects, the distinction of power in the form of force from power in the form of authority should not be problematic. In such cases power will always take the form of authority; only in the most exceptional cases will moral agents act together without any morally identifiable intent, or any consequent moral responsibility; act, in other words, as a grouping of bodies without reason or responsibility (and even here the cosmic concept of a creator God could turn the resulting release of power into an instance of authority!). But when moral agents act upon each other it is entirely possible that what might be seen as an exercise of power as authority, when looked at from the point of the moral agent who initiates the action, may be in fact experienced as an exercise of power as raw force from the point of view of the moral agent acted upon, the receiver or the patient. If I am physically restrained from doing the evil act which I fully intend to do, then what I now do instead of that evil deed – pace my prison cell, fuming – will seem to me, and indeed be, the effect of power as force and not of power as authority, even though my jailer, who was inspired by ethical motives in so restraining me, will see from his point of view an act of power as authority. Yet, had I been persuaded by cogent reasons to love my enemy instead of doing him the injury I fully intended to inflict, or had I been persuaded to lock myself away voluntarily until the likelihood of inflicting injury was over, I should presumably see the resultant love, or even the confinement, as an exercise of power as authority from my point of view also. In both cases it could clearly be said that power was exercised upon me, and in both cases it could be said that the power exercised was from the point of view of its source or original agency power as authority; yet in one case the further effect which this exercise of power produced, now through the intervention of my agency, could be seen as an exercise of power as force, and in the other case as an exercise of power as authority.

It would not do to oversimplify this distinction between instances in which actions of mine which result from influences of other moral agents upon me are effects of power as force and instances in which they are examples of power as authority: as if the former were always cases of use of physical force and its attendant fear, and the latter always instances of the use of language, any language other than that which threatens physical force and thus induces fear. All kinds of discourse can be used in order to reduce the operation of the truly moral factor in the agent to whom it is directed. In fact, one modern philosopher has maintained that all human discourse is so used. Already in *Madness and Civilization*, his first major work, Michel Foucault argued that, by identifying certain patterns of behaviour as madness, others as sanity, the whole of human behaviour was being manipulated, governed in ways which by-passed people's own appreciation, people's own perception of values which would then be to them moral ones. Power to Foucault, far from being just physical force, is an operative system of knowledge carried by language itself, to which all are induced to submit by giving it, for example, the status of 'science', the modern resort of certainty. Foucault's later work generalised further: we are all trapped by what he called 'power-knowledge', a creation of human discourse, a secretion of language itself, and made up of systems of ideas and images which, by being embedded in language itself, actually rule and limit our lives and all our expectations of life. It has been said that Foucault's *Discipline and Punish* is essential reading for any who would understand how power really operates, and in our terms it seems to operate in human discourse itself more to diminish than to enhance that personal appreciation of, and commitment to, value in which the moral factor properly consists.[8]

So in the social dimension of power, in cases of moral agents acting upon each other, it is necessary to become quite critically aware of the precise ways in which discourse is used by some in order to elicit action on the part of others, before

deciding where on the range from force to authority the resulting effects of power may lie, particularly from the point of view
of those in receipt of the influences of others. Foucault's analysis may be morally pessimistic, his description of human manipulation overdrawn, but it does raise critically the question of
the kind of discourse which could enable people to come to
their own personal awareness of, and commitment to, value,
and thus make operative in social life the moral factor which
presages the presence of power as authority at the expense of
power as force.

It is obvious that in common parlance people use our terms –
power, force, authority – with what can only be called bewil-
dering interchangeability. People talk of wave-power as an
alternative and very 'green' form of energy; Dylan Thomas
entitled one of his poems, 'The Force that through the Green
Fuse drives the Flower'; there is the force of instinct and the
power of persuasion; the phrase 'the powers that be' has as its
equivalent in society 'the authorities'. Such usage may illustrate in its way the rightness of seeing power as something that
oscillates between its twin forms of force and authority. At any
rate little more can be done just now to recommend this
suggestion for an initial and generally identifying definition,
than to illustrate the fact that the terminology, devised from
modifications of D'Entrèves and Weber does apply, particularly at the social level, and that the definition does serve to
identify the cases and questions with which a treatise on power,
particularly in its social manifestations, might be expected to
concern itself. For example, case studies in social existence,
from which it is obvious that power is operative at some part of
its reach as force, certainly raise again the question as to
whether any human society can be realistically expected to
cohere without some element of force, or whether all human
societies should be expected to aim at the elimination of force
in favour of the consistent and comprehensive experience of
authority. Such macrocosmic questions are sometimes
deployed on the microcosmic scale of, say, the theory of penal
institutions: whether prisons should have a retributive or a
rehabilitatory purpose, or must always have a mixture of both.

But, before these issues arise, it is necessary to make some opening observations about types of human society and types of Christian church.

TYPES OF SOVEREIGNTY, TYPES OF CHURCH

Power is one of the original features or factors in this universe, so named because it effects things, or, more mildly put, because it enables states of affairs to come about. So, like other terms for original features of the universe – more general terms like 'being', more comparable terms like 'causality' – it must be used analogously because of the variety of different categories in which it is manifest. Or it is like light, in this respect at least, that, just as the refraction of light reveals the range of colours in the rainbow, the analysis of power proves it to be deployed along a range of appearances of which raw force is one extreme and pure authority another, and shades composed of mixtures of these in various proportions take up the middle space. Now it may sometimes be thought – especially if but little thought is given to the matter – that different points on the range of power's appearances would correspond to different forms of government in human society; that something very like a hereditary monarchy claiming the divine right of its kings would correspond to unqualified force, whereas the most highly developed democracies would surely approximate to the status of power as pure authority. A very little reflection, however, is all that is necessary to show that this correspondence need not hold, and very little historical experience is all that is required to show that it does not hold. An equally thoughtless impression is often held, and indeed may often be created quite deliberately, that Christian churches of their nature exercise power as pure authority; for, although some of their officers may have sinned in the use of force in the past, and some indeed may do so again, Christian churches of their nature dispose of 'spiritual' rather than 'temporal' authority, and this, however it is to be further defined, operates at the moral level, at the opposite extreme to that of force. It needs a little more reflection to see how misleading this second impression can be; hence it is worthwhile to take these impressions in order, and to devote some thought to each in turn.

Many studies in political and social theory make the point that particular forms of government cannot be made to correspond with particular forms of power as force or as authority. D'Entrèves in his own way makes the point fairly frequently. But Bertrand de Jouvenel makes the same point in a way which is particularly valuable for this present inquiry into the nature of power and its relationship to Christian ethics. 'The differences between forms of government in different societies', he writes, 'and the changes of form within the same society are but the accidents, to borrow the terminology of philosophy, of the same essence. The essence is Power.'[9] In order to be able to use the valuable material in de Jouvenel's work, I take his 'essence is Power' in the sense of the basic definition or description already offered. He would want to say more about power in essence, more than that it oscillates between force and something else; he would want to say that it has some intrinsic inclination towards the extremes of force. But, since he also calls for a corrective to this inclination from the realm of moral value, it should be possible to leave his additional view of the essence of power without comment for the moment, in order to avail of his analysis of differing forms of government as accidents that can leave the essence of power untouched.

De Jouvenel, then, in the course of his book, provides many illustrations of the lack of commonly expected correspondence between a form of government and a form of power. The expectation that the absolute monarch must exhibit power as force is defeasible in theory by the medieval view that such tyrannical government had to be exercised for the obviously moral value of the common good; otherwise it ceased to be justified and could rightly be overthrown.[10] And it is defeasible in practice in de Jouvenel's view in the example of princes praised by men of such credibility as Kant for taking into account not merely the common good of the people, but the people's own freely expressed views about the same.[11]

Much of this matter was discussed in the past by political theorists when they wrote about the *summa potestas*, or, in later

English, the issue of sovereignty, its nature and locus. This was thought from Roman times to be the power behind the laws or the power that issued in the customs and laws of any particular society; and when theorists speculated about its 'location', they really looked for some person or body who could be seen as source of rule rather than its subject, some person or body who was in that sense *ligibus solutus*. Now this last Latin phrase might, of course, be taken to suggest that there may be found in any and every human society a power which is absolute, in the meaning of arbitrary, above and beyond all law. But the vision behind the theory of *summa potestas*, sovereignty, ran quite contrary to such a prospect. The search for the *summa potestas* is, as to location, the search for those who lawfully exert power, rather than those over whom it is lawfully exerted, and the presumption is that the search ends with those from whose judgment there is no further appeal. But notice the repetition of the word 'lawfully' in that last sentence – the implication is that the behaviour of the holders of the *summa potestas* is itself conditioned by the law; and this was recognised to the point where a Byzantine emperor could be considered *nomos empsychos, lex animata*, in loose translation, the law incarnate.

The Romans had their own views about the *summa potestas* residing in the people, although the *imperium*, the actual government and practice of that power, might not be entrusted too lightly by too many of them to the people as a whole. That idea, when its time had come, gave rise to the various forms of modern democracy. So it is the vision of the 'essence' of power that shines through this ancient idea of the *summa potestas* and not, to continue with de Jouvenel's distinction, clear directions concerning the 'accidents' of the practical modes of its exertion in society. The vision, in reality, is of people ruling themselves by means of the law; even in the case of the Byzantine emperor, who must live by the same law as he promulgates and enforces upon the people. And, since people who rule themselves by law, even if through an intermediary, will do so in their own best interests, for their own common ends, power as force will scarcely be necessary, and power as authority must win the day.

Now, of course, the question is ready to burst from the lips of every *realpolitiker* within hailing distance of this present discussion: yes, but who is there to see to it that the Byzantine emperor does live by the law of which he is the supreme source for his society, that he does not rule arbitrarily in his own interests and subdue others by force to his own selfish will? The point of this particular part of the argument is not that this is not a real question, but that it can be posed equally well to any form of rule or *imperium*, any kind of government. De Jouvenel, after all, was writing in the shadow of a modern nation state, the megalomaniac leader of which had persuaded the majority of his people to place such effective power in his hands, and to co-operate so much in its further exercise, that minorities within the country, and other sovereign states outside it, experienced the fullest brunt of power in the most destructive form of force that the modern world has so far witnessed. The question must then be put to any form of government; and, to anticipate a little, it must be asked of divine, as well as of human, governments. It is asked of divine government, in the form: does God command what is good, or is something good because God commands it?

This is not the place or the time to enter any further into the practical questions concerning the means by which power in its various governmental forms, or 'accidents', can be prevented from embodying naked force, can be nudged towards the status of authority. Is the choice of rulers made by the people, or by God, better in this respect than the process of selection by primogeniture or, as Plato seemed at times to wish it, by selective breeding (the aristocratic principle)? Does the modern theory and practice of the separation of powers by which the *summa potestas* is distributed between a legislative, a judiciary, and an executive, provide with sufficient assurance the checks and balances which would prevent power turning into raw force? Political experience makes any simple answer to such questions hazardous indeed. A particularly dominant political party in a modern democracy can so monopolise the business of government over such a length of time as to virtually elide the separation of legislative and executive power; and the recent series of appalling miscarriages of justice in England illustrates the ease with which a judiciary, whether by its own ineptitude or for more sinister reasons, can become a tool for the extraction of retribution from innocent members of easily identifiable minorities. This is not to say that practical means should not continue to be sought to prevent power from deteriorating into naked force, and that some of these do not already succeed in this better than others have done. Separation of powers can certainly be recommended, but the point remains that power in essence is something that oscillates in practice between force and authority, and that oscillation cannot be plotted in any close alignment with the different 'accidents' of actual forms of government.

It is, of course, difficult to state the essence of power in this way without the accompanying moral preference for power in the form of authority, or as much in the form of authority as human ingenuity can contrive and human limitation can accomplish; and it is to this end that the tortuous struggle for democracy, and the insistence on separation of powers, and so many other detailed and practical experiments have been aimed. For it is in the presence of power as authority that human creativity and its consequent freedom can flourish. Nevertheless, as already remarked, de Jouvenel himself took a pessimistic view of the essence or nature of power. Impressed or, better, depressed by the 'natural history of its growth' the detailed story of which takes up most of his book, and more particularly by its most recent demonic manifestations in Nazi Germany, he came to see the force element having such natural attraction for the egoist in all of us that power must always swing in that direction. That is why all actual forms of government seem at times to be equally susceptible to the corruption of authority by force; and the only way in which we could save ourselves from this, he thought, was by looking again and again to those moral rules or values against which all human law must be measured.

But that, of course, is to do no more than tell people to do occasionally what one sees them fail to do so frequently. It leaves us no further on than the recognition that power is some primordial, effective or enabling entity which oscillates between its two forms of force and authority in its empirical manifestations, and that people prefer, or ought to prefer, the latter form of it over the former. It remains a moot point as to whether this inclination towards the force end of the spectrum of power is a merely empirical matter or belongs more to the very essence of power. De Jouvenel himself might be reluctant to use the term 'power' at all at that end of the spectrum where pure authority is to be found. But that, too, is a moot point, and it could scarcely prevent from using his excellent material and analysis someone who wants to see power as in essence something which does oscillate between its two manifest forms as force and authority.

This leads to the second questionable impression outlined above: that churches of their nature wield spiritual rather than secular power – even if some of them sometimes overlooked this distinction in the past – and that spiritual power, a moral entity by nature since it comes from God, inevitably yields in practice power in the form of authority and never in the form of force. The fact that some such impression as this is wide-spread – it takes the form quite often of the view that organised religion is a source, if not *the* source of morality in society, that if people gave up their religion they would go to the dogs – does not prove it to be any the less misleading. For amongst the factors that count against this impression there is not just the fact that in Western civilisation Christian churches have con-stantly engaged with secular powers on similar if not identical terms, there is also the fact that the terminology and under-standing of power in the West is common to church and civil society. That in turn did not happen by accident, because of a temporary coincidence of kinds of governmental structure in church and civil society in the age, let us say, of the Holy Roman Empire. No, the common terminology and under-standing is due to the much more essential factor that the essence of power is the same in church and state, and reveals in its usual oscillation between the forms of force and authority the same non-alignment with the 'accidental' forms of different ecclesiastical governments. And, far from there being a tendency of ecclesiastical power to stick at the authoritative extreme of the oscillation, there is one factor common to all Christian churches, namely, a common understanding of the doctrine of devine revelation, which tends to keep the power exercised in these churches closer to the opposite extreme of force.

The clearest and most substantial statement of the right of the Christian church to engage with the secular government on its own terms is contained in the Bull *Unam Sanctam* of Boniface VIII, issued in CE 1302. Spiritual power, Boniface declared, is as far superior to earthly power as spiritual things are superior to temporal things. But it was obvious that he was not thinking of two quite different genres of power, the exercise of which could neither mix nor collide, for he used the metaphor of two swords, the spiritual and the temporal, declaring that both were controlled by the church, that one was wielded by 'kings and soldiers', but at the wish and by the permission of the church authorities for, as he put it quite bluntly, 'sword must be subordinated to sword'. This is the clearest statement to the effect that the head of the church has power over the head of civil government and over the civil government's exercise of power. For this was Christendom, the *respublica christiana*, the Christian commonwealth; and, as there was little notion of a law that was purely secular rather than religious in origin if not in content, so the distinction between 'spiritual' and 'earthly' power referred mainly to the different wielders of power, and perhaps to some differences in the ends for which it was wielded, but not to any real difference in its nature and exercise. 'The distinction between "spirituality" and "temporality" is not a distinction between two organizations', is how D'Entrèves puts it, and he adds two further examples: 'It is precisely because society is and must remain one, that Henry's claim to full sovereignty sounds like both a reminiscence of Boniface VIII and an anticipation of Hobbes.'[12] In other words, Henry VIII's decision to make himself head of the church as he already was head of state, was still an entirely logical one in view of the development of a civilisation which came to exemplify such a unitary view of power.

The same unitary view would seem to be exemplified in the

Treaty of Westphalia of CE 1648, which ended the long saga of
the post-Reformation wars that ravaged Europe, and particularly in its stated principle; *cuius regio eius et religio* (religious
allegiance should be regional). This principle tends to reverse
the rule of secular and sacred prince in the process of exercising
the *summa potestas*, a fact which owes more than a little to
Luther's appeal to the German princes; and it might in this
way be thought to be a step on the road towards Hobbes'
Leviathan, in which the reversal of priorities between secular
and sacred princes was complete to the point of the disappearance of any vestige of power in society for the latter.
Hobbes recalls the metaphor of the two swords, but only to say
that the metaphor for two governments in one human society,
one temporal and the other spiritual, served merely to make
men 'see double' and to mistake their lawful sovereign. A
church, to Hobbes, is identical to 'a civil commonwealth,
consisting of Christian men'.[13] The unitary power is now
wielded solely by the secular head of state.

This potted and extremely patchy history of relations
between church and civil society in Europe is meant to show
that we do not deal with the fluctuating interactions of two
separate and different 'powers', but rather with the same
language and imagery of power, the same idea or essence of
power, animating two governments, each assuming different
practical forms in the course of time, and all of this providing
for the historical spectacle of fighting, interfering, treating with
each other, of merging, and, at times, if only in the theory of
Hobbes, all but disappearing, the one into the other. The same
impression of a common language and imagery of power, a
common essence of power, emerges from a brief sampling and
survey of different contemporary forms of government in
Christian churches themselves. There emerges also some confirmation of the view that the oscillation of power between the
forms of force and authority fails here also, in ecclesiastical
structures, to align itself to changes from more obviously
imperial to more apparently democratic forms of church
government.

Take first the oldest surviving form of Christian church

government in the West, that of the Roman Catholic Church. According to the *Code of Canon Law*,[14] the power of governance, or the power of jurisdiction, 'which belongs to the church by divine institution', is capable of being exercised by those who are in sacred orders. Note this confinement to sacred orders, although it is allowed that lay members of the church can co-operate in the exercise of this power (canon 129). This power of governance is 'divided into legislative, executive and judicial power' (canons 135ff.), but this distinction does not lead to any provision for a theory or practice of the separation of powers in the Roman Catholic Church: the distinction serves only to assert the fulness of power in all forms of its exercise for those for whom its sovereign status is claimed. So only clerics can obtain offices the exercise of which requires the power to govern, the power of jurisdiction (canon 273), and a person becomes a cleric for this purpose by reception of the diaconate (canon 265). When the issue of sovereignty, the *summa potestas* or, in the English translation of the Code, the 'supreme authority' of the church is raised, the locus of this is first said to be found in the office of the Roman pontiff. 'Consequently, by virtue of his office, he has supreme, full, immediate and universal ordinary power in the Church' (canon 331). That this power is judicial and executive power, as well as legislative, is clear from the whole context, even if it is not already clear from canon 333: 'There is neither appeal nor recourse against a judgment or a degree of the Roman Pontiff.'

It is next said, however, that the College of Bishops is also the subject of supreme and full power over the universal church (canon 336). How are these two claims reconciled? Well, the Roman Catholic bishops of the world are subject, as a college, to this supreme power only when in union with the head of the college, the pope. Furthermore, he chooses the ways in which the college can act, and no informal consensus of the college can achieve the status of an act of supreme power unless he proclaim, or at least accept, it freely. The most solemn form in which this collegial power is exercised is that of an ecumenical council; but this must be convened by the pope, he must preside over it, set its agenda, approve its decrees, and transfer, suspend or dissolve it (canons 337–41). It would take a canny lawyer to estimate the real amount of supreme power left over for the college of bishops when that of the Roman pontiff is subtracted in any one instance of its collegial exercise, or in all.[15]

There is another college with which the papacy is closely involved, the college of cardinals. Suffice it to say here that it is the college which elects each pope; but it is the pope who selects all those to be promoted to that college, and who creates each cardinal by decree (canons 349, 351). Even in the case of the college of bishops, though some others might have a right to present lists of candidates for a vacant episcopal office, it is the Roman pontiff who freely appoints bishops or confirms those lawfully elected (canon 377); and in any case he can exercise ordinary power over their individual dioceses. This last provision is said to 'reinforce and defend the proper, ordinary and immediate power which the bishops have in particular churches' (canon 333). It is not necessary to query this claim in order to appreciate the awesome extent of the sovereignty which Roman Catholic constitutional law confers upon its supreme pontiff.

But if this picture of *summa potestas* reminds us of the most impressive forms of imperial power from the past, it is all the more necessary to remember that neither this picture in itself, nor the accompanying conviction that this power is in the church by divine institution, presses this picture of power inevitably in the direction of pure force. For power which is possessed by the grace of God is quite a different matter from power which is possessed by divine right or, worse still, by the alleged divine status of the one who wields it. For power exercised by divine grace is wholly compatible with its being exercised, as canon 129 says of supreme papal power, 'in accordance with the provisions of law'. The requirement of legality avoids the arbitrariness which is the hallmark of force, and the presumption must be, of course, that the illegal use of supreme power would involve the withdrawal of divine grace. If there is some reason to believe that some Christian churches exercise their power in the form of force, the reason will not consist in these particular contours of the institutionalisation of sovereignty. The contention that forms of government cannot simply be aligned to points on the spectrum of power remains intact, and the real reason for power in a Christian church assuming the form of force may, when it is found, point the finger of suspicion at churches other than the Roman Catholic Church.

Now if the 'accident' of this imperial form of government in the Roman Catholic Church – 'accident' also in the sense of being a contingent historical development rather than the result of a divine decree – fails of itself to reveal whether social relationships within that church are instances of power as force or power as authority, there is clear need to look further into the actual details of governing theory and practice in the church (and later in other churches). There is a particular need to keep in mind what has been said above about physical and verbal means of interaction between personal agents, and about different kinds of discourse with their very different effects upon the operative moral factor, and most especially in relationships between the officers of good order and those governed by them.

So the point has been made that even where a form of sovereignty, any form of sovereignty, acts in accordance with law, and hence not arbitrarily, its claim to represent authority rather than force is still based upon the extent to which the moral factor is allowed to operate in the society so governed. And this means in effect that the laws which the sovereignty imposes and which both sovereign and subjects have to obey must, to the personal knowledge of both, be validated by their perceived relevance to a 'common good,' to a value or set of values embodying the well-being of all and perceived by all to do so. This was the conviction that underlay the medieval view that an unjust law did not morally obligate, and that the revolt against a serious and persistent sovereign impetrator of such unjust laws was a moral right of all subjects. The means by which sovereign governments are replaced may have changed with the coming of representational democracies, and previous societies may have had no clear direction on this delicate point.

Nevertheless the basic principle remains the same throughout such changes. Any rule, even the rule of law, must be such as to facilitate rather than suppress the moral agency of its subjects, their ability and human need to evaluate, that is, to make their own moral assessment of the moral values to which the laws must be directed, and which the same laws in their own way embody.[16] Legislation which does not secure this general moral factor and, *a fortiori*, legislation which is so conceived as to positively prevent it, must be seen to inhabit a part of our spectrum which is closer to force than to authority. Reminded of the basic definitions and of their further implications, return now to further considerations of Roman Catholic constitutional law, and to similar constitutional law from some other Christian churches.

The Roman Catholic Church speaks of a 'deposit of faith' which has been entrusted to it by the Lord. Behind that image of entrusting lies a common Christian doctrine of divine revelation; but it is the content of the 'deposit' which merits attention at the moment, rather than the precise mode of its origin. The phrase most frequently found in the section of canon law (canons 747–54) which concerns the promulgation of this 'deposit of faith', this 'revealed truth', is the phrase 'matters of faith and morals' or 'doctrine concerning faith and morals'; and the canon law is certainly not shy about this church's claims concerning the 'morals' part of the 'deposit'. 'The church has the right always and everywhere to proclaim moral principles, even in respect of social order, and to make judgments about any human matter in so far as this is required by fundamental human rights or the salvation of souls' (canon 747). The section goes on to claim the prerogative of infallibility for both the pope and the college of bishops in union with the pope (the holders of *summa potestas*, as we have already seen) in the instances of their most definitive teaching on 'faith and morals' for the whole church; and it requires from their subjects a response of 'divine and catholic faith' for such teaching. The adjective 'divine' here implies the divine origin of the doctrine or ruling; it makes the idea of divine revelation directly relevant, as the condition under which such rulings are

promulgated. The precise nature of the process of divine revelation thought to be involved is not always clear. There is
reference in the present context to 'the word of God' in the
deposit of faith, presumably a reference to an original verbal(?)
revelation contained in scripture and handed down in tradition (canon 750); but other church decisions refer to a divine
law allegedly revealed in nature. For purposes of present
analysis, however, this does not matter; nor does the implied
distinction between matters of faith and morals,[17] for most
beliefs have the most practical of consequences, and believing
this rather than that is itself a 'practice' which may well be
enjoined upon us.

We are in the presence of rulings for conduct, the content of
which comes from divine revelation and the office for the
imposition of which is itself divinely instituted, according to
canon law. This is made finally clear from those canons which
state that, even in cases where the 'assent of faith' is not
required, subjects of the Roman Catholic *magisterium*, whether
in the form of pope and college of bishops, or of individual
bishops, are to offer 'submission of intellect and will' to the
former, and 'submission of mind' to the latter (canons 752–3).
What is finally clear is this: that, when the wielders of the
summa potestas in this church promulgate a ruling as in content
divinely revealed (and presumably most essential matters of
Christian life, of faith and morals, are such), there is no role for
the rational wills of the subjects other than simple assent,
instant consent.

One would not wish to say that every instance of a moral
ruling being handed down from some authority human or
divine, someone with good reason believed to possess particular
experience or expertise in the matter, automatically robs the
recipient of such exercise of personal assessment and choice, as
to render the ensuing effect an instance of power as force rather
than power as authority. Not all such discourse need be seen as
Foucault tended to see it; and we shall shortly see, in the
analysis of the anatomy of morals, the essential place of the
master/apprentice relationship. But the combination here of
claims to infallibility in relation to divine origin, and demands

for submission of mind and will ... this combination certainly suggests such refusal of personal assessment on the part of the recipient moral agent as to make the end result an example of the exercise of power as force rather than authority. And this is true before any thought is given to threats of punishment, physical or spiritual, by which such moral rulings in this church might well be accompanied. These latter, of course, need to be considered later.

There is not the space, and probably not the need, to survey all the range of forms of Christian ecclesiastical government the world now knows. For purposes of the present analysis of power, it should be sufficient to offer an example at the opposite end of the range from that occupied by the Roman Catholic *imperium*; it should then be easy enough, for anyone interested in doing so, to deploy combinations of relevant characteristics amongst those other forms of Christian church government which, by mixing, diluting or strengthening in various degrees the contrasting features of our two examples, place themselves at different points on this range of Christian structures. The example that suggests itself here is that of Presbyterian churches and, in particular, the Church of Scotland. In these islands it would then be possible to plot the analysis of the Church of England between the Church of Scotland and the Church of Rome, which is the dominant ecclesiastical power in the Republic of Ireland.

According to the Westminster Confession of Faith,[18] the subordinate standard of belief adopted by the Church of Scotland (subordinate, that is, to the supreme rule of faith, the Word of God contained in canonical scriptures), 'There is no other head of the Church, but the Lord Jesus Christ' (xxv, 6); yet the Lord Jesus 'appointed a government, in the hand of Church officers, distinct from the civil magistrate. To these officers, the keys of the kingdom are committed' (xxx, 1–2). The confession contains no further guidance on the protocol of church government except to suggest that 'for the better government, and further edification of the Church, there ought to be such assemblies as are commonly called synods or councils' (xxxi, 1). It is this factor which makes Cox in his *Practice and Procedure in the Church of Scotland*[19] declare it a principle of Presbyterianism that it be 'conciliar in polity'; and Cox's collection of the constitutional documents, on which the particular structures of this church are based, reveals the following deployment of 'synods or councils', now called 'courts'.

First, at parochial level, the lowest court operates, made up of one teaching elder or presbyter (i.e. one ordained to the ministry of Word and Sacrament), and a number of ruling elders or presbyters, who are ordained for life to that office, and it is called a kirk session. The next court is the presbytery (The Right Reverend The Presbytery), responsible for an area covered by a number of parishes, made up of the teaching elders or ministers of the relevant parishes, and some others, a representative ruling elder from each parish, and such others as will make this group up to the number of the teaching elders. Next in order of superiority is the synod, which includes all the members of a number of presbyteries and 'corresponding members' of adjacent synods. Finally, the supreme court of the Church of Scotland is the General Assembly, normally meeting once a year and made up of equal numbers of teaching and ruling elders sent by all the presbyteries of the Church.

Individual parish congregations issue a call to a prospective teaching elder or minister, but it is Presbytery which acknowledges the call and ordains to the ministry of Word and Sacrament; just as it is Presbytery (as *episcopos*) which proposes ruling elders to be ordained to that office, to individual parishes. This Church of Scotland is not, then, a true representative democracy. However, apart from the fact that the lay/clerical distinction would be quite controversial in Presbyterian circles and much resented by many Presbyterians,[20] the governing power could not in any circumstances be described as a clerical monopoly, as is the case in Roman Catholicism, since in the lowest courts the ruling elders must outnumber those ordained to the ministry of Word and Sacrament, and in the three other courts parity of numbers is always maintained. The Presbyterian Church is therefore conciliar in polity as the *Westminster Confession* suggests a church should be, rather than properly democratic in structure, and the extent of its conciliar nature is emphasised in the so-called Barrier Act of 1697. This was designed to prevent hasty changes of a substantial nature, but it succeeds simultaneously in preventing power from coagulating at the top, for it proposes that any acts which the General Assembly (The Venerable) might wish 'to be binding rules and constitutions of the Church' should be remitted to the presbyteries, which would report to the General Assembly of the following year and reveal a 'general opinion' in agreement, or not in agreement, as the case might be.[21]

Where, on the range of power between the forms of force and authority, might this model of church be found? It is scarcely necessary to repeat the point that it is not the kind of governmental structure involved – in this case a conciliar one – which determines that location, but more the answer to the question concerning the presence or absence, and perhaps the 'quantity', of the properly moral factor, the genuine exercise of people's freedom of will in pursuit of their common good. Looked at from this perspective, does the Presbyterian polity fare any better than the Roman Catholic?

'The Church of Scotland acknowledges the Word of God which is contained in the Scriptures of the Old and New Testaments to be the supreme rule of faith and life.'[22] This church takes as its subordinate standard the Westminster Confession; it recognises liberty of opinion on matters which do not concern the substance of the faith; it claims the right to modify, interpret and formulate its subordinate standard in accordance with the Word of God; but it insists that it is itself the sole judge of this agreement. Hence the one to be ordained to the ministry of Word and Sacrament, as well as professing belief in those points, promises to be subject to 'the superior courts of the Church',[23] the supreme court being, of course, the General Assembly.

It is difficult to avoid the impression that, despite the most obvious differences in governmental structure, the answer to our question about force and authority must appear very similar in the case of the Presbyterian Church to what appeared in the case of the Roman Catholic. We are dealing not with human discovery, it would appear, but with divine revelation. The content of this divine revelation concerns 'faith and life', a phrase which is surely very similar to the Roman Catholic 'faith and morals'. As with the Roman Catholic phrase, we may be left in some doubt as to the nature and extent of divine revelation in that which concerns moral rules for life: many Protestants, suffering from phobia of natural theology – either because they wrongly believe that its defenders base it on something other than divine revelation, or because they estimate at close to nil the ability of the fallen mind to perceive that revelation any longer – refuse to entertain the traditional Christian idea of a natural law morality; but they do speak of 'ordinances of creation', and these do seem to have some revealed quality about them. But what is left in no doubt whatever is this: the church is 'sole judge' of the agreement with the revealed Word of God contained in Scripture of any doctrine concerning faith and life.

In short, the church is ruled by divine revelation, yet it can define the content of revelation, if only by judging all doctrinal formulae purporting to present that content. This basic similarity between Roman Catholic and Presbyterian surely forces out to the margins of theological interest such well advertised disputes as those concerning scripture and tradition,[24] and threatens to reduce to little more than a slanging match the dispute as to who places what above the Word of God. For both proclaim themselves 'dependent on the promised guidance of the Holy Spirit' (or words to that effect) in issuing doctrine consonant with the Word of God, as well as the true interpretation of that Word. Neither is there much point in one side proposing that it is fallible, while the other pretends that in some recurring instances of teaching at least, it is not. For the question we all have to ask is this: how are we ordinary mortals to know? In both cases we are faced with a church which proclaims itself the sole judge, under the guidance of the Holy Spirit, of doctrinal presentations of divine relevation; in both cases a supreme tribunal for such judgment is pointed out to us. How could we ever know that they were wrong? Even if they told us that on some occasions they had been wrong we would be in no better position ourselves than if they told us they had never been wrong; for since they are sole supreme judges in the matter, we have only their word for it that they were wrong, if they say so, and if they say so, they could of course be wrong in saying so; so we are really no better off than if they had calmed our little minds by telling us that they are never, and never had been, wrong at all.

The point, perhaps too provocatively put in these terms, is that the combination of the idea of divine revelation with an idea of power structure in human society claiming to be sole judge of any teaching which purports to put before us the content of such revelation, is itself one which places the power of that structure closer to force than to authority, for the reasons already given in the analysis above of the Roman Catholic case, and irrespective, as has been said too often already, of the precise form of structure involved.

It is scarcely necessary – and there is not enough space in this book – to offer further examples of Christian church structures. This is not because Roman Catholics and Presbyterians are thought to occupy the extremities of a range of structures, from the imperial to the democratic. There are churches whose governmental structures would place them far to the 'right' of Rome, and others well to the 'left' of the Church of Scotland. No; it is unnecessary to consider further examples of forms of Christian church structure for the simple reason that the analysis of these two very different church structures yields such similar results for the placing of the power they exercise on the range that stretches from force to authority: the role played by claims to interpret divine revelation, which both believe themselves to have in some sense in their possession, is common and crucial to both, and that is presumably common to all Christian churches, whatever their concrete structures may be. Hence it is necessary now to say no more than a very little about ideas of divine revelation and what these may do to power exercised. At that stage it should be quite possible for anyone wishing to do so, to conduct a similar analysis of any other Christian church.

The theology of revelation flashed like a meteor across the Christian sky in the 1960s. Not much, if anything, had been seen of it before that – Christians had always taken for granted that revelation happened, that records of it were kept, but little or no analysis of the phenomenon itself ever seemed to have been thought necessary. This meteoric theology of revelation seems to have fizzled out as abruptly as it erupted on the scene, at or about the point marked by H. R. Schlette's *Epiphany as History*, which was published in English translation in 1969. It is neither possible nor necessary to try to summarise here the trajectory of that meteoric theological event,[25] but it would help our purpose here to say something about the theme with which it began and the theme with which it ended.

The topic first claimed attention with what can only be called an attack upon the propositional view of revelation. This view was more implied in traditional ways of referring to revelation, rather than expressed in any explicit attention to modes of divine revelation, for such attention, as has been said, was largely lacking up to this time. It is called a propositional view of revelation because the impression conveyed was that God communicated in propositions or their equivalent: statements, teachings, formulated truths, doctrines or, at any rate, words. Beginning with what proved to be a very persistent attack upon this view, the movement fizzled out in suggestions that what we really have under the rubric of divine revelation, and all that we have, are historical events read in the light of faith. The events needed to be read in the light of faith if they were to prove revelatory of God's ways with the world, for the simple reason that in themselves, as part of the messy, shuffling motion of human history, they could not stand out sufficiently to convince those unwilling to risk believing in their divine origin. The wandering of Abraham, the Exodus from Egypt, the conquest of the land, the Davidic dynasty, exile and return, the promulgation of the Torah, the life, death, and even the resurrection of Jesus as historically verifiable by witnesses of his 'appearances' – none of this need of itself be any more revelatory of special divine intervention designed to direct our minds and wills, than any of a hundred counterparts claimed for each event on that list. Even the sight of someone walking about and eating some days after he was known to be dead, apart from the fact that it has been claimed more than once, fails in and of itself to reveal his divine status, much more his status as saviour of the race. Hence the necessity of faith, and the final truth of the traditional contention, to which Protestants have given a rather exclusive focus, that we must be saved by faith.

The impression conveyed by the most common official language used of the divine revelation in those churches the structures of which have just been passed in review – and in most, if not all, Christian churches – is one that coincides with what has been termed the propositional view of revelation. The Roman Catholic authorities speak of a deposit of revelation containing the truths of the faith. Both churches speak of the things to be believed as being contained in the Word of God, though the Presbyterian churches look for that Word only in the Scriptures,[26] and insist that, where there is difficulty in attaining to the true and full sense of a scripture passage, recourse should be had to other relevant passages where the matter is made clear. Nevertheless both churches offer creeds, confessions, and other solemn formulations or church teachings as being in agreement with, or proposing the content of, the divine revelation contained in the Word of God in scripture. It is for such propositional forms that the churches claim the prerogative of the sole competent judge, the last court of appeal on earth.

This combination of impressions given and claims made is dangerous; it ices over a natural incline that descends from power in the form of authority towards the extreme of force. The impression is conveyed that divine revelation is propositional in form. That, in moral terms, already favours the form of precepts, laws. Add claims on behalf of ecclesiastical bodies to be 'sole judges' of the content of such legal formulae; add, further, an institutional hierarchy of courts; arrive at the adjective 'supreme' for one of these on earth; and the prospect of the regulation of human behaviour in a manner which does not really allow for the operation in individuals of the properly moral factor, is all the more imminent. It is worth noting that, if God dispensed with these mediating ecclesiastical courts and decreed himself directly that we were to act in a particular way simply because we were so commanded, the result would be the same. There would then be propositional moral revelation to individuals, and in this form it would prevent them from appreciating moral value for themselves and pursuing that value because of such appreciation, i.e. acting on their own valuation. It is worth noting further that a Christian body with no hierarchy whatever, which faced the world with unquestionable divine commands, in a similar understanding of revelation in moral matters and of its own role as transmitter of this, would similarly act to the detriment of human morality, and invoke the spectre of force in human affairs.

And would things be any different if the idea of revelation were to be adopted on which the recent theological movement spluttered out? Possibly so; perhaps because revelation could no longer be taken so literally as in the so-called propositional view of it. Faith would now provide the fundamental idea. Some people experienced something in certain events of an otherwise common-or-garden variety, which they believed to be a specific pointer to God's general way with the world. We need not inquire here as to how some arrived at such a conviction, when others who encountered the same events just as closely just as clearly did not; and perhaps no satisfactory result awaits such inquiry, nothing other than an appeal to divine activity both additional and similar to that which the same faith allowed in the case of the select events. This amounts to saying that faith is circular; but that in turn does not amount to saying that faith is unverifiable. If, for example, a particular faith were to offer salvation, together with a tolerable description of the salvation envisaged, then it would be deemed to be verified if some at least were saved in this way, and falsified if none ever were. Science is circular in a similar fashion. But the point of interest in the present context is this: the term 'revelation' would now function as a cipher for the conviction of some people's faith that the power active in the events selected was God; in short, the term would function in order to convey the conviction of a faith that was ever in the process of verification, as more people for a longer time tried to live that faith out of their own conviction and in ways successively adapted to their own inevitably changing circumstances. That is the point of interest in the present context for this reason, that the image of the leadership in a group of believers understood on this model of faith and 'revelation' could well be different from the image of leadership based on the understanding of revelation as a body of divinely authorised propositions committed to a church which was appointed sole judge of its content and interpretation, with a leadership exercising, as it inevitably would, a special role in such a judicial process.

To put the matter in another way: if faith is the fundamental term, and revelation language is used simply to convey the conviction of believers that the power active in select events is that of the one, true God, then every formulation of the faith will be seen as a human artifact; the scriptures too will be thought human witnesses to the events which their writers and receivers believe to be special instances of God's ways with the world, and not as containers of divine revelation in the form of God's Word(s). The scriptures may be considered as all Christian churches consider them, divinely inspired human compositions – in a somewhat similar manner to that in which, on the first revelation model, churches and their offices may claim to be under the guidance of the Spirit in expounding the truths of revelation, the content of God's own word – and hence as possessing an authority to which no other witness to God's selected and alleged acts may aspire. But they would then be human documents for all that, with all the strengths of the time and place of their production, and some at least of the inherent limitations.[27] The same could naturally be said for any and all subsequent attempts to expound the faith to later generations, whether as exegesis of the scriptures or as doctrine purporting to be in agreement with their contents, whatever the claims made for further guidance of the Spirit in the course of this unending process.

Such a view opens onto larger prospects for the participation of all ordinary people in the decisions as to how to live a faith and subsequently to give an account of it, than does the view of an already formulated and entrusted body of revealed words or truths, to be interpreted or reformulated by supreme ecclesiastical courts, and then imposed with God's own authority. A God believed to be active in selected events – if only as a means of drawing attention to God's precise ways with the world in all its parts and events – could be thought to be guiding and enticing, inspiring or even empowering, rather than defining and, so, legislating. People could believe themselves engaged in discerning the spirits, the power active in these events, and, if convinced that this power was good, indeed divine, could then take as their first task to live out such concrete inspiration, so that when the time for definitions came, as no doubt it often would, all could be seen to have opportunity to test and to vote for the suggested formulae; the consensus of all could be seen to have a role to play – whatever the constitutional arrangements concretely designed for this role-playing – rather than confinement of such prerogatives to some. On the former idea of revelation and its official interpreters, on the other hand, the supreme judicial body in the communion of believers, no matter what its nature and composition, would have to expect from all to whom it addressed its teaching, simple and unquestioning obedience to its edicts, and these, no matter how in the concrete they might be enforced, would of necessity represent the exercise of power as force rather than authority.

Something of this matter must be raised again in discussion of powers secular and powers sacred, and the relationships between churches and states. For the moment the matter serves only to illustrate the nature of power in its range from forms of force to forms of authority; and this chapter on the anatomy of power may conclude with a summary of its main findings.

The definition or description of power which is being sought is a very basic one indeed, one which would be capable of identifying the phenomenon in all the great variety of its manifestations, but by no means one which would attempt to say the last word on the subject. Power, then, is that which makes things happen, which enables states of affairs to come about. On a little further reflection it appears in a variety of forms, from naked force to pure authority, with mixtures of these in various proportions covering the rest of the range between. The criterion which distinguishes power in the form

of force from power in the form of authority, which determines
its place on this range for any particular exercise of power, is
the operative presence of the properly moral factor. That
factor in turn can be described for the moment as the operation
upon the state of affairs brought about by power of the free or
creative will of a rational agent. The point at which the matter
becomes complicated is precisely the point at which its social
dimensions begin to appear, the point, namely, at which moral
agents act towards one another. At that point one man's
authority can become another man's force. A powerful initiative designed to create or to change some state of affairs can
originate in the free creative will of one moral agent, but it can
affect other moral agents caught up in this process in such a
way that in the latters' engagement their own wills tend to be
either activated or inhibited, freed or chained. If free or
creative willing is induced by the initiatory action of another,
the resulting responsive activity will itself be power in the form
of authority, if inhibited it will be to that extent enforced or at
best an act of pure conformity, and an instance of power as
force. Hence, even in the more complicated social dimension of
its presence and exercise, the distinguishing factor for power,
the criterion which decides that its exercise is a form of force or
of authority, is still the operative presence of the properly
moral factor. To a fuller analysis of the anatomy of this factor,
to the anatomy of morals, the next chapter is devoted.

Meanwhile, it must be noted that there is no linear correlation between the different types of structure according to
which social interactions in the largest human societies are
regulated, between types of government or states, in short, and
manifestations of power as force or as authority, or varying
mixtures of those. Democracies can as easily force their minorities as enlightened monarchies can induce the free co-operation
of their subjects. It is far too easy to make too much of this point
and to ignore so many and such impressive practical issues that
go to make democracy preferable to monarchy. A system
which allows its people to judge their leaders at regular inter-
vals, and to remove them from power by peaceful and constitutional processes, has clear advantages over a medieval system

in which only the right of revolt was suggested as a remedy for the enforcement of unjust laws upon unwilling subjects. Similarly, the separation of powers whereby the legislature, the executive arm and the judiciary, are functions of different bodies within the body politic can, where it is properly managed, go far towards preventing governments from resorting unnecessarily to force. And a combination of such features can multiply the benefits to morality and authority in social life. Nevertheless, the point about the lack of linear correlation between forms of government and forms of power does keep in play the necessary conviction that it is the properly moral factor, and in the end it is that alone, which makes the difference between force and authority, and that the practical arrangements just mentioned are valuable primarily because they do so much to facilitate the proper operation of this factor in social affairs. Certainly they can never replace it.

Once it is realised that constitutional factors do not of themselves determine the prevalence in any society of force or of authority, it appears that other factors may operate in society to do so. This point has been illustrated in this chapter from the practice of churches rather than states: but, since churches imitate states in their structures, and operate within states towards those who are otherwise members of these states, the point is far from being of purely ecclesiastical relevance. In general terms, the point is this: if the beliefs on which I am to act or the rules of my behaviour are simply revealed to me, if they are put in such a way that I am prevented from judging them, much less arriving at them, then I am once more in the presence of force and not of authority. This will be true whether it is God or some body claiming to broker such revelation on God's behalf, which operates on such understanding of revelation. It will also be true whether the enforcement entails penalties physical or spiritual, and even in the case where no penalties whatever are involved. For, once more, under these conditions the properly moral factor cannot operate. To this factor, and to a further analysis of its presence in churches and states, we must now turn.

CHAPTER 2

The anatomy of morals

On the most elementary account of it, morality combines the features of a distinction between good and evil with a sense of obligation to do the former and avoid the latter. The distinction between good and evil, since it is a cognitive kind of operation, an attempt at telling the difference between good and evil, inevitably contains the usual suggestions about objectivity; that is to say, it suggests that the difference corresponds in some way to what we call reality, and is not entirely an imaginary thing. The sense of obligation, on the other hand, immediately on being 'sensed', raises the question of freedom. As paradoxical as it might seem at first blush, I should consider myself to be and to act as a truly moral agent if, and only if that which I feel obliged to do, I am nevertheless free enough not to do, if I choose not to do it. Such is the most elementary phenomenology of human morality that one could easily offer at the outset of any discussion of the matter.[1]

And yet, however transparent the claim of this opening account to represent our most immediate and universal experience of ourselves as moral agents, it can seem to be controverted at almost every turn of contemporary literature on the subject, particularly the literature emanating from Christian sources.

At times the controversial point would appear to be similar to the point that Cantwell Smith and some others used to make about religion. Many peoples, these would say, had, or have, no such word as 'religion' for the simple reason that they would see no difference between what they would call 'life' or 'living', or some such hugely comprehensive term for all that they were and did, and what we in later Western history would call 'religion'. Their life in all its concrete comprehensiveness was their religion; their religion therefore indistinguishable from the whole of life. Bernard Williams comes as near as any modern moralist to the expression of a quite similar view concerning morality.[2] If we misconceive morality as, in Williams' words, 'a peculiar institution'[3] alongside other institutions of our individual and social lives, then, he would argue, we are better off without it. We should do better to drop the special subject called morality, and spend our time instead in answering some question as highly unspecified as, how should we live? Stanley Hauerwas and Charles Pinches present a similar point of view on morality, although it is on this occasion confined to Christian living. Their way of putting the point is to insist that the following question really makes no sense: 'now that I have become a Christian, how should I best express my Christian commitment in my moral life?'[4] The question makes no sense, presumably, because it subtly persuades us to assume that the moral life of a Christian is somehow distinguishable from the totality of Christian commitment; and that assumption is plainly false if, as our authors would contend, the Christian commitment finds its full expression in nothing short of the totality of the lives that Christians live.

There is much to be said for the point made by Cantwell Smith and Williams, at least as a general point about religion and morality respectively; but its deployment in the case of Christianity is more questionable. As a general point about morality and religion respectively, it extends the reference of these terms to the whole of human life, and refuses to have that reference restricted to any single compartment of the whole business of living. Understood in this way the point does not deprive us of the use of the terms 'religion' and 'morality', as the fact that it is urged in both connections surely proves; although the language of those who put this point would sometimes appear to suggest such deprivation. However, if the point is equally true in both respects, in respect of both religion and morality, then we may conclude that we must describe the whole of human life as both religion and morality; and, if we are to agree that the terms 'religion' and 'morality' do not have the same connotation, even if we insist with Cantwell Smith and Williams that they have the same unrestricted denotation, then we must agree that we must use 'morality' to describe human life in one respect, 'religion' to describe that same totality in another respect, and that there are no doubt still other respects in which the same totality may be described, each of which will correspond to a difference 'logos', a different angle of perception with its differing discourse, a biology, for instance, or a sociology, rather than a theology or an ethic. Religion then is human life in its relationship to the divine.[5] Morality is all of human life in relationship to what? or in respect of what? It is such questions that a chapter on the anatomy of morals may be expected to answer; but not by dropping the term 'morality' just because it may suggest to some an unwelcome compartmentalisation of human life.

But what happens when Hauerwas refuses to distinguish between morality, or moral life, and the *Christian* religion in action? In 'Virtue Christianly considered' he and Pinches are less concerned to set right the claims of a 'virtue' approach to morals, and much more concerned to convince their readers that the Christian virtues, far from being thought to build upon Greek notions of virtue, for example, must be thought to provide a radical alternative, hence a radical challenge to Greek virtues; and the surviving accounts of Greek virtue, from Aristotle for instance, should then be used only in the course of this operation of displacement.[6] Now, unless they wish to suggest that 'Christianity' also really refers to the whole of human life (surely an impossible extension of Rahner's concept of the anonymous Christian?), and thus mean to do no more with the term 'Christianity' than to replace a potentially compartmentalising term (morality) with a term now innocent of such compartmentalising tendencies, they must be taken to propose some purely exclusivist Christian view of truth and goodness, something similar to the kind of exclusivist blast with which Dietrich Bonhoeffer opened his *Ethics*. Beginning with the suggestion that the Christian faith invalidated all other knowledge of good and evil, Bonhoeffer continued, 'Christian ethics stands so completely alone that it becomes questionable whether there is any purpose in speaking of Christian ethics at all. But if one does so notwithstanding, that can only mean that Christian ethics claims to discuss the origin of the whole problem of ethics, and thus professes to be a critique of all ethics simply as ethics.'[7]

Of course Hauerwas and Pinches may simply wish to do for Christianity what Williams did for human living in general, that is, to prevent the use of the term 'morality' from suggesting that only a part or compartment of living (in their case, of Christian life) was covered by it. But then they have even less right than had Williams to remove the general term 'morality' from the discourse. Christianity refers to a particular way, amongst others in human history, of relating to the divine. It may attempt to declare that it is *the* way of doing this and that, of course, would predetermine the answer to any moral question such as, is it right or good to do so? But at what cost? At the cost of what could only be described as complete amorality. Note this, however: the amorality now in question could not be confined to those parts of human behaviour, such as prayer and ritual worship, which most directly attempt to secure or to maintain relationships with the divine. Christianity, like any other religion worthy of its name, refers to a whole way of living in the world. Hence the refusal to allow any distinction between Christianity and morality would mean that, for Christians at least, one could only 'show' examples of Christian living; one could not tolerate the question as to whether this was a right or a morally good way of living. The logical conclusion to this train of thought would be that no action of a Christian could be subjected to any criterion of right or wrong. In fact no action of any human being could be queried in a moral fashion; for Christians could scarcely endorse the application of moral criteria to the total life styles, and all particular parts of these, in the case of other religious bodies, or in the case of agnostic or atheistic humanists, yet refuse to submit their own life style and any and all of its behaviour patterns to the same moral criteria.[8]

Christians have no more right to reduce the term 'morality'

to a status of virtual disappearance under some such phrase as 'Christian life', than had Williams in respect of human life in general. The appeal to the alleged compartmentalising tendencies of the term is no more persuasive in one case than it is in the other. In both cases the proper procedure is to extend the denotation of morality to the whole of human life, and then to ask what makes the whole of human life moral, or the whole of Christian life moral, morally good or morally bad or, most likely, morally mixed; and to see this as a similar but different procedure from that of asking what makes the whole of life religious, or irreligious as the case may be. This will mean that life as religion can be subjected to moral criteria, that relations between humanity and the divine can be subjected to moral criteria, and to that extent the divine can be subjected to moral criteria. Therein perhaps lies the first lesson for those who seek to lay bare the anatomy of morals, a lesson unwittingly taught by those who challenge its distinctive terminology, the lesson, that is, that any attempt to make it disappear behind allegedly more comprehensive terms such as 'human life' or 'Christian living' will only serve to show how utterly comprehensive its real range of application truly is, once its distinctive connotation is understood.

It is rather a pity that in matters such as this the example of Socrates in Plato's *Symposium* is not better known and more frequently followed. When Socrates' turn came to speak of Eros he echoed the wisdom of Greek myth in not counting Eros amongst the gods. The full relevance of Socratic Eros to the anatomy of morals must wait a little yet; for the moment it is necessary only to note that, just as a Greek god may be erotic (in an ancient and fuller sense of that word than is now current) but Eros is not a god, so the Christian God may be love, but love is not God,[9] and the Christian God must be moral, although morality is not, and cannot be, God. That last identity cannot hold; that is to say, God's being and doings cannot without further ado be identified simply with the good and the morally good – they may be good and morally good, but they could be evil. God is morally good, we do believe, but moral goodness is not simply God.[10]

Perhaps the moral philosophers criticised above were just carried away by their fear of compartmentalisation, and the point they really wanted to make was at once a lesser and more serious one. Perhaps they simply wished to isolate and then attack the view that morality is identified by the verbal indicators of specifically moral language, in particular the language of 'ought', of obligation, of normativeness. Now it is as obvious that the language of obligation is the commonest means of passing moral judgment on human activity – you ought to do this, you ought not to have done that – as it is that various groups for quite varied reasons would want to regard such a means of moralising as being applicable only to quite restricted parts of human life.

So, for example, a moral philosopher who prefers to theorise in virtues-language might claim that those who favour obligation-language must necessarily omit much that really belongs to morality, because all that truly belongs to morality cannot be stated straightforwardly as a set of obligations on anybody and everybody. Hauerwas and Pinches in 'Virtues Christianly Considered' take this view. And it is quite common to hear Christians say that they should not feel themselves to be subject to 'oughts', rules, norms. The great Kant, whose moral philosophy is so often summed up in the adage 'duty for duty's sake', if only because his is quite the most adamant resistance to acting morally for any ulterior purpose whatever, when he comes to consider what he calls 'the holy will', describes this precisely by the lack of any sense of ought, any sense of an imperative in its willing. Imperatives expressed as 'oughts' come into play only when misguided human wills are torn between their duty and some of the many ulterior motives which, in their fallen state, they find attractive. Hence, for the holy will, as Kant puts it, 'there are no imperatives: "I ought" is here out of place, because "I will" is already itself necessarily in harmony with the law. Imperatives are in consequence only formulae for expressing the relation of objective laws of willing to the subjective imperfections of this or that rational being – for example, of the human will.'[11] The more common Christian version of this preference for an end to the language of obligation takes the form of the advice to 'love and do what you will' – a highly irresponsible piece of advice, given that there are so many kinds of loving, including, of course, many ways of loving God, and some of them at least do more harm that good. Kant, to be fair, was more specific about the conditions under which he thought he could dispense with imperative terms.

The opening move in this chapter offered an elementary account of human morality in terms of distinction between good and evil accompanied by a sense of obligation. Now that we have argued the need for a distinctive account of human life as morality, we need a distinctively moral terminology, a set of linguistic or logical indicators which will let people know that it is human life in its moral aspect that is talked about. Of the terminology used in the opening account, good and evil are equally patient of moral and non-moral meaning, as are other pairs used to make the necessary distinction, such as right and wrong (a good apple or an evil eye, the right or the wrong key). It is not a good idea, therefore, to give up the language of 'ought' at this point; and yet it is necessary to see if its opponents have a point worth taking.

The arguments are confused and confusing, as is so often the case in ethical contexts, but, amongst the considerations which appear to be urged upon us by those who resent the language of obligation, the following at least are consistent and clear. The language of obligation appears to some to suggest the imposition upon the human will by some external source of the details of our moral behaviour. This might even happen on the Kantian account, for all Kant's wish to avoid heteronomy in morals, for the free (one might even say free-floating) rational will from which our duties derive can seem as external in Kant's philosophy to our empirical willing and doing, as the Platonic Forms did when some middle-Platonists lodged them securely as Ideas in the mind of God. Such imposition *ab externo*, it has been noted in another context, is calculated to reduce the moral status of the recipient agent. There are other versions of externality than those just mentioned: there are times when natural law theorists create the impression that the details of our moral behaviour are dictated by the physical or biological patterns of nature. The imposition in this case can be helped along by the veiled threat that nature interfered with will take its due revenge. The phrase, frequent in that tradition of natural law ethics, 'the law of God and of nature', merely compounds the sense of externality or heteronomy, and increases the anticipation of imposition by threat.

What is at the heart of this antagonism to the language of obligation? Is it perhaps the assumption that 'oughts' must always, and sooner rather than later, find their proper expressions in the promulgation of laws? Quite possibly. Consider the more specific objections made under this general heading. One objection, noted already, disputes the ability of 'ought' language to cover the whole of the moral life, on the grounds that there are some genuine moral commitments which cannot be made binding (by law presumably) on every member of a particular society, yet they represent no less a set of moral values for that; quite the contrary in fact. A larger objection focusses less upon the propensity, peculiar to laws, of affecting all potential subjects equally, and more upon the externality of the source, as already hinted; but again this appears to be a feature of promulgated laws: they do come from a source beyond the will of the individual moral agent, and in this, as well as in the suspicion that this source may well take steps to enforce what it has promulgated, lies some reason to suspect that they may be more conducive to the decline of truly moral living than to its genuine increase.

If this is right, if at the heart of the antagonism to the language of obligation is a suspicion of law, sometimes expressed as a rejection of legalism in morals, might one not imagine that one hears the rumblings of a return of the old debate about law and morality, of which the famous Devlin–Hart disputation was but one of the more memorable episodes?

Hart, it may be remembered, set out his case for the separation of law and morality by putting firmly to one side the questions he was not about to try to answer. First, the question, has the development of law been influenced by morals or, for that matter, the development of morals been influenced by law? Here the question concerns the material contribution which moral precepts may have made to promulgated laws of the land, and vice versa. Second, the question, must some reference to morality enter into an adequate definition of law or legal system? Here the issue is that discussed in the first chapter: government and its rule of law may tend towards the extreme of force unless its aim is towards a value, a good that is common and freely received as such. Third, the question, whether a particular legal ruling, validly arrived at and promulgated according to the constitution of the society, is open to moral criticism? It seems clear from a reading of Hart's argument that however one answers these questions, and even if one were to answer the third question in the affirmative (on the grounds, presumably, that some damage could be done, or was actually done to the moral fibre of the individual or of the society as a result of passing, however validly, a particular law), it could still be argued, as he does in fact go on to argue, that immorality as such ought not to be made a crime; in other words, one ought not to make morality as such into law.[12]

Lord Devlin, in the now famous Maccabean Lecture to the British Academy of 1958, had argued that the relationships which constitute a human society or, as he put it, the bonds which hold it together are, at least in part, made up of its common morality, and that that morality is therefore the business of the law, even to the point at which the criminal law can prosecute and punish breaches of that morality *as such*.[13] The practice of making morality into law in this manner constitutes, in Devlin's view, an essential part of the protection of society itself, and hence the protection of human beings, who can live and thrive only in society. Devlin refused to set any *a priori* limits on the extent to which the law could be used to embody in its own particular mode the morality of a particular people; and he refused also any facile distinction between public and private morality. He preferred to believe that morality could be said to have simultaneous individual and social implications, or a combination of these, and often perhaps a clash of public and private interests attached to it, but it could not itself be subdivided into public and private spheres.[14]

In Devlin's view of the matter none of this committed him to such conservatism as could outlaw in advance any changes to the moral principles and the laws of a given society, and certainly none of it committed him to the endorsement of majority opinion as arbiter of moral right (however quaint his reliance on the feeling of the ordinary Englishman may now seem to some who have experienced the full brunt of English justice). Further, though he would set no *a priori* limits to the legislation of morality, he never argued that the law should offer a comprehensive coverage of all moral beliefs adopted in any society, and he pleaded to the end that the real debate should centre on the range of extent of moral beliefs which should be made the business of the law; this rather than the increasingly sterile debate as to whether or not morality as such should be the business of the law.[15]

The advance thesis of Hart's attack upon this position contained the concession that one does indeed find in all social moralities such universal values as individual freedom, safety of life, and protection from deliberately inflicted harm. Yet Hart disputed Devlin's contention that even these values attracted the protection of the law precisely because of their moral status, and because morality was one of the necessary bonds of society without which people could not live. On the contrary, according to Hart, 'the preservation of any particular society is of value because, among other things, it secures for human beings some measure of these universal values'.[16] For a society in which those values went missing would be of no practical use; it would represent neither an empirical nor a logical possibility. From this rather nebulous distinction between himself and Devlin he argues that individual divergences in values other than these essential universal ones, must not be prohibited; and that all values including, one presumes, the essential universal ones, must be protected, as moral values, by means other than the coercive methods adopted by the law of the land. This in turn yields the position upon which Hart finally takes his stand, namely, that such universally essential features of social living as safety of life and protection from deliberately inflicted harm can, and must, be enforced by the law, but not as moral values. Presumably the other essential universal moral value mentioned by Hart, individual freedom, is secured precisely by not enforcing by law any more than the essential minimum already described under the other two values? Presumably also, the final reason why this minimum of universal essential values must be enforced, but not as moral values, is that, once the door is open to legislating moral value as such, it cannot easily be closed upon so few of them?

However that may be, Hart's position does seem to distil into the doctrine that the criminal law should be used only to protect others from harm to their persons or property. Devlin argues quite convincingly that the harm of which Hart speaks in this connection must be confined to bodily or physical harm if Hart's case is to succeed, for if the law could be seen to protect from moral harm also, or could be reasonably interpreted as doing this – as in protecting minors from corruption, for example – the contention that morality as such could not be the business of the law would have to fall.[17] Hart is indeed quite vulnerable on this point. But is he not even more vulnerable on a point which Devlin failed to take up, the point at which Hart himself describes protection from deliberately inflicted harm and safety of life as values which form an essential and universal part of social moralities? What can it possibly mean to say that a law is designed to enforce the moral value of my protection from harm, that its full force can be brought to bear on any who deliberately do me such harm, but that it is nevertheless not as a moral value that my safety from harm is thus secured?

It is in answering that question that the real strength of Hart's position appears, however much the question might seem at first sight to point to his Achilles' heel, and it is also in answering that question that the crucial difference between Hart and Devlin emerges, though neither of them proceeded to focus the issue in this precise manner. For Hart finishes up the argument of the section which deals in these essential and universal moral values by taking up again a topic which concerned him frequently in the course of his book, the topic of coercion. At this point Hart is concerned only to argue that his refusal, after Mill, to allow the coercion of which the law is capable to enforce the conventional morality of society, does not entail indifference to that morality or to any other. For, he rightly points out, there are other and more suitable ways of sustaining the whole social morality which, he agrees with Devlin, cements any society. Similarly, at an earlier point in the argument Hart had analysed the coercion involved in legal enforcement into its main constituent types, coercion by threat and coercion by actual punishment; and he had shown how coercion by threat would at most induce conformity, and actual punishment would add to a piece of wickedness performed a piece of evil unwillingly endured, two minuses attempting to make one plus. But in the first context he failed to apply this reasoning about coercion to the universal essential values, and in the second he excludes protection of people from infliction of harm, explicitly arguing that coercion in this case is good, even if it induces mere conformity out of fear – (whatever, in other words, might be the dispositions or motives of the ones thus induced to abstain). Further, although he had said, quite rightly concerning the case of actual punishment for breaches of the rest of society's morality, that two evils do not add up to one good, he seems to invert that judgment in the case of laws that prevent harm to others and secure the safety of all: for he suggests that it is the sight of the harm done to others that most commonly persuades us of the rightness of making those who inflict it suffer also, or at least of preventing them from enjoying life as a consequence of their actions.[18]

Now this can hardly be persuasive. Whatever good is done in the course of preventing people by threat from harming others, it cannot at any rate be moral good: for the threat in this case is as likely to induce conformity rather than a truly moral response, as it would be in the case of social moral values in general. And it is no more likely that two evils add up to one good in the case of punishing those who inflict actual harm, than it is in the case of punishing those who are found in breach of any other kind of rule or law.

In essence the celebrated debate between Devlin and Hart centred on one issue: should the law of the land, or should it

not, make morality as such its business? Devlin had clearly
said, yes; Hart then wished to say, no. Hart's strategy was to
find the forms of behaviour which the criminal law in particular prevented or protected, and which could not themselves
be described as moral goods (or evils). Had he succeeded, law
and morality could be deemed to be distinct and we, incidentally, would have before us one powerful and paradigmatic
case for the exclusion of law, itself the quintessential use of the
language of obligation, from the realm of morality. However, it
is difficult to avoid the conclusion that as long as the argument
was conducted in these terms, Devlin had the better of it;
Hart's own inclusion of safety of life and protection from
deliberately inflicted injury amongst the essential and universal values of social morality surely lost him his queen in this
particular game of chess.

And yet the tournament was not over. For even the most
casual observer would have noticed the prevalence of the
language of coercion on both sides of the question from the
beginning. The Maccabean Lecture from which it all began
was, after all, entitled 'The Enforcement of Morals', as was the
book with which Devlin sought to end it all, or at least to move
from conflict to co-operation. Hart, too, in his opening formulations of the divisive question, offered three versions of it, two
of which explicitly invoke enforcement, in name or in kind: 'Is
the fact that certain conduct is by common standards immoral
sufficient to justify making that conduct punishable by law? Is
it morally permissible to enforce morality as such?' Only the
third version of the question might be thought to overlook the
element of enforcement: 'ought immorality as such to be a
crime?' – but only if one ignored the way in which the law
defines a crime.[19]

In philosophical as in military matters it is far from idle to
speculate on how a particular campaign might have been
altered or might have been continued. If, in the present case for
example, the factor of enforcement by punishment or by the
threat of punishment had received the benefit of a more central
analysis and exposition, it is arguable that we should then see
the real strength of Hart's case, and the beginnings of an

answer to Devlin's final request for a reasoned decision on how much of human conduct could be made the business of the law. But even more than this, we should see such analysis of the nature of morality flowing from Hart's own contrast between truly moral behaviour and mere conformity as would really help us to situate properly in relation to each other morality, on the one hand and, on the other, laws promulgated in societies with whatever means of imposition any of these societies might wish to invoke. The campaign then might have been conducted or carried on along the following lines.

The principle invoked by Hart that the threat of extraneous punishment induces conformity rather than truly moral behaviour, and that this is undesirable for both the individuals and the societies concerned – provided this principle is generally invoked and not, as Hart appears to wish, invoked only for the rest of social morality after the essential values of safety and protection from harm have been subtracted – can imply that promulgated law, in the manner of its execution if not in its spirit, tends to reduce morality perhaps to vanishing point, that in that sense it cannot be said to make morality its business, and that it should therefore be restricted to as small an area of human behaviour as is compatible with the protection of society itself from violent destruction; thus acknowledging that societies are sustained on the whole by shared moral values to which, being moral values, people freely and willingly adhere, or are induced to adhere both willingly and freely. The extraneous nature of the punishment needs to be stressed. The term is used to denote a punishment inflicted in addition to the damage that may accrue from the very performance of the immoral act itself. The difference may be elaborated in this way: to point out to a moral agent the harmful effects intrinsic to the very action contemplated, however forcefully this is done, is in fact to enhance the operation of the agent's rational will and the element of real choice which is of the essence of morality, for it further informs the agent's mind on all the implications of the contemplated action. However, to threaten punishment additional to this, to threaten an extraneous evil, is to induce fear of another, to invoke an exercise of what in the final chapter was called force, and that is to threaten to oust morality from the event, at least as far as this agent is concerned.

Therefore it is the enforcement element attached to the law that ensures, but only in so far as it actually affects the subjects of the law, that the law is not concerned with morality as such. That would appear to be the truth that emerges from the Devlin–Hart debate, and it would prove each of them partly right. It would also yield a paradigmatic case of the correct account of the relationship between morality and the language of obligation, the standard linguistic forms of which occur in promulgated laws. Law does, and must always, make its business what would be morally right for people to do or to refrain from doing. That is always true of law, in any form of human society which proposes itself to be essential to human living. It is true of the laws of churches and of states – although it is not true necessarily of other inevitably rule-making voluntary societies such as tennis clubs. This is the part of the truth that Devlin protected so well on his side of the debate. Far from it being the case, then, that law and morality as such are incompatible, the law must seek to enshrine moral precepts as such. This must be taken to mean in turn that laws are a perfectly acceptable way of formulating morality. Indeed they probably provide an indispensable means of formulating morality at the social level at which human life is always lived.

Yet Hart has pointed up the fact that law habitually avails itself of a penal system as a means of enforcement, and he has pointed unerringly to the quite literally demoralising tendency of the apparatus of extraneous punishment and of its ever-present threat. Hence the pointedness of his question – whether or not he himself realised this, for the italics are not his – 'is it *morally* permissible to *enforce* morality as such?' If enforcement, as Hart often argues, is really incompatible with 'morality as such', then he must surely be right to answer 'no' to this question, and that is the part of the truth that he protected so well on his side of the debate. But then it is the means of enforcement, and not the law itself, which is inimical to morality as such, and the next question must surely be: is it, and when is it, morally right to enforce conformity to a law, knowing that the price to be paid is a possible reduction of human behaviour to an amoral level?

It is probably worth saying that the very promulgation of a law, even with threat of punishment for any breach of it, can perform that educative function in society which enhances freedom and morality. For there is nothing inherently objectionable about the idea that people who have little enough time, or little ability to think through the implications of many aspects of human behaviour, should be prepared to learn from those entrusted with legislative responsibilities, provided, of course, that their right of assessment on their own account continues to be respected. There is some point in saying that the penalty attached to a law can itself perform a part of that educative function – its weight can alert people to the seriousness of the moral obligation in question, for all moral obligations may be equally moral, but they are not equally serious. The point, in any case, is that laws promulgated with penalties threatened may perform functions other than exciting fear, and they may not inspire fear at all in a majority of people. The question then may be formulated: when is it morally permissible to promulgate laws with penalties and incur the risk by so doing of rendering some responses amoral?

The answer would appear to be that this may be done only in the case of behaviour which by threatening people's safety, be exposing their very lives to injury or danger, would threaten the very possibility of moral living itself. In these cases a society is surely morally justified in taking the risk of forcing amoral (but not immoral) behaviour, since the alternative is a threat to life or livelihood, or to its necessary means and supports, the essential physical basis of all moralities. To this might be added cases in which the morality of the young or otherwise vulnerable is corrupted, for here also there is a direct threat to morality as such, and a case for risking amoral conformity as an acceptable alternative. But the extension of laws-with-penalties beyond this basic area would not be justified, on both the grounds that the rest of social morality (i.e., over and above Hart's universal and essential social values) is a constantly developing, and not a static, entity, as we must see, and that the risk of reducing people to an amoral conformity has no similar justifying cause in these further cases.[20]

To return to the central theme of this section. The antagonism to the language of obligation cannot attach itself reasonably to the expectation that such language must sooner, rather than later, form itself into promulgated laws, for it has just emerged that there is no incompatibility between law and morality, but only between enforcement, or force and fear, and morality. Recourse to force and fear, therefore, is what those who place the highest value on moral living should abjure when at all possible; threats of extraneous punishments like prisons and hells is what they ought to avoid like plagues, but not the formulation of laws. It is, after all, the connection of force and its attendant fear with a common experience of law in human societies – mainly criminal law, one might add – that persuades people to keep such legislation to the essential minimum, and this in turn may be at the source of the impression, more often stated or assumed than it is analysed and defended, that law, the paradigmatic form of the language of ought, cannot really be made to manage a morality as extensive as a whole of human life. The fact of the matter is that, taken merely as a form of linguistic construction, once it ceases to trail behind it the fear of coercive punishment, the ought-language of law is as capable as any other linguistic form of doing just this. Human life is so infinitely variable in its experiences and responses that there would need to be as many ought-systems as there are people and each would need to be infinitely complex, if indeed it could ever be produced in final form.[21] But something similar would be true of any other linguistic form in which one tried to express at once the variety and comprehensiveness of moral lives. How many stories would one have to tell, and how many times modify them? And there remains the fact, as well known to parents of young children as to churches and states, that basic and essential moral values seem to need the clear and uncompromising expression of precept, even if they do not need the attendant threats for non-compliance.

But what of the larger source of antagonism to law with its characteristic categorisation of oughts and ought-nots, thou shalt and thou shalt not? What of the source of antagonism to the language of ought which stems from the suspicion that, with respect of all ordinary human life and the everyday world in which it is lived, the formulated obligations are themselves extraneous? Do the precepts, the moral imperatives, our stated and defined duties, come into and upon our ordinary world from some source outside of it, are they imposed upon life rather than emergent from it, much less identical with it? The spectre of Williams' morality as a peculiar institution that we would be better off without, is not so easily exorcised.

The sense of the adventitious nature of moral duties with respect, that is, to ordinary life, derives from many different contexts. It is most obviously present when the moral duties are described literally as the will of God. Kant is the most determined opponent of this form of heteronomy. He considered, and criticised, the two forms of 'the theological conception which derives morality from a divine absolutely perfect will':

because we have no intuition of the divine perfection and can only deduce it from our own conception, the most important of which is that of morality ... our explanation would ... be involved in a gross circle; and, in the next place, if we avoid this, the only notion of the divine will remaining to us is a conception made up of attributes of desire of glory and dominion, combined with the awful conceptions of might and vengeance, and any system of morals erected on this foundation would be directly opposed to morality.[22]

Kant is correct on both scores: on the second, on the issue of force and punishment, we are already convinced. But even if, on the first, God could be conceived to keep up the continuous moral advice which alone could clarify the details of our moral duties in the ever-changing circumstances of life and history, we should still be conformists rather than moral agents. The only escape from conformity would be to do something (that God commands) because we ourselves chose it as our good, with some of our own reasons for so choosing, and then we should be judges of moral good in the same way, though not of course to the same degree, as God is. There is no human morality whatever, and human life is mere mindless conformity, where the human rational will is not active in the pursuit and discernment of value.

But when Kant himself sought the source of moral imperatives, he looked towards a free rational will that seemed in the end as vague in our concrete experience as the always difficult to discern will of God. And since Kant – and Iris Murdoch is right about this – is the single greatest influence on all subsequent moral philosophy in the West, it would not be surprising to find in many other quarters an equally nebulous impression of the source of our moral duties. To take but one example, Moore's famous adage about not deriving an 'ought' from an 'is', however defensible on the grounds that no empirical description of the way things actually are can of itself and without more ado yield an implication as to how they ought to be, nevertheless did leave the source of obligations adrift in some unspecified will, and the obligations themselves seemingly bereft of verifiable content. So morality seemed relegated to a shadowy world, away from the world of empirical fact, attached somehow to a will; 'a shadow', in Iris Murdoch's pithy phrase, 'clinging to a shadow'.[23]

One can vindicate law as morality. One can reject coercion, force and fear, and conformity, yet leave intact the initial phenomenological account of morality with its reference to the sense of obligation and the consequent validity of ought-language. But can one then give an account of what the opening description called the objectivity of moral distinctions, of their origin and place in the real world of our daily experience, without creating further impressions of heteronomy or of shadows? The suggestion to be made here is that one can do so if, rather than regretting the language of obligation, one analyses the phenomenon expressed by 'ought' and places it at the very centre of a philosophy of human morality.

THE GENESIS OF MORAL VALUES

It might be said of Iris Murdoch herself that she was not altogether successful in giving to moral discourse a form of epistemological realism, a modicum of transcendence of the subjective realm where it too often declines into a shade. She tries to abjure the false transcendence of these nebulous wills imposing moral obligations from some vantage point beyond the empirical realities of life, and yet to seek in moral good an escape from ethical (emotional) solipsism, an escape to a vision of reality as it really and palpably is. Oddly enough, given the title of the book, *The Sovereignty of Good*, she fails to find this transcendence and realism in dealing with the concept of the good as such, which she insists on leaving indefinable, non-representable, 'invisible', and so instead of the good she looks to beauty, while declaring at one point that she is not sure if this is 'an analogy or an instance' of the good.[24] In more concrete language this would mean that art is the analogy or the instance that could show us moral goodness (and moral evil?) in the realist and transcendent terms that Iris Murdoch rightly requires; morality in the very warp and woof of life itself and yet exercising a kind of authority over life. So she takes art as her instance throughout the book, and since Plato is her guide it surely is an instance rather than an analogy. The artist is the paradigmatic instance of the moral person, then? Most likely so. But in order to construct an account of the anatomy of morals in this way, it is necessary to go back again to the beginning, and perhaps necessary to go back once more to Plato.

Take a text from Plato like a scripture, and consider the rest of this chapter a commentary on it.

This reality that gives their truth to the objects of knowledge and the power of knowing to the knower, you must say is the idea of the good, and you must conceive it as being the cause of knowledge and of truth, in so far as known. Yet beautiful as knowledge and truth are, you must think of the good being more beautiful than either of these.

This passage goes on to say, in a sentence that has had a truly incalculable influence upon the development of properly theological thought: 'the good itself is not being, but is beyond being (*epekeina tes ousias*) and superior to it in dignity and power',[25] but this is not of such immediate concern for present purposes. What is of immediate concern is the first impact of the previous passage, the impression which it conveys that the good is the cause both of truth and of our knowledge of truth, such as it is, and that beauty, and degrees of beauty, somehow supply the marker-dye by which we can detect both goodness and truth. What sense can be made of such a radical and intriguing suggestion? And how can it help to outline the anatomy of morals?

If moral duties are to be seen to arise within human life itself in the world of our experience, if they are not to seem rather shadowy entities somehow emerging from an equally shadowy source, then both elements in the opening elementary account of human morality – the knowledge of good and evil, and the sense of the obligation to do good and avoid evil – must be seen to simultaneously characterise all ordinary human life (at least) and the ordinary world in which it is lived. It cannot be that we should first have a description of human life in this concrete world, a description entirely construed in terms of Moore's 'is', a description which could be thought at some point to be complete in itself, on which we should then super-impose a set of moral obligations.

To put the point in alternative terms: of the twin elements in the opening elementary account of morality, it is the freedom-respecting obligation to do good and avoid evil that makes what might otherwise seem a purely cognitive element, the distinction between good and evil, of one piece with morality, rather than just an additional piece of knowledge as infor-mation. The two elements are then neither separate nor separ-able. The *sense* of obligation contributes as much to the know-ledge of what is morally good and morally evil as the discriminatory power hinted at in that phrase 'knowing good and evil' contributes to the sense of obligation. If we could describe this complex but unified operation of being 'obliged' towards, bound for, as sailors might say, what we could then detect in this very process as being morally good – obligation, it must be remembered, is not determination, it leaves freedom intact – and of being obliged away, from bound away from, what we could detect in this very process as being morally evil, then we should have a description of moral obligation in its

broadest reaches which could well do duty for a moral description of human living in this world. For the sense of obligation,
after all, is itself an empirical datum; the phrase denotes an
awareness of being driven towards the achievement or acqui-
sition of that which we in the process discern to be good for us,
thus making it morally good for us. It names a kind of impulse,
a drive or power (what Plato named Eros), evoking and
uniting with a power of discernment as its necessary adjunct
and instrument.

Looked at in this way morality, on the most elementary
account of it, is a way of living. It is life itself looked at from a
particular perspective, the moral perspective from which life
itself in this empirical world, and the world itself in so far as it is
a human or personal creation, is a driven but discerning
pursuit of goodness. This is the truth that is contained in the
work of those recent moralists who were consulted a little
earlier: not that we should prefer to speak of life rather than
morality, but that we should discover how best to speak of
morality as life itself in one of its primary aspects; and not that
we should abjure the language of obligation, but that we
should so discern the nature of obligation as to see in it a
fundamental factor in the business of living and the very factor
that makes living moral.

Looked at in this way morality, even on the most elementary
account of it, is also a way of knowing our world. To be bound
for or to be bound to what will be good; to be bound to this in a
discerning mode, to be always actively involved in bringing
about what we hope will be a better world – that is clearly a
process of getting to know one's self and one's world. Indeed
this may represent our most basic means of knowing and our
most foundational knowledge of the world, compared to which
other forms of knowing, other contents of knowledge, may well
be ancillary, if not perhaps even peripheral. At this point
something of the sense of Plato's contention that the good is the
source of truth and of such knowledge as we may possess begins
to come across. But for the moment it is only necessary to
remark that what now begins to emerge is no less than a kind of
theory of truth itself, that is reminiscent of a variety of modern

philosophies. Marx stated it as follows in his *Theses on Feuerbach*: 'man must prove the truth ... of his thinking in practice. The dispute over the reality or non-reality of thinking that is isolated from practice is a purely scholastic question.' Gilbert Ryle stated another version of it in his presidential address to the Aristotelian Society (1945–6), when he claimed that 'knowledge how' is a concept prior to 'knowledge that'. Knowing-how is taught and learned by doing things, just as practice is a matter of doing things also, and morality is all about doing things as creatively as possible. Being bound to do good and avoid evil, and so doing and avoiding, that is morality. If knowledge and its verification as truth is a matter of doing in some inevitable sense, as Marx and Ryle from their very different perspectives both suggest, and if all our doing is to be located in the realm of morality, as those who equiparate morality and life itself were seen to insist, then it follows rather clearly that morality is indeed the basic way to knowledge and truth, and the first part of Plato's odd paragraph is fully borne out.

It would not be possible to plot here, even in the broadest outline, the alternative epistemology which takes 'knowing-how' to be prior to 'knowing that', much less to pass in review all the many philosophies in which this thesis, or something very like it, has appeared under so many beguiling forms.[26] It is only necessary to remember that 'knowing-how' is a matter of doing, and doing in turn, at least in the case of the principal agents of whom we are cognisant in this world, is a moral matter. From this there flow a number of consequences of some importance in the present context.

First, on the very broadest canvas the world appears to be a vast and complex vista of events which give rise to the things we know, including these things we call ourselves, and which we know moreover only in the process of interacting with them; this rather than appear as a world of constituted things, which we come to know in a rather more contemplative mode, and then decide somehow what to do with, or to, or about, much as we might rather incidentally notice what so many of these things are already doing to, or with, or about each other. So does the world now seem, from the original Big Bang, as largely general in its all-originating role as it proves incredibly specific in evolving the determinate quantities of particles and their interactions – the very thought of its awesome and continuous creative turmoil makes one wish for the seventh day and God's rest. The corresponding microcosmic scheme is well caught from each individual's point of view in Gerard Manley Hopkins lines from *Inversnaid*:

> Each mortal thing does one thing and the same:
> Deals out that being indoors each one dwells;
> Selves – goes itself; *myself* it speaks and spells,
> Crying *what I do is me: for that I came.*

Second, an account of reality cast primarily in terms of act and action, of event seems always to require an image or idea of a prime mover, not in the sense of the first cause in a chain of agents, but in the sense of some immanent power setting and keeping the whole in motion, driving or drawing it all in all of its vast and variegated range as well as in its local and individual endeavours. This is the place of the Platonic Eros, a fundamental image in the whole of Plato's philosophy, but to which he specifically devoted *The Symposium*.[27] It is not easy to translate 'Eros' or to give in a short space any adequate account of its general nature. It can be translated 'love', but it must not then be divided against itself, as erotic rather than agapeic love, for example. It can be translated 'desire', but its universal range would then carry it far beyond the borders of the psychological, within which desire is normally known. It seems to be an idea or image as necessary to a certain view of 'reality as process' as it is difficult to define; and it is as inevitably anthropomorphic as any other of our key ideas and images of the real.

It is its anthropic form that concerns us most at the moment; for its explanatory role in the anatomy of morals, and more particularly the light it can throw upon the sense of obligation. Put simply if, one hopes, not too simplistically, Eros in the human form is what humans sense as moral obligation. In all its felt and hinted forms – and it goes no doubt by many names, from the survival instinct to the ambition of Icarus – it is that which drives or attracts (not different powers these, but different appearances of the same power in a spatio-temporal continuum), it is that which binds (and gives the word 'obligation' from *ligare* in Latin), binds us to all that we may then will and maybe do and be. But it binds us as the indeterminate beings that we are, and not as it might bind other beings; so that if our awareness of Eros is our sense of obligation, it is simultaneously our sense of what we call our freedom. This indeterminacy, too, is manifold in its manifestation. At the bio-evolutionary level it is manifest as a certain lack of specialisation of the organs, attributes, and various appendages of *homo sapiens*, so that the latter is not confined to any particular ecological niche, but is relatively superior to other species in powers of adaptation and adaptibility; at the psychic level, it is manifest as reflexive consciousness which, by managing to make an object of its own self can then make an object of every other thing, and in the abstraction and distance from them so gained can compare and contrast them, and substitute symbols for them, and so talk and communicate, discuss and decide, and, in the dark hole which that distancing opens up, contemplate the annihilation of all, and even of self, face death in short, and so give to the binding felt, to any thing or any self, a profound pathos.

To approach the matter from the human awareness of Eros, from the human sense of obligation, is to open up the prospect of a positive and fulsome account of human freedom, which must otherwise seem negative and jejune. For on this approach it is the idea of creativity that comes to the fore: Eros, the power of obligation, driving this distinctive yet indeterminate being to keep going on and to make itself whatever it can then imagine in the rather more determinate world which in this very process it comes to know, and comes to refashion in its own imagined image. Outwith this understanding of the sense of obligation, freedom becomes as shadowy as the will and its obligation were, in Iris Murdoch's phrase, in a moral theory which sought both of those outside (or hidden somehow on the inside or other side of) the concrete and comprehensive phenomenon of human living in the world of 'is'; or, as she puts the matter in another happy phrase: 'The agent, thin as a needle, appears in the quick flash of a choosing will.'[28] Freedom, in other words, is otherwise patient of only a predominantly negative description in which it is barely distinguishable from randomness,[29] and characterised largely by absence of countervailing influences such as those of force, fear, and passion. And it makes all reference to obligation look like a form of enforcement, and seems to justify those who resent its use in moral theory.

The focus on creativity, to which the analysis of moral obligation as Eros leads, sets in relief in turn the relevance of Plato's, and Iris Murdoch's, recourse to the idea of beauty, and the relevance of the reference to art. Beauty is a matter of form, a question of pattern, order, or internal finality, as Kant might say. But, as Kant would also insist, in the *Critique of Judgment*, it is, as distinct from the pattern or finality in nature which the scientist seeks and believes can be found, a pattern and a finality created by the imagination of the artist within the relevant creation. Therefore those who believe in God represent the universe as just such a creation of order out of chaos,[30] and represent the scientist as the discerning admirer lost in contemplation of the masterpiece. And those believed to be themselves made in the image of God, and who are thus also under the impulse of Eros, create in their lives, and at least in those parts of the world touched by their lives, that internal finality, that order and pattern which is their part of the beauty of being. How each is enabled to envisage the beauty to be created is a question which may be postponed for the moment, until some other questions are answered: namely, is every human agent an artist, then? And is morality art?

The short answer to both questions is, yes. As Plato in the *Symposium* remarked that some were called poets particularly, but only by conventional restriction of a term that applies to all art; as Ricoeur showed in *The Rule of Metaphor* that every sentence consists in a combination and tension of terms, in which they focus each other's indeterminate range of reference and thus release meaning, but the poet manages this to quite a new and revealing degree; so everyone is an artist engaged in creation, the creation of beauty, but the ones we call artists are the inspiring leaders in this active and universal enterprise. To say that *goodness* is what our sensed obligation, our sometimes quite conscious Eros, aims at and drives or lures us towards, can tend to be somewhat tautological and that is precisely why the image or idea of Beauty is pressed into service in order to provide criterion and context.

One can scarcely create much more than a crude impression in this context of the distance one has to travel in order to escape from Moore's 'no ought from an is', and to find the spring of morality at the heart of reality, at the very centre of life. Nothing short of a fully alternative epistemology would suffice, along the lines so long ago drawn by Plato in that paragraph already quoted. It would begin with Eros, no more at first, perhaps, than a name for human being itself in its need and desire to be, and to continue to be (for its self-reflective consciousness can sense its death), to live and to live more fully. This conscious Eros, this sense of obligation, thrusting and enticing to action, to being (the *actus purus* of the Medievals), and to all the more characteristic actions that flow from and enhance being, is itself a heuristic device. For in the profligate thrusting of activity, which is called life, and which it instigates and to some extent directs (for it is the Eros of an entity with some distinctive structure, despite its unspecialised status,[31]) – first the play, the preparation, the practice game, the trial, then the real thing – lies the simultaneous discovery and establishment of truth and falsehood, good and evil. The elements of the opening, elementary account of morality really do not fall apart, any more than does knowing good and evil separate itself from knowing things. Reacting and acting, this conscious and reflective thing, simultaneously erotic and discerning, attains in the very furtherance of its well-being, and even in its failure to further its well-being, all the knowledge it will ever be able to take as truth (Plato's 'in so far as known'). All knowledge in origin and essence is the knowledge of good and evil, the knowledge which, according to the Genesis myth, the first parents of the race sought in paradise. But this account of it does not make knowledge either solipsistic or static.

The first thing that the Eros-driven quester, the lover of *sophia*, the philosopher discovers is that its well-being is bound up with that of all others, so that knowing them in this interactive fashion requires the discovery and the maintenance of their integrity; knowing, always a moral enterprise, must undergo the discipline of the real in order to reach fulfilment, or suffer the consequences of phantasising. It is this fact that gives to 'knowing-that' the quasi-independent status we seek for it in referring to the need for objectivity, and in seeking to ward off the distorting effects of the selfish desire for short-term pragmatic relevance. It is this fact also which gives permanent importance to the natural law tradition of ethical theory, a theory which stresses the need for the closest attention to the given contours of reality. The second thing that the Eros-driven quester discovers is that the openness and indeterminacy of its kind requires it to be creative. Neither words nor things, neither events nor absences, are pre-selected or pre-arranged for people in any absolute way by genes or instincts. And in that creativity lies their freedom and the final essence of their morality. Of course their creativity may be stunted by those who would force conformity on them by injury or threat thereof, or by more subtle psychological means, but this would represent the stunting of their moral obligation rather than its release, and there are other factors of which this could be said, which any standard textbook of ethics could enumerate.

The endemic creativity of human life points unerringly to imagination as the highest human faculty of truth, and to art as both its commonest and its highest expression. Those who rightly resent the conclusion which now seems to emerge, that truth is as much made as it is discovered – like those who rightly reject the cruder forms of pragmatism on the grounds that truth could be forced by those who could bring events or situations into being willy-nilly – are thinking of fabrication rather than creation, for creation respects the integrity of the material it works just as much as it reaches for interactions, relations, and forms which have never been before.

How is morality learned and how is it taught? It would be possible to begin the answer to that question at the more exotic end, to speak of intimations or even visions of Beauty in differing forms that people do actually have, and that do draw from them lives of dedication, and at times lives of greatness, which in turn inspire countless others. For Beauty in its transcendant mode can and does appear in the most ordinary of mortal things. Dante saw the vision of the young Beatrice Portinari, and its affective power was sufficient to carry him through hell and purgatory to the *Paradiso* on the wings of some of the greatest poetry ever written. But he was a poet. Patrick Pearse saw it somehow in the messy history and the current suffering of his own country, of a colonised Ireland in the opening decades of this century, and for him it took the form of the vision of a sovereign nation of free people contributing to a world of sovereign nations their own distinctive culture and service. And he was just a schoolteacher. Yeats, however, was there to see and to tell how terrible such Beauty can be as the vision of it reaches such absolute status. In his commemoration of Pearse's rebellion, *Easter 1916*, he marvels at how such ordinary men as those he had saluted so perfunctorily on the streets of Dublin, had been 'changed, changed utterly', so that 'a terrible beauty is born'. But then he had noted too, in his attention to the beauty of Helen of Troy, the propensity of such absolute perfection for the bringing about of the final sacrifice of some and the utter destruction of others: in *Leda and the Swan*, his poem on the conception of Helen when Zeus comes on Leda as a swan ('the brute blood of the air') he has the lines:

> A shudder in the loins engenders there
> The broken wall, the burning roof and tower
> and Agamemnon dead.

Beauty does certainly appear to otherwise quite ordinary individuals in the midst of otherwise quite ordinary lives, and in different forms it does approach the status of an absolute; but absolutes are better left until later, in books as well as in life, for, since absolutes essentially partake of the nature of the divine, they are lords of death as well as life. One has to learn to die before having any dealings with them, and that in turn can be done only by learning in certain ways how to live.

The more general answer to the question about learning to be moral, then, would take up again some passing reference to games and to imitation, and develop these perhaps in theories of story-telling and the example of good lives. Professional moralists have taken to the story with gusto in recent times; and none with more gusto than Christian moralists and Christian theologians in general. Such has been the enthusiasm that some, who could not tell a decent story to save their lives, have failed to be persuaded that the best service they could render to this newly discovered enterprise is to cease to write about it at such length in the tortuous anti-style of Teutonic prose. The 'showing' of Christian lives – which incidentally is the substantial motivation behind the otherwise questionable Catholic commitment to canonisation – the power of example which is scarcely ever absent in some degree in any human life, the more artistic mimesis of all of this in stories and novels, and perhaps predominantly in the theatre, all of this can easily illustrate the general answer to the question as to how morality is taught and learned. But two points, in the nature of caveats, must be made.

First, neither the exemplary life nor the novel, nor the play, can be taken as invitations to conform. Even from the point of view of art, the didactic novel is the poorer for being didactic. It was put as an objection to legislation that since it sought to impose the will of another, whether of God or some human power, even if on occasion it did not do this by treat of punishment for non-observance of the law, it would nevertheless tend to diminish rather than procure the morality of its subjects, and would make of them mere conformists. The same objection would naturally apply then to these preferred forms if conformity remained the intention behind them. But if in life and in art – and every life is really an art form, however flawed – they serve to illustrate, that is, to enlighten and to inspire that creative process by which each individual Eros seeks to image forth its own life in all the inevitable responsibility of its growing, creative freedom, then morality is indeed being taught, and learned.

Second, however, the preference for 'showing' lives and

telling stories, for writing and performing plays, must not be allowed to overshadow entirely that more prosaic contribution to the teaching of morality which takes the form of making rules and laying down laws, in short, codifying human conduct. With these forms the risk of conformity is very high, with the concomitant loss of that creativity and freedom in which the essence of individual morality is most surely found; and the risk is highest of all where threat of punishment is added in order to induce fear and force compliance. Yet it has been argued already that this humble contribution must also be allowed. The law may be an ass, but in rough terrain and for more menial tasks an ass may prove more useful than many a more sophisticated means of making progress. The penal enforcement of some laws, it has been noted, can be a moral option in essential societies, even though that threatens the very possibility of a moral response, on the grounds that only by such means in some cases can the conditions be secured upon which the future growth of any moral harvest may depend. Parents know this as well as do the elected guardians of states. For the rest rule-making, even without extrinsic sanction, is justified on the same grounds as the imaginative in general is thought to require the occasional, perhaps frequent, and maybe even constant, aid of the analytic. As people can be taught to analyse poems without replacing them with, or reducing them to, the inevitably more abstract and general definitions or concepts with which analysis works, and as this may be thought a help to the reception of the full imaginative impact of the poem, so moral lives, whether fictional or fact, can have their impact enhanced by the presence and the focus of general moral definitions, the conceptual analysis which these employ, and the generally directive propositions in which they can be crystallised.

So, in answer to the question, how is morality learned and taught?, one can mention the great symbolic ideals of Beauty, Truth, Justice, Freedom ... which do appear to people, always seething with the hidden and awful power of the absolute; one can mention lives and stories and plays and their power to draw the individual Eros towards some concrete goals, and to repulse it from others; and one can mention the more prosaic rules, the beginners' kit for would-be creators; those three. There are palpable dangers with the first and third of them, more hidden seductions perhaps with the second; and so all three may be simultaneously required. But there is a still more practical answer to the question – and, after all, morality is a most practical matter – and it is at this stage that the contribution of Alasdair MacIntyre comes most properly into its own.

One often gets the impression from commentators on MacIntyre's work that the focal point of that work consists in his preference for communities over isolated individuals as the necessary context for moral formation and the moral quest. It is not an accident that this impression is given by Christian commentators so enamoured of the very idea of *koinonia* that they talk as if the primary purpose of the Christian faith were to create community; hence the very fact of being a Christian community, rather than, one must suppose, a poor isolated Christian, would somehow give assurance of moral progress or at least moral rectitude, an assurance otherwise bound to be lacking. This is often done while explicitly acknowledging the fact that Christian communities differ within themselves and amongst themselves and are frequently unfaithful, sometimes quite seriously unfaithful, to the moral values they are supposed to represent.[32] The lack of fit between the thesis and the admission of failure is presumably thought to be overcome by some implicit conviction of God's special presence to the Christian community – but this, of course, is just what moral terms prevent one from simply assuming. For it makes as little sense to say that a community represents moral values by which it does not live, as it does to say that God can be trusted to keep these values in a community in which they may not be presently detectable. In any case, it would make as much, or as little, sense to say that kind of thing of an individual as of a community. Moralities and communities come about simultaneously and by the same processes of interaction: it is neither communities in contrast to individuals nor individuals in contrast to communities that create morality.

Now of course MacIntyre, especially in *After Virtue*,[33] excoriates moral individualism, and insists upon the formative role of tradition-bearing communities upon the development of human morality. But what he excoriates in moral individualism is not the individuality of the moral agent so much as the rationalist criteria on which recent moralists have operated: the criteria of reason and truth in the rationalist age were universal, impersonal, and objective. Kant's main moral maxim provides a perfect example: act only upon that maxim which you can at the same time agree to be a maxim for all rational agents. Now that is not the moral stance of an individualist, in any moral understanding of that term. It has the totality of moral agents in view, the community of persons, the kingdom of ends, as Kant would say. But it, and similar moral criteria of the rationalist age, do suggest that we learn and teach morality by arriving, much as the scientist is supposed to do in his discipline, at the universally valid laws of human behaviour; and, like any other rational quest, this one too can be accomplished by any individual endowed with reason, provided only that reason is used effectively and people do not rest satisfied with unanalysed and unsupported opinions passed on by the ignorant to the gullible.

The real thrust of MacIntyre's work became most clear in the course of his Gifford Lectures at the University of Edinburgh,[34] and especially when he described morality as a *technē* (in Greek), an *ars* (in medieval Latin). He noted the place, in Aristotle in particular, of *orexis* (desire), or better *prohairesis* (desire guided by reason) – versions no doubts of what here has been called Eros. He comments upon the commitment which these require, but adds to this immediately the need for initiation. How and by whom? Well, since we are talking of a *technē* here, by a master craftsman, an artisan – remember that for Aristotle the criterion of prudence was in the end the prudent man. So, summing up the Greek view of the matter, MacIntyre writes, 'it is by the ability to teach others how to learn this type of knowing-how that the power of the master within the community of a craft is legitimated as rational authority'.[35] It is correspondingly the role of those most adept at 'knowing-how' to live good lives, and capable of forming the apprentices of each new generation, that gives the practical answer to the question as to how morality is taught and learned.

This turn to a practical answer to the question about teaching and learning morality brings back to mind the interpersonal dimension already examined in the anatomy of power, and the consequent possibility that one person's authority may prove to be another person's force and the diminution, or the death of morality for that one. Little can be added on this point in this particular context – although it will be worth returning to the matter in more detail later – but perhaps two preliminary notes can be entered. First, references to *technē* and *ars* may themselves be taken to suggest that the interpersonal relationships here envisaged are construed from proven ability or expertise on the one side, willing apprenticeship on the other, and that initiation rather than raw instruction is the model in mind. Second, and particularly in view of the fact that morality is not compartmentalised, but covers the whole of human living, the able ones envisaged in this context are to be found in every part of every human society, in all the trades and crafts and professions, in every walk of life; for all go to the pursuit of life and of life more abundant, and all are equally intrinsically moral enterprises. The most general role of master-craftsman belongs to every parent and, put into praxis, it forms the family. In the wider society the role can belong not only to the charismatic or elected leaders of the whole society who are entrusted by office with the business of legislating, judging, and executing, but also to the proven experts and leaders in all the myriad ways of 'making a living' or making life in this world. Together they fashion a community into a creative source for the moral formation of all its subjects, for they know how to link past and future, how to direct the traditional training, the practical wisdom they have received, towards new and unexpected ways of reaching the ultimate *telos* of this essential human craft. It is this process, finally, involving each individual in his or her own changing role, that fashions communities into the character-forming, virtue-laden entities that they then become.

Nor is the theorising, the conceptualising element, ever entirely absent from this communal tradition-making. Of Plato, Aristotle, and Aquinas MacIntyre writes:

For them, of course, every moral agent, no matter how plain a person, is at least an incipient theorist, and the practical knowledge of the mature good person has a critical theoretical component; it is for this reason that both Aristotle and Aquinas agree that we should study philosophical ethics, not only for the sake of theoretical goods, but so as ourselves to become good.[36]

And, as in every other *technē*, there are some who become particularly, though not exclusively, expert in the philosophy of morals, and who make of this their distinctive contribution to the goal of all humanity.

MacIntyre, finally, suggests that Aristotle needed a *telos* which related the soul to something outside itself and beyond the world; otherwise we should be faced, he thinks, with a Hobbesian 'perpetuall and restless desire of power after power, that ceaseth only in death'.[37] He believes also that Aristotle needed the Christian conviction of the human inability, without outside help, to keep evil at bay. He believes equally, however, that Christians need Aristotle: 'take away or reject the Aristotelianism in the Thomist account, but leave the despair of moral achievement and the gratuitousness of grace, and what is foreshadowed is Luther',[38] and in the end, perhaps, the utter exclusiveness of Christian morality which, as was argued above, may issue in no morality at all? The questions now arising concern the relationship of morality to religion, or the secular to the sacred, and, for Christians in particular, the question as to whether there is such a thing as a Christian morality.

POWER AND MORALITY: AN INTERIM CONCLUSION

There has been a significant overlap in the descriptions of the anatomy respectively of power and morality over the course of these two chapters: they are not necessarily at odds with each other, as had been hinted at the very outset. The overlap occurs at that end of the range of manifestations of power at which it takes the form of authority. An exercise of power in the form of authority, in short, is a passage in morality.

The overlap is perhaps not quite so easy to detect, and its implications for both power and morality not quite so easily drawn, when people persist in thinking of morality primarily, if not exclusively, as that which is embedded in codes of law, and in those grandiose abstractions which we call moral ideals and name as Truth, Justice, Freedom, and so on; even if we do think of both laws and ideals as operative entities with respect to human behaviour, and not as theoretical entities confined to the appropriate texts. On the other hand, the overlap is easy to detect and its implications more easily drawn when morality is viewed from the actual process of the genesis of moral values. It is probably as difficult to describe this genesis as it is to define moral value.

But say for the sake of argument that moral value is not to be defined primarily by either laws or named ideals, although both of these will find a role in the genesis of moral value; say instead that moral values are to be defined as actual states of affairs, brought about, or to be brought about, by the free creativity of moral agents in pursuit of their well-being. Then, at the very least, moral values will appear as concrete realities, actualities, persons and things seen for what they are, namely, agents in continual and mutual active relationships, by which they maintain and further their very existence. The 'no ought from an is' adage, beloved of some moral philosophers, must be treated with great caution. It can only mean that if one issues a value-free description of some state of affairs in the world – and it has been conceded that this can of course be done, for to say that morality is co-extensive with at least human life is not to say that life and the world cannot also be described in non-moral (physical, biological) terms – one cannot deduce an 'ought' directly and without more ado from this. One can in addition gain guidance from value-free descriptions, but even that does not result automatically in a moral imperative.

It may well be true, as has been claimed, that for humans this process of coming to know reality always involves activity, doing, agency, and hence human initiative, creativity, choice; in short, morality in practice. But that process can begin and end in awareness of the way things are, in short, in some value-free descriptions. To these, as long as they remain so, the adage 'no ought from an is' applies. But that is all that can be said for the adage. It would be a mistake to conclude that 'oughts', moral values, are not also 'is's'; persons and things in active relationships embody values, *are* values, in so far as the states of affairs are brought about by, maintained, adapted or allowed by these moral agents. This act of composition in which I am now engaged, and the whole set of relationships with publisher, students, readers, which it sets in motion, is at once an 'is' (or partly a 'will be') and an 'ought', a value (or at least, if I get it wrong, a disvalue). The tongue-lashing I just delivered to my son for apparent failure to reach a higher academic standard, and the relationship that now exists between us, are no doubt more of a disvalue.

The general idea that moral values are first and foremost actual states of affairs comes easier to a metaphysic which, instead of seeing reality made up of discrete entities or substances than rather accidentally acting upon and relating to each other, sees reality as a set of active relationships, a process in essence, which crystallises into and then around individual centres of agency, and does so increasingly as these individuals are themselves more highly centred in highly centralised nervous systems and brains and their accompanying reflective consciousness. From this perspective it is easier to understand how states of affairs which make up our empirical world, in so far as they are affected, created, modified, accepted, allowed by personal agents, are moral values and furnish the primary denotation of that term. (And if the whole of reality is created by a personal God who exercises minute providence within it, all states of affairs that make up reality are moral values or disvalues.) No doubt moral values in this primary denotation, created and appreciated as such, can be codified for purposes of communicating them to others (do not speak sarcastically and dismissively of your son's efforts); and they can be generalised by means of general nouns designed to denote truth, justice, fairness, and so on, and to draw attention to such aspects of concrete active relationships or states of affairs. But these codes and named ideals are then secondary expressions of moral value, and not their primary instances. Moral values are generated in the very process of bringing about the states of affairs that make up reality. If an 'ought' cannot be derived from an 'is' in the restricted sense of our adage, it certainly does not follow that an 'is' cannot derive from an 'ought' and continue to embody it in the world. To point to moral values is to point to process-realities that exist. So the account of the genesis of moral value coincides with an account of a certain kind (creative, person-originated) of genesis of life and of other existences.

The recent work of some developmental psychologists, provides remarkable confirmation of this view of the genesis and primary nature of moral value; as well as confirmation of much else that has been said above: for example, the coincidence of the genesis of morals with the genesis of community (or inter-subjectivity), and the innate role of driving emotions (or pre-conceptualised motivations) of the kind generally characterised above as Eros, in this process. Because this recent work concentrates on infancy; because it studies the human being from the moment of birth (and in some respects before birth), it is of the utmost relevance to an account of the *genesis* of morality. It is even remarkable for the manner in which it foreshadows the belief that codes and general nouns are derivative and ancillary forms or morality. For these, since Kant especially, are characterised as rational principles, i.e. regularities arrived at by reason, which records patterns of actions, catalogues their effects, and thus arrives at guidelines for future human action which individuals can then be asked (and in some cases forced) to adopt, if only in order that human communities could live in peace and co-operate towards progress.

Now the recent work in developmental psychology does make to seem derivative and ancillary those rational and putatively universal principles and precepts; and not least when it criticises the older standpoint of the empiricist tradition in developmental psychology. According to this older standpoint, 'The human newborn is inferred to be a disconnected, irrational and amoral bundle of biological reflexes, open, somehow, to be trained in the ways of society by the intelligent, selective behaviour of adults.'[39] In other words:

In the experimental cognitive tradition of psychology, a single attentive subject perceiving and thinking before choosing to make a response is the basic given. Explanation of psychological functioning has to be in terms of how the subject conducts, associates, and remembers experience as processor of stimulus information.[40]

Even Piaget, the single most influential figure, certainly in educational theory, to this day, is 'this century's greatest rationalist among developmental psychologists. He portrays the child as an autonomous experimenter who acquires representations of objects in the world and who gains rational awareness by recording the effects of his acts.'[41] The social dimension of this process occurs and increases as the child assimilates adults' representations for the objects and acts it has recorded in its own way. The process is complete when the child learns the language of its society, the repository of the truth, scientific and moral, which is at that stage in the community's possession.

Social life is just a particularly fertile milieu for practice with representations. At the start, symbols, as components of private thought, are not exchanged directly; it is only gradually that the infant's images (singular and egocentric) become the preschool child's pre-concepts (partially socialised representations/fantasies) and then the adolescent's concepts (general and communicable – about truth). Concepts are expressed in language and, more concisely and elegantly, in formal mathematical systems.[42]

It is not that previous work in developmental psychology ignored the community dimension. But it was invoked at a point of, and for the purpose of, teaching the child the agreed symbols (mainly words) for the stimuli which the child had in its own way recorded, the available generalisations for patterns in these which it was seeing; and of course such teaching greatly expanded the child's purchase upon all of this general knowledge, including knowledge of acceptable patterns of behaviour. However, what the previous work failed entirely to explain was how communities rather than just individuals develop in the first place, and how meanings, truths, and values came to be communal possessions in the first place.

It is not even that previous work in developmental psychology ignored emotions and affections. In Piaget's words, 'affectivity regulates the energetics of the action while intelligence provides the technique', and in general, 'affective schemas do not achieve the same degree of generalisation and abstraction as logical schemas except when they are regulated by reversible operation of reciprocity, etc.; i.e. when they thereby become moral schemas'.[43] In short, affectivity, emotion needs the control of rational generalisations – in the case of morality this would be the principle of acting on a maxim you would wish all other agents to act upon, as Kant might say – so that the whole affective and motivated side of the developing human being is second-rated and suspect in the task of arriving at truth and goodness. That however fails to do justice to the community-building and simultaneously heuristic power of the most formative and comprehensive of human emotions. And it increases the failure to explain how communities of co-operation and common rules for action ever come about at all, rather than individualism and total permanent competition. It fails in particular to reckon with what has been called Eros in these pages, the sense, the feeling, the emotion of being driven, drawn, bound from, or to, what will be good for the co-operative questers in their common environment; a sense or feeling that makes to be outward bound a being already endowed with reflective consciousness; a sense or emotion that is a veritable shape-changer, now named as desire, now as aversion, now as love in one of *its* many modes, now as hate, now as sadness at loss, now as joy in possession; but always in essence combining with each level of elementary awareness in order to promote well-being, and simultaneously knowledge and understanding, or alternatively ill-being, ignorance, and misunderstanding; always the emotion of this structured thing in this structured world, and hence discriminatory, though not deterministic, from the outset.

The more recent work in developmental psychology, in which an Edinburgh colleague, Colwyn Trevarthen, plays a pioneering role, paints a very different picture from that of the older experimental cognitive psychology. The infant, from the moment of birth at least, proves itself in possession of a dual 'self and other' organisation in the brain and mind. This dual starting state, this elementary possession of 'self' and 'virtual other', is the origin and foundational form of reflective consciousness, and the precondition for the actual intersubjectivity which occurs as soon as the umbilical cord is severed and the infant encounters a separate 'other'. Hence in a piece entitled 'Signs Before Speech' Trevarthen wrote: 'The peculiar features of human signing are adapted to exchange of meaning in a community of minds *motivated to transform reality together*'[44] (my italics). Here already in this brief sentence are adumbrated the connections between meaning (knowledge, truth) and the *co-operation* of conscious, personal agents; meanings achieved and agreed in praxis; community achieved simultaneously.

The detail follows in the work of Trevarthen and others; the evidence of the neonate preferring (choosing in that sense) a caring adult, expressing that preference in expressed emotions, soliciting supportive emotional response; genuinely communicating with gesture and voice and facial expression long before speech; initiating action and eliciting co-operation.

It is obvious from the first protoconversations at 2 months, through the games of mother with child, to the role-taking fantasies of 3- to 5-year-olds who rapidly absorb both the language and conventions of their culture, that children actively seek co-operation. They 'worm' culture out of their companions within a succession of special relationships that are regulated by emotion. They reason in a common cause with others and trust that social moves will assist their minds to grow freely.

Even though an infant shows signs of a rational individuality, of a cognitive mind that in isolation can rehearse a stock of experience, solve problems, examine arguments for inconsistency or promise, the ultimate reference for meaning is what makes sense to a community of individuals used to working together with common cause.[45]

There are many summary conclusions offered by Trevarthen and his collaborators, but one from an earlier work will suit best the present purpose, since it has been more than vindicated by all the research of the years between:

I claim evidence that human infants are *intentional, conscious* and *personal*; that above all they have a faculty of *intersubjectivity* which is in embryonic condition in the neonate and rapidly developing active control over experience after that, and which soon becomes the central motivator and regulator for human mental growth . . . Infants are intentional because they are capable of formulating forms of actions that are measurably aimed at specific external goals, these goals being not immediately present to cause the actions reflexly. They are conscious because they carry images of external goals through perception within a complex space that is full of many events, selecting objects of adaptive value. They are personal because they are appealing to, conscious of and expressive to other human agents and the intentions of these agents.[46]

Now this surely is an account of the genesis of moral value which corroborates the analysis offered above of both morality and power as authority,[47] and it does so in the particularly persuasive manner of describing the development of human beings themselves as social creators of the well-being and truth they then possess and enjoy together. The priority of moral value meaning actual states of affairs brought about by humans in co-operative community is confirmed; as is the derivative and ancillary nature of moral value expressed in the form of rule, code, generalised maxim. The latter form of expression is useful and necessary in the ways that have been allowed already, but they are, no less than the concrete states of affairs which provide the primary denotation of moral value, the creations of the cultures in which they arise. Further, general rules do not offer the prospect of secure movement to a given action or piece of contemplated behaviour, for the simple reason that they have already abstracted certain features thought valuable, or an anti-value, from concrete activities that already revealed a certain family resemblance amongst themselves. But concrete instances of contemplated or actual

behaviour are always more complex than the abstraction describes, and so it is common to find that application of a rule
requires a further piece of evaluation on the part of the agent,
or that more than one formulated rule applies or, more crucially still, that rules which do seem to apply are not always
simultaneously capable of fulfilment.[48]

The resulting issue of objectivity or verification of moral
valuation (and even of the concomitantly 'created' meaning or
truth in a culture) is too large for this context. Suffice it to say
that the truth of a moral proposition, in whatever form, will
refer primarily to the well-being or the increase or decrease in
well-being which its observance brings about, and that also
will inevitably be a matter of evaluation by those in the best
position to evaluate it, that is to say, those whose well-being is
in question. The 'objectivity' of a moral proposition will refer
primarily to the fact that the given structures of agents and
their objects, which offer them a certain guidance in their quest
for betterment, were actually enhanced by being developed or
changed, and thus contribute more to the general well-being,
and that also will be a matter for further evaluation. In this
theory of morals – and of knowledge as such, since all knowledge on this theory of it results from the doing that is part of
the quest for well-being – there is never any escape from or for
the evaluators. But then there never was any escape from the
judgment of the perceivers, even in more theoretical accounts
of the nature of knowing, when the issue of its truth and
objectivity arose. Skinner's Box was never more than the final
illusion of naive materialists.

Next, this excursus on recent work in developmental psychology corroborates the view that morality coincides from its
very genesis with power in the form of authority. Human
beings create morality in the very course of developing or
creating themselves, their lives, and their world. From the very
beginning they do so in a social web of enablers and depend-
ants, masters and apprentices, in which the former have power
over the latter. But the only form of power which is compatible
with the genesis of the human is power which elicits and

promotes the growing moral creativity and freedom of those who seek its benefits from infancy.

Finally, however, the use of the work of developmental psychologists to illustrate and support the analysis of the anatomies of authority/morals seems to emphasise, if anything, the naturalism of what is being described – something generated by and with humans in their own world. Is morality purely secular then? And is power as authority, the exercise of which fully coincides with human morality, purely secular also? How does sacred power, if it does, enter the picture?

CHAPTER 3

Powers secular and powers sacred

The task of identifying powers secular and powers sacred, and of then appreciating the differences and similarities between them, can coincide with that of discussing the relationship of morality and religion, and of deciding where that relationship lies on a range between the extremes of overlap and incompatibility. Naturally, if powers sacred can only appear in the form of power as force, the relationship of religion to morality will occur at the extreme of incompatibility; if powers sacred can be discovered which manifest themselves as power in the form of authority, the relationship of religion to morality will involve overlap.

The issue of distinction and relationship was raised by some observations of Alasdair MacIntyre's on Greek and Christian morality in the course of the last chapter. MacIntyre felt that the true and adequate goal of moral striving must be found in the human soul's relationship to something at once outside itself and beyond the world; he also felt that our common experience of the human inability to keep evil temptations at bay pointed to the need for something like the faith, hope, and charity which Christians call 'infused' virtues. These observations call for a number of comments.

First, even were such elements absent, the resulting morality need not necessarily be deemed lacking in properly religious dimensions. The Stoic philosophy, after all, arguably the single most influential moral theory in the history of Western civilisation, was set securely in a theology of the cosmos characterised by a wholly immanent divinity. The Stoics were atheists only in the sense in which the early Christians were called atheists – their God was unintelligible or unacceptable to their critics, who therefore called them atheists. So, whatever might be said about the individual soul's relationship to something outside itself, it was not in Stoic theology related to anything beyond the world, for there simply was not anything beyond the world; everything that existed, including God, was within the world. Something similar could be said about the other element, the persisting human inability to avoid evildoing. Moralities could surely be found with religious dimensions which did not press this inability – although here one would need to know how great or small this inability was thought to be, and how intractable; Pelagius had much place for persistent inabilities also. Yet there is scarcely a morality to be found which did not catalogue 'infusions' of divine aid in a variety of forms. Hence Greek morality did have a religious dimension even where some of the elements enumerated by MacIntyre were missing. But perhaps his point is rather that such morality could not fully be itself unless these precise elements were present, and it was Christianity in fact which supplied them?

Second, then, the precise elements were present in Greek pre-Christian settings for morality. One might speak more accurately of their equivalents, since they were not necessarily present in their Christian forms. Nevertheless, it would be foolish for Christians to try to pretend that they had invented the idea of a fall from paradise or from a golden age, and that Christianity alone had tried to describe, and to supply the remedy for, the ensuing and inevitable evil. For one thing, some of the Christian theories of fall and original sin have done serious damage simultaneously to the perception of human morality and to the human image of God. For some of these have actually suggested that people are to be held responsible, and punishable, for sin or evil which they did not, and could not voluntarily commit, and as a consequence they have sometimes painted a gruesome picture of a God who actually punishes the souls of infants for such 'sin'. In addition, if Christianity did actually have a remedy for the ensuing and allegedly inevitable evil which no other moral or religious

system before it possessed, then there would certainly be some
noticeable decline in the quantity of evil during the Christian
centuries, at least in those areas where the majority of citizens
over many, many generations had been baptised. But no such
decline is in evidence as yet;[1] so that Christians might be well
advised to look again at some of their theories of original sin,
and to look elsewhere for evidence of their moral successes.

In actual fact, however, the image of evil apparently
indomitable in this world, and at some basic level apparently
even intractable, was constant enough with Plato, and
attempts to wrestle with such a problem of evil form a substantial part of the long tradition of philosophy to which he
gave his name. Much the same variety of explanations for the
persistence of an evil apparently so ineradicable – explanations which ranged from the very nature of a material
universe to a fully developed demonology – were at the
service of Christian and Platonist theologians alike during all
those early centuries in which their respective institutions
coexisted, sometimes peacefully, sometimes not. On the other
side of the coin, the side of religious remedy for the moral
disease, although the non-Christian philosopher may not
have operated with any image as potentially crude as that of
'infusion' when dealing in matters affecting the human spirit
and will, there can be no doubt about the fact that, during
the long tenure of a philosophy which pre-dated Christianity's birth and formed much of the religious environment for
its growth, the Good and the Beautiful, in source if not also in
sense divine, was commonly thought to evoke the very Eros
which was itself the engine of human moral progress, the goal
of which, according to Plato, was the *homoiosis theo*, the like-
ness to God in so far as that is possible for God's creatures.[2]
That is quite the equivalent of 'infused' charity on any
neutral assessment of such matters. And Plato's description of
the Good as *epekeina tes ousias*, beyond being, entered the
common theological tradition called Christian Platonism as a
key term for the degree to which the goal of human life,
consisting in some sort of union with the divine, was beyond
the empirical world.

If we were to seek a distinction between powers secular and powers sacred by seeking a more general distinction between secular and religious moralities, we should find no such distinction in the sources of Western civilisation, nor at any point in the course of its history until we come very close to contemporary times. And it is very doubtful if we should fare any better with this particular approach in any other civilisation before the modern era dawned and, more particularly, before some of these civilisations came under the influence of one or other of the forms of late Western humanism. Nor can the issue of relationship between powers secular and sacred, morality and religion, be decided simply by reference to the past.

The past has offered us the highest insights into the anatomy of morals, and none more so than Plato; it has offered us insights into the nature of power exercised as authority, if only in the insistence that the *summa potestas* belongs really to the people, even if they might never as such exercise *imperium*. And the ubiquity of religion in both theory and practice might then indicate the happiest of relationships. But the same past also offers us too many examples of power exercised and institutionalised as force, and such similarity of ecclesiastical and civic institutions as to give abiding relevance and significance to the question: just what are the essential traits that define a sacred power or a religious dimension to morality, and (once the definition and identification takes place) is this compatible with secular power in the form of authority, or must it always appear as power in the form of force and thus be the enemy of true morality? One can begin by taking the usual philosophical line, discussing the definitions, and analysis, of the relationships between religion and morality; but, given the topics of the title of this book – power and ethics – it would make sense to move rather quickly thereafter to an inspection of the powers, and more especially the authorities, their practical forms and theoretical underpinnings, that have been introduced already in the chapters on power and morality, and to ask how the definitions and relationships arrived at theoretically are, or can be, instanced there.

MORALITY AND RELIGION

It would take at least as long to describe the anatomy of religion as it has taken to describe the anatomy of morals, and it would probably cause an unnecessary delay in the argument of this book. A short-cut to a brief discussion of the general relationship between morality and religion is therefore justified, one that is already well marked by considerations of 'absolutes', 'an absolute', or even 'the absolute'. In other words, a short-cut to an answer to the question of the relationship of morality to religion is sometimes sought by raising the issue of moral absolutes, on the grounds that 'the Absolute' is often used as a title for the object of religious belief, and that if there are moral absolutes, these must then relate somehow to the religious object, either deriving from the divinity or revealing themselves as characteristics of it.

The claim that there are moral absolutes takes two forms: it is sometimes a case about propositions such as 'thou shalt not lie', sometimes a case about named ideals such as justice or goodness itself. In neither case is the meaning of the word 'absolute' as clear as its users might wish. In the case of precepts, norms, and ethical propositions one might take it that an absolute rule is one which permits of absolutely no exceptions. If that is so, then it would have to be said that no human proposition can do more than give a false impression of being absolute – and a proposition received by humans is as much a human proposition as one engendered by humans. In every case a closer analysis of the proposition would reveal that one is really being asked only to do better than one has done, or less harm than one might otherwise do; in other words that the realistic content of such precepts is very relative indeed. If someone urged you to tell the truth, the whole truth, and nothing but the truth, another way of saying that you must never tell the least lie, even by omission, then you know that that is impossible. For you never know the whole truth about anything, and a good deal of what you know about everything is no doubt faulty if not false. You are really being told, then, that if you speak you must speak out in each situation as best you can. That partial truth will then be a relative value, relative to your condition and the situation in which you find yourself. It may often involve a clash with other relative values, and face you with an anguished choice between them; to tell the truth as best you know it at a particular time might endanger the life of an innocent person; to refuse to tell it might endanger your own. However, if you are told 'thou shalt not kill' and this is represented to you as an absolute injunction, then you will know that this also is impossible. For all your life you live at the expense of other lives. As old Heraclitus said: 'each one lives the death of others and dies their life.'[3] Or the earliest surviving fragment of Western philosophy: 'But from whatever things is the genesis of the things that are, into these they must pass away according to necessity; for they must pay the penalty and make atonement to one another for their injustices, according to time's decree.'[4] You are then really being told to wear others down as little as possible, or to replace them as slowly and as gently as possible, and to give of your own life also so that they may live more fully; and perhaps to try to make the latter process compensate for the former (make atonement to one another for the 'injustices'). After all even God does not appear to be able or willing to prevent the deaths of those to whom believers say he gives life; and Christians in particular affirm that God suffered death in some sense in the effort to save humankind from a fate worse than death.

There is a lesson to be learned about the limitations of doing ethics entirely through the construction and analysis of propositions, precepts, rules, commandments, laws. It strengthens what has already been said about legislation in civil society; it supports the disdain with which sensitive moralists regard the mediocrity of a moral life that consists solely in avoidance of any breach of commandments; and it suggests ways of bringing, what are sometimes relegated to the peripheral areas as 'counsels of perfection', back into the mainstream of moral life and thought. For the formulated precept can never do more than offer the most general guidance for moral behaviour, and so secure the least amount of conformity which is compatible with the very possibility of moral life within any human community. The so-called Ten Commandments provide a classic example of a code of precepts, its necessity and inherent limitations: telling you to worship the true God, not false ones, and to make time for this; to respect parents, not to kill or bear false witness, not to steal or covet a neighbour's wife or a neighbour's goods. This code offers a modicum of protection to human life, to human reputation (and thus to morality itself, since honour has always been at the centre of moral motivation), and to property (which then included wives). But it is perfectly clear that it and all future codes would need to leave to more creative and imaginative formulations, and hence more continuously creative ones, by far the greatest amount of the detail of moral duty. The making of morality as a mental exercise issuing often in words, is a matter of envisaging the creative furtherance of what is perceived to be good, of continuously deciding how to do and make better than before, or at least to do and make differently in the inevitably changing circumstances of a moving world.

What of values, then, rather than precepts, as possible candidates for the adjective 'absolute'? Are there absolute moral values? Moral values really refer to states of affairs brought about by rational agents in their creative freedom. A writer does a fair day's work for a fair day's pay, and that is distributive justice, in so far as it is justice; for values, like love, 'must be made real in act', as T. S. Elliot might say. The value called justice is an abstraction from such states of affairs, and if it can be filled with any content other than that of the state of affairs just mentioned, this can only be done by the usual means of making progress in morality, i.e. by envisioning further states of affairs, patterns of behaviour, in which a greater or a different justice can be realised. Of course, the value of justice can be made to stand as a cipher for some state of affairs in which the very perfection of justice is realised, but at that stage of development the cipher would reveal the influence of the Eros-thrust upon the human imagination, driving it to envisage an ideal beyond its present powers of supplying concrete detail, and achieving the status of an absolute only at the expense of its impotence to give concrete direction to life.

Justice as a perfect ideal might be delineated in a cluster of sentences such as 'give to everyone according to each one's dues', 'from each according to ability, to each according to need', 'each ought to act and experience according to the place of each in the overall order of things' – where terms like 'dues', 'needs', and 'the order of things' positively cry out for further definition. Much the same points could be made about goodness or the good as a moral value, for it is a class noun, that is, an abstract term for all moral values together.[5]

Creativity remains the common factor in morals, and perhaps in that factor lies the clue to the encounter of morality and religion. When Eros drives the general-purpose agent called *homo sapiens*; better said, since this agent is self-conscious, hence conscious of Eros, when Eros draws this agent, but draws this agent indeterminately because that form of consciousness creates a distance in which self and things can be taken or left, dealt with or not, this way or that, creativity and a unique way of knowing coincide. In this creativity the content of human morality is progressively construed, and any possible encounters with religion detected.

Creativity is featured in every aspect of human behaviour and at all levels. The commonest bodily movement becomes the dance, and the influence of the dance returns to make more graceful all ordinary movements. The most basic need for food and drink gives rise to the ritual of the meal, the art of cooking and the rules of etiquette, from the most elementary to the most elaborate. Food is tastier then and nourishes more than the body. Sounds are made into music, words into poetry; song at first always combined them both. Learning is easier then as more is learned, as more than mind is drawn into the experience, emotions are played upon, fine sensitivities aroused. Seeing things gives rise to etching and painting and sculpting, which in turn enables people to see things better and, beyond that, to envisage their ideal and perhaps future forms. Sex is socialised, channelled into love and loyalty, and becomes infinitely more pleasurable in the process. Shelters become palaces, and even weapons become works of art symbolising the constraining of conflict itself from random brutality. And all in the service of a web of more beneficial relationships, themselves created out of the otherwise random instances of give-and-take which would yield and characterise haphazard confluences of human beings rather than ordered societies.

Creativity characterises all of human being, and consists in the fashioning of the given towards a purpose, the ordering of things to an end, as an older formula might have put it.[6] Art it is, a *technē* to the Greeks, creating order out of relative chaos. But the word 'relative' there is crucial. For, although the given is made to look relatively chaotic by the new order imposed upon it in human art, the given in human experience is never simply chaos. Far from it in fact; the striking thing about the given at every first encounter with it is that it already seems to be a process of maintaining or advancing order over chaos quite similar to that which human beings seek to bring about in the creation of their lives and world. The evolutionary hypothesis has enhanced rather than diminished that impression. But from the earliest awareness of the order of the seasons to the most modern of mind-boggling insights into the surging power of 'superstrings' holding everything together at the most elemental depths of what is called universe, the impression is the same: a creative process going on and on, order out of chaos, a kind of art.

It is not necessary to decide which is the hen and which is the egg here; whether it is this process in nature which, in some sense of the word, causes the process to be repeated by that self-conscious instance of nature that styles itself human, or whether this whole discourse is inescapably anthropomorphic, an imposition of the categories of the human upon the processes of the pre- or non-human. In fact it may not be possible to decide definitively – and that may be the reason why the existence of God cannot be proved in any finally cogent manner. But the similarity of the processes inevitably makes one think of a creative thing, an ordering entity, an artisan of some kind, within or behind the whole swirling universe. One may think of it only to deny it; one may end up believing in it, but in either case the sense of creative power as exhibited in the universe is at the origin of all religious faith, and must always be its heart and centre. No religion, however historical in its foundation upon a 'special', a new, an allegedly definitive revelation, can ever entirely supplant the clue of the resilient creativity perceived in this natural universe, can ever entirely refuse to consider the birds of the air and the lilies of the field, the sun which warms the good and the bad, the rain which refreshes alike the just and the unjust (so, love your enemies). '*Si Adam integer stetisset*,' if Adam had not fallen, even Calvin must allow, the knowledge of God the creator from the creation would have fully sufficed for final human happiness. Scripture resupplies, but it does not supplant, such knowledge. It is Calvin's assessment of the Fall, not his theology of creation, that puts him at odds with other Christians, and other religious people still, on the perennial powers of the natural universe to reveal God to those who can see it.[7]

The content of human morality consists in that very creativity to which humans are bound by Eros, a living dynamic complex of act and apprehension. Obligation is thus compatible with freedom, for creativity is a combination of just those elements. But freedom, for human moral agents, is never total since *creatio ex nihilo* is not within their power. The creativity already involved in the given-in-evolution-process is ever a constraint upon the Johnny-come-lately creativity of human being. To some extent this is a deterministic constraint; for the material universe in its generality and particulars sets some inevitable limits upon finite agents – there are always some things one simply cannot do (like revising yesterday's actions), and some things it will force one to do willy-nilly (like dying). To some extent the given represents more a form of guidance; for if one follows the lines along which things are naturally developing, one may find creative ways of relating to them for the benefit of both parties in the enterprise, the given and the moral agent – much ecological damage provides a negative illustration of this factor. Moral action is always a mix of being determined, directed, and free, but it is the incidence of (directed) freedom that makes our actions moral to the extent that they are moral.

Now the given, the whole evolving universe in which moral

agents live and move and have their being, always influences human morality in extensive and significant ways. For Albert Camus the overwhelming indifference of the universe not only coloured the emotions, but shaped through that colouring the possibilities of moral response, principally through the levelling realisation that for those who live under a universal death penalty, nothing made any lasting difference – think of Mersault's final meditation in *The Outsider*. For Bertrand Russell, the spectre of raw invincible force as matter rolled on its relentless way, could make cowards and partners in cruelty of human agents or it could inspire them to a lonely heroism that needed no final hope.[8] In both of these cases the human moral agent is something of a rebel against a reality which disappoints the very highest expectations that moral commitment itself arouses – the expectation that human creativity will continue to count for something, at the very least. But those who are enabled, either by the analogue with human creativity which the universe appears to offer, or by some more positive 'revelation', to believe in a transcendent moral agent can then see in these cosmic creative processes the action of this divine agent, can take that mixture of determinism and direction as a kind of guidance from God, and can see in their own creativity a kind of co-operation in the divine creation. That at least lends a context for a larger and longer significance, or for hope in this, for moral agents and for all that they do. Perhaps the best illustration of this point that the history of Western literature can offer is Boethius' *The Consolation of Philosophy*;[9] all the better for present purposes because of the fact that, although Boethius was undoubtedly a Christian, readers of this classic text have found difficulty in detecting any specifically Christian theme in its construction. So it stands all the more prominently as an impressive monument to the ability to theists in general to construe as divine providence all that would be otherwise accounted deterministic fate or blind chance.

Religious faith can and does arise out of morality: in this basic and elemental sense that, driven by Eros, human agents learn about their world in the course of dealing with it, and are often led to see processes within it which, by analogy with their own creativity, they suspect to be creative, in the fullest sense, the sense that these represent the activity of a transcendent creator. If the genesis of morality and the genesis of human knowledge coincide, as the preferred epistemology in this argument suggests, it should cause no surprise to find morality as a source of religious faith, provided that the dogmatism of the atheist and the elect are both equally avoided. Even in those instances in which religious faith arises in an individual through the more particular means of an allegedly special revelation or the particular preaching thereof, it is difficult to envisage the content of that faith being in the least intelligible, unless its would-be recipients can be put in touch with some implicit awareness of cosmic creativity and the power of the accompanying analogy to give some content to the very term 'God' – appeals to consider the birds of the air and the lilies of the field are neither as fanciful nor as optional as they are sometimes made to seem. Correspondingly, the most cursory search through the intellectual baggage of the dogmatic atheist will often uncover some sort of ultimate or most general source or principle which governs in its way all things and events, and from which it is difficult to withold the title 'divine'; in Bertrand Russell's piece it is matter that is omnipotent – and the practice of making things into absolutes, some of which demand the sacrifice of human existence itself, must be noted later.

The analogy with which the religious believer operates will carry on to the point of attributing Eros to God also, if only to explain why God would get involved with a world such as ours. The Eros will not now take the lesser forms it often takes in humans, much less the distorted forms of gluttony or lust. To the best of their gods at any rate believers will attribute the highest moral perfection conceivable. The goal of human life may then be described as Plato's *homoiosis theo*, or as Matthew's gospel has it, 'be ye perfect as your heavenly father is perfect' (Matthew 5: 48); and indeed it may well be thought, as Platonism increasingly insisted, to entail a return to God from which all things originally came.

At this point the whole of morality may be seen as the plotting and the acting out of one's relationship to the divine. And it is precisely for this reason that, at this point above all, it is necessary to keep religion and morality distinct: religion is life in its relationship to the divine; morality is life as the free, creative uncovering of the good of the agents involved, which in that process, and in that process alone, becomes morally good. Perhaps the simplest way to retain that distinction is to return once more to the problem of discerning the details of our moral duty. Reference has been made to a certain determinism and a certain guidance with which the given, the world, precedes our moral agency. The former, the determinism, acts as a simple limitation on moral progress and, as such, contributes nothing to it, with the possible exception of the quality of attitude and emotion we are able to forge in the encounter with limitation, and the manner in which we can extend that quality to the rest of moral life – see Bertrand Russell again. The latter, the guidance offered by the way in which things around us, and even our own natures, operate and evolve, can never be more than guidance. This guidance was canonised most of all by the Stoics whose immanent God was also called *physis* or Nature, but the Stoics themselves read the guidance offered by nature in such widely different ways that even they offer no support for making it into anything other than guidance.[10]

How might the regularities of nature and the directions of its evolution be made into more than guidance? Plainly, if simple and detailed conformity to these is urged upon us as our moral duty. Perhaps the classic case of this in modern times has been the Roman Catholic church's official teaching on contraception. Based on a desperate attempt to maintain a distinction between 'artificial' and 'natural' means of planning conception, this piece of proposed morality sought simple conformity of human behaviour with the physical forms and processes – and, one might add, vagaries – of the reproductive system. From its very promulgation in the Papal Encyclical *Humanae Vitae* in 1968, it was widely seen to be mistaken, and it has been ignored by virtually all married Roman Catholics in the world.

Nevertheless it does stand as the most significant example of the most characteristic abuse of what has been called natural law moralising to this day. It brought a very great deal of unnecessary suffering on the few faithful ones who did try to live by it during their reproductive years, as on many others who suffered the painful wrench of conscience in risking, in this instance, the rejection of their spiritual leaders. The sighs of these suffering ones were too often met by celibates, sometimes in very high places indeed, explaining that, if it were up to them, if it was their law, they could do something about it, but since it was the law of God there was nothing they could do except to urge its victims to pray to God for strength and the grace to endure. This response, in addition to showing its maker more compassionate than God, confirmed the view that human morality was here reduced to simple conformity, in this case simple conformity to natural processes. But that, of course, is not morality at all. On the contrary, it is in the freedom of the human being either to maintain or to modify such regularities or, more usually, to creatively manipulate these in a manner that maintains them by modifying them, that human morality consists. In this view of the matter the 'ordinances of nature' or the 'natural law' do no more to dictate the details of our moral duty to us than do allegedly verbal revelations of divine rules and precepts. It is not in such dictation of the details of duty that the relationship of religion to morality ever consists.

The moral enterprise itself, then, may encounter or indeed engender religious faith along the way, in something like the manner already described; and if it remains true to its erotic nature, to the relatively free creativity in which its very essence consists, it can never entirely rule out the prospect of belief in a creator God and of the higher and further hopes for its own future that such belief can make possible. But – and here is the need to keep morality and religion distinct in any theorising about them – the moral enterprise can be conducted by those who, however intensely they might feel the wish intrinsic to such an enterprise for a world founded and guided by a supremely good moral being, see no cogent reason for belief in such a God and, for the kind of good reasons we can all imagine, refuse also the invitations of believers to accept any one of the more particular revelations of God alleged to have occurred during the course of human history.[11] The moral enterprise can be conducted by these on equal terms, in fact on the same terms, as it is conducted by believers of one kind or another.

Whatever it is that religious faith might supply – and an example will be provided in the chapter on the Christian experience of power – whether it be a higher hope, a deeper inspiration, a general but distinctive direction, a further relationship, this will affect an enterprise that is truly common in all its essential features to believer and non-believer alike. This is shown to be true as much by the daily co-operation of believers and non-believers, as by any adequate analysis of morality itself. And when non-believers criticise religious folk for the alleged damage done to human morality in the name of God, they do not have in mind any of the details of moral duty which they happily acknowledge as a common inheritance open to common deployment and development; they have in mind rather a kind of abuse of authority or, in our adopted terminology, a kind of power, whereby moral precepts are dictated by God through some human intermediary, evoking conformity in place of a truly moral response, keeping people in the position of children who have not yet reached the use of reason. However, it must be obvious by now that whatever account we are to give of sacred powers in moral matters, it cannot be thought to put people in possession of moral precepts already formulated by God as laws or commandments and entrusted to these people together with the task of enjoining conformity to them, almost always with the implied threat of otherwise angering or alienating God. If it is the moral enterprise itself that offers along its way the possibility, though not the necessity, of the most basic and foundational religious belief on which all more developed religious belief must somehow build,[12] then the only kind of sacred power one can envisage is, surely, one that is in line with morality, that is to say, power exercised as authority, and not power exercised as force, for the latter is the very antithesis of morality and works always to its destruction.

THE POWERS THAT BE

What if one were to turn from such general considerations concerning religion and morality, if one were to turn to more concrete instances of the exercise of morality, and, more particularly, to examples of actual moral leadership or, to what is in effect the same thing, to concrete examples of power in one's social experience exercised in the form of authority? Would that turn make any easier the detection of a distinction between powers secular and powers sacred, and a consequent clarity with which each could thereafter be identified? In view of what has been already said about the general relationships between morality and religion, hopes cannot be very high. For it appeared that the moral quest, which is itself in method and substance the quest for all knowledge, may or may not evolve a kind or level of human faith in reality, present and future, to which the adjective 'religious' might be properly thought to apply; and there does not appear to be, or to be readily available, any criterion by which one could decide when such a level of evolution would or should emerge. The matter is complicated further by the fact that atheistic or agnostic humanists who would abjure any religious faith whatsoever, are often accused by religious people of idolatry, that is to say, of presenting ideals for human behaviour, or other controlling entities, which because of their 'absolute' status more than amply fill the space emptied by refusal of belief in the true God. Humanists in turn, especially since Feuerbach, are accustomed to accusing religious believers of using religious imagery merely to mask, sometimes admittedly from themselves also, the most secular, if not the most selfish, of concerns. And religious groups have accused other religious groups with whose image of the divine they did not agree, both of idolatry and of being atheists in reality, albeit with some grudgingly allowed moral pretensions. Hence, in theory at least, the line between human moralities and human powers which exhibit the religious dimension, and those which do not, is not easy to draw.

All the more reason, one might impatiently interject, to get on with some inspection of actual moral powers; one could

scarcely fare worse, and one might well do better! Now that is
all very well, but given the analysis of morality and of power
exercised as authority adopted in previous chapters, where in
the survey of instances of the latter in human society could one
begin, or, to put the point in a more crucial form, when could
one possibly end? For, on the analogy of the arts and crafts of
old, when we speak of concrete instances in human society of
power in the form of authority, we are speaking of masters and
apprentices. And, since morality is coextensive with human life
itself in all its mesmerising variety, how numerous and how
varied these intertwining circles of masters and apprentices
must turn out to be.

Parents are placed in the position of masters by the very
biological facts that make them sources of a new life which
needs to be nurtured towards the point, quite distant in the
case of human neonates, at which it can survive without them.
Do they mediate morality with a religious dimension, do they
exercise authority on behalf of the sacred, are they in that sense
sacred powers only when they teach their children to say their
prayers, to recite their creeds, and to participate in overtly
religious rituals? Or is there in the very depths of the existential
relationship between parents and those they bring to life a dark
intimation for the latter of a graceful and empowering dependence of cosmic dimensions, of which parents provide not only
the paradigmatic instance, but the lasting symbol systems of
Earth Mothers and Fathers who are in heaven? Or is the truth
more complex still, and somewhere in between?

At the larger end of the social scale one meets the *imperium*,
the government of each empire, kingdom, or state, the highest
power in each of the largest social units that comprise the
human race. This, too, is a moral power, and quite frequently
power in the form of authority, and not just when it is actually
legislating. Its general programmes for health and social
welfare, its regulation of industry and commerce, and all
programmes adopted for the common good are, both in theory
and realisation, moral values, states of affairs envisaged and
brought about for human well-being. At the most abstract
level of all a government may adopt a system of moral valu-

ation which can have the most profound and practical effect on the society it leads. A government, for example, which regards the creation of material wealth as the primary function of all significant bodies under its control, even if only in the belief that all other goods and forms of well-being will flow from this and eventually flow to all, may well imbue a large part of that society with quite a different moral perspective than would a government which regards material wealth as the mere practical condition of, if not merely one of the by-products of, the securing of more important forms of the general well-being. The government is a moral master, a power exercised in the form of authority. And, as in the case of parents, one may ask if it exercises this power with religious dimension only when it mentions God in its Constitution, has a Department of Religious Affairs, or otherwise engages in the promotion or control of overtly religious beliefs and practices? This question can be left to the next section, for there are examples of governmental theory and practice, in both civil and ecclesiastical forms, that have been looked at already and could be revisited with this question in mind. But in-between parenting and governing there are myriad forms of mastery and apprenticeship in human society, to which the question about secular or sacred might with equal right be put.

What about people such as captains of industry, officers of trade unions, and those often faceless but always very powerful ones who manage the money markets? It is incontrovertible that they, like all other human beings, are in their vocations part of the moral quest with all that is entailed of personal responsibility. They are also 'masters' in that they mould the behaviour of others in these walks of life, and influence the attitudes of others still in the broader society within which they operate. Does their moral authority reveal the religious dimension only when they for some reason decide to appeal to an existing religious tradition for some moral guidelines that it happens to contain, guidelines which would promote, for instance, a 'green' approach to production methods, or an investment policy that would shun countries or companies in which human rights are more than usually ignored in practice?

Or could it happen that, inside the very single-mindedness with which they pursue their purpose of making raw materials into (still material) human products a face like that of Mammon might begin to form, and to force them into thinking that human life might not be fulfilled in service of such a lesser god? Or the ecological backlash of mistreating the good earth as 'raw' material might haunt them sometimes with the suspicion of a higher hand already somehow guiding reality to a more comprehensive well-being?

If creativity is of the essence of human (and divine) morality, and art in all its forms is at least the analogue, and at best the paradigmatic instance, of the making of morality, what about artists? Especially those artists who are 'masters' with apprentices either formally or informally so designated; but all artists in a way, for they bring out something of the artist in all who are able to appreciate their work? If knowing always entails doing, and if doing creatively, that is, in such a way as to advance the given, is the characteristically human form of doing, then the creative work of the artist reveals that coincidence of the moral and the cognitive which the analysis of the anatomy of morals suggested. As Simone Weil put it, it is 'art which teaches us that the mind can descend into matter, *and that the ideal can pass into reality*',[13] (italics supplied for present purposes). Novelists, playwrights, poets, painters, musicians, sculptors ... are thus by their very calling entrusted with a role in the moral education of society, and could be allowed to deny that role only upon a very superficial view of the making of human morality, to which their own capacity for creative vision of reality would itself give the lie. Any art form which is truly creative facilitates a new vision of the world, orders human experience in new and promising ways and thereby educates in the business of ordering their lives all who are privileged to encounter it.

But who are the religious artists and which is religious art? Unless the question can be answered in the simplistic way in which a similar question about captains of industry can be answered, by pointing to a borrowing from existing religious traditions themes to be, in this case, 'illustrated' by the artist or the art under consideration, it can prove a very difficult question indeed. Artists may be the first to point to their experience of a source of their inspiration beyond themselves and perhaps beyond the human; but they can also prove to be as reductionist about religious themes as the most secularist of social scientists. The relationship between the priest and the artist has seldom been without its problems in any culture; that may be because the priest, the professional believer, must be dogmatic, or at the very least didactic, whereas the artist wishes only to entice, having been enticed, or to open up to the possible corroboration of others' vision a very personal revelation which gave demanding insight without office; it may be that the artist by nature wishes to discover, to see, rather than be told. But the causes of the strained relationship have gone deeper in modern times. In fact ever since Giotto in his 'Flight Into Egypt', for instance, painted a very human matron holding a very natural child on a very secular donkey the suspicion has been growing that artists of all kinds merely make use of traditional religious symbols as familiar, and therefore potentially evocative, ciphers for a human condition deprived of any divine dimension – therein lies the reductionism.[14]

Artists in the modern world may well line up against the pervasive and crude materialism that has invaded recent human history, and fly a defiant banner for the spiritual dimension, but a spiricual dimension does not necessarily entail a religious dimension, and the puzzle remains as to when, if ever, the artist–moralist master reaches and represents the latter dimension.

A further example. If the suggested coincidence of the origins of knowledge and of morality – the point of all pragmatisms and of all preference for praxis – is at all acceptable, then the leaders in the sciences must accept that they have a special role also in the mastery of morals, that their educational task cannot stop short of the human will and emotions, and be thought to affect only the intellect. This point could perhaps be accepted most easily in the case of history, if history is a science rather than a modern and highly erudite form of story-telling. David Hume, who thought that religion was naturally bad for

morality, thought a knowledge of history of the highest importance for it, on the grounds that a knowledge of human nature
which ignored the history of human kind would prove to be
extremely defective.[15] But the confinement of this point to the
case of history, even if history is a science, could scarcely be
allowed, if only because we should then be faced with the
continuance of the rather puerile pretence that the quest for
scientific knowledge and technological advance is itself morally
neutral, and only when questions arise about the practical
application of the advances in science and technology, do
moral issues also arise, so that these are not strictly speaking the
business of the scientist as such. The scientist in the laboratory
is engaged in a process of the creative manipulation of the real,
to its maintenance, enhancement or destruction, and this is as
much a piece of implicit moral decision-making, and as much
an authoritative analogue and instance of moral living, as is
anything that the same scientist might do outside of academia,
or as the more facile phrase has it, 'in the real world'. This
point must surely no longer be lost in a world which is so
thoroughly the creation of science and technology.

And where, if at all, does religious belief enter for this latest
group of moral masters? Only where its object is a 'god of the
gaps', and only for as long as some gaps do remain in our
knowledge of the world and our ability to manipulate it for our
purposes? Or will science once again recapture the ambition of
its Western origin, before some accidents of Western history
forced those mutually constraining distinctions between
science, philosophy, and theology? Will it recapture the
ambition to seek the *physis tōn ontōn*, the nature of things, but in
that extended meaning of the word 'nature' in which it comprised the genesis of things as an essential part of the understanding of them, and hence comprised their ultimate source
and goal?[16]

The enumeration of these groups of masters and apprentices
which make up the middle ground of human society, and
which illustrate in their activities the genesis and furtherance of
human morality, on the understanding of morality as a *technē* or
art, and one which is at once the product and the creator of

human community, could go on and on; and the issue of the presence or absence, necessity or unacceptability, of a religious dimension, the issue as to whether the various authorities thus described are sacred, in the sense of being mediators of a religious dimension to morality, or whether they are on the contrary purely secular, could be postponed indefinitely, postulating an uncertain end to such enumeration. But a book of limited length must be satisfied with the examples offered, with a summary of some common clues to the puzzle of the relationship of secular to sacred which they offer, and with some supplement containing an analysis of the theory and practice of *summa potestas* in churches and states, where the relationship of sacred and secular is often more explicitly treated. Before moving to such a summary and supplement, however, one more question does occur concerning the pullulating groups of moral masters or authorites: was the group of those who might be called professional ethicists omitted merely for reasons of space? Is there room for a group of people whose professional service to a human society would consist precisely, not just in philosophising about the nature of morality, but in actually formulating moral rules or guidelines, defining virtues and vices, deploying the content of moral ideals? Or is it the case, as the omission so far might suggest, that the genesis of moral value, in whatever form it is thereafter expressed, must be left to those groups who are active in each walk of life?

If only because so many professional moral philosophers spend so much of their time in dealing with specific moral rules or propositions, and in analysing virtues and ideals by means of propositions concerning specific conduct, it must be necessary initially at least to count them amongst the groups who may be moral authorities in society, and then to attempt some account of their specific contribution to a general but very varied task. Professional moralists themselves, it has been noted, often nowadays seek to demote the propositional forms of moralising in favour of story-telling. Apart from the fact that this move would put most of them out of business, since they could not tell a decent story to save their lives, there is a case to be made for a group of people who try to work out a description of moral values for society in a predominantly analytic and propositional mode.

The case is in two parts. First, there is the case for doing ethics through the construction and critique of propositions such as 'it is wrong to lie', 'killing another human being deliberately is never justified', 'rebellion against a government is justified in the following circumstances'. The case at this stage concerns the contribution which this kind of activity makes to the necessary process of legislation in societies, civil or ecclesiastical. A traditional convention in the Roman Catholic church combined in one person the moral theologian and the canon lawyer. And that process of legislation itself, it has been argued, is moral in both form and content, as Lord Devlin saw. It represents the most fundamental means towards the making and re-making of the basic morality of any human society. Second, doing ethics in analytic and propositional forms is not restricted to the service of legislation. There is a more general relationship between this way of doing ethics and the more imaginative and practical ways outlined above in the cases of other groups; this is part of a still more general relationship between the human imagination as the primary 'faculty' of truth and the more analytic, conceptual, intellectual 'faculty', a relationship much discussed in a growing modern literature on imagination.[17] Suffice it to say here that the literary critic, the teacher of history, and a host of other commentators on the primary works of art and craft and technology, do resort to proposition-type formulae quite regularly in the course of attempting to distinguish the good from the bad, the better from the worse, in the works with which they deal.

It is perhaps necessary to add that the critic, the analyst, the dealer in propositional forms, must have participatory experience in the matter so treated, or must at least engage in a genuine team effort with those who do have participatory experience, with all the genuine mutuality of dependence which a team effort entails. No one can arrive from outside the participatory experience with a list of precepts and expect to be taken seriously. The celibate cannot offer precepts for married life to the married; the minister of religion cannot arrive at the medical clinic with preformed rules for medical procedures, derived without further ado from some allegedly general moral principles. Imagination and critical analysis can go hand in hand in this way also, each making its necessary contribution to cover the native shortcomings of the other. The operators of the analytical and propositional mode, then, make a twofold contribution to the genesis of morals: they help generate basic legislation, and they offer to the imagination-at-work the necessary critique of analysis and assessment. But what, as a distinctive group, do they contribute to the present question concerning the relationship of sacred to secular? Probably only their more philosophical insights, the kind of reasoning and analysis that occupied the last section above, on morality and religion. When they are drawn to consider the nature of the moral quest itself, to which in their own particular way they do contribute, they may have much to say about the point at which it reveals or fails to reveal, or seems to reveal in a particularly problematic way (problematic, that is, for those who like clear analysis and cogent propositions), a moral source to all of reality known to us.

What might be said in conclusion to this short section? That power in the form of authority, that moral mastery or leadership good or bad, takes myriad forms in human society; of course. But what on the issue of distinction and relationship between powers secular and powers sacred? Only perhaps that, in the concrete contexts of particular walks of life and the circles of masters and apprentices peculiar to each, the same kind of point can be reached which is reached in the general pursuit of the moral quest, the point at which creative efforts at well-being and the concomitant knowledge of the nature, the depths and heights of our common world which this engenders, tempt one to think, to believe or, at the very least, to hope (though hope at this height is no little thing) that the whole of reality might be moral in its beginning and end; that, in Platonic language, something which might be called The Good (One) is the cause of all truth and knowledge. The analogy that allows this belief or hope to come to expression is the Eros-like striving that becomes palpable in every extensive evolutionary account of our world before it becomes aware of itself as sense of obligation in reflective self-consciousness; a common striving, a terrifying mixture of co-operation and competition – the act of loving and the act of killing visually indistinguishable for a moment as a lioness mounts a zebra's back and mouths its neck – with maintenance of life, life more abundant, higher well-being, the constant motivating force. The belief finds its final form in the conviction or the hope that whatever is the most general source of all this pullulating and striving universe, is both moral and good and capable of working effectively through the creation so that 'all will be well and all manner of things will be well'.

Analogies limp, as the old Latin adage has it, and this one can limp badly in both legs. First, the Eros-like striving which we detect in all the world can be presented as a proof of God's existence, and then it stumbles and falls. Worse still, this abuse of the analogy can mislead people into thinking that morality is the bequest of religion, whereas in truth religion is a function of morality. That latter conviction represents, perhaps, the acceptable substance of the claim made by some Christian ethicists that Christian life and morality are indistinguishable; for, once the moral quest has realised its religious dimension, the whole of human creativity can be seen also and truly as the service of God and a co-operative promotion of the divine plan necessary for its achievement.

Second, and before that sometimes too cosy perspective can be reached, one must explicitly recognise the fact that the general analogy has its countervailing features. The world which offers images of striving after well-being and the concomitant guidance for human creativity in and for the world, also faces all of its moral agents with the brute force of limitation, disintegration, destruction. It was the universal death penalty that caused Camus to describe the human person as *The Rebel*, rebelling for the sake of its very humanity against the idea of God, as against any alleged absolute that might attempt to take the place of God. So it is that the moral quest, which is itself the quest for knowledge, if it were to focus rather exclusively upon limitations as such, and in particular on the final limitation of death, could as easily arrive at a God whose hallmark was omnipotence indeed, but power in the form of force rather than authority, and thus the enemy of morality. If that were to happen, then Camus is correct. Since morality, free and responsible creativity, is of the essence of being human, one would be left with no option but to rebel against such a God; just as in any of the master–apprenticeship relationships in any walk of life, one would have to rebel if the master were to exercise power as force, rather than exercise power as authority in order to develop the personal creativity of the apprentice.

The moral quest, the human quest which is simultaneously the quest to be, to make, and to know, is not only at the source of whatever basic religious belief is possible (and thereafter essential for the assimilation of more elaborate and particular religious systems), it is also discriminatory with respect to a worthy object of religious service. But if some Omnipotent Being whose power is exercised as pure force is found unworthy of human respect, the escape from such a prospect cannot be found in avoidance of a focus on limitation, disintegration, death, and destruction. Unless the religious person is to yield to the atheistic humanist critique of religion on this further ground – it is really but an extension of the humanist complaint that divine dictation makes human moral development impossible – it becomes necessary to show how the limitations under which we labour can either be overcome or at least made to serve some truly moral value. Death itself is commonly treated in both of these ways; but it would be impossible to go any further into this matter here. Suffice it to say that only when these things are done is it possible to accuse the secular humanist in turn of foreshortening human prospects in a misguided attempt to protect what is essentially human.

Not much more can be done at this point than to conclude that the prospect of religious belief or hope arises at some point of the moral quest; but that that point cannot be determined in advance, and that it may be recognised differently in the different concrete contexts in which circles of masters and apprentices pursue the quest in the different walks of life. Only observation can tell the point at which secular pursuits – and all pursuits initiated by human beings are in origin secular – shade into pursuits of the sacred, when powers secular become powers sacred. Usually we come upon the scene when that point has already been passed, but it is always possible to retrace the steps, and we are often nowadays forced to do just that by the determined efforts of secular humanists to persuade us that the point must never again be reached. That is not to say that one could not begin with religious belief, in general or in a particular form, and seek out from that starting point the relationship of religion to morality, sacred to secular powers. In effect something like that will take place later in this book. But it is morality that defines the human spirit, the human being, and so it is moral criteria in the end that decide the possibility and the acceptability of the religious dimension of morality itself.

Before coming to the second part of the book, and beginning with the examination of a particular religion, it is worth looking at some of the largest powers in human society, at governments of churches and states, their explicit theories and practices, in order to see what further light can be thrown on this tangled issue of the distinction and relationship between powers secular and powers sacred.

STATES AND POWER SECULAR

Is there, either in fact or in theory, a state which exercises purely secular power, a church which exercises purely sacred power? Take the first part of that question.

There can scarcely be any doubt about the fact that the political philosophy which envisaged the most thoroughgoing secular society ever conceived was that of Karl Marx. Some models of British sovereignty may be thought to come close, but these do not seem to have aimed at the provision of such comprehensive accounts of the human condition, and so they need not be seen to rule out all imaginable access to sacred power in every possible realm of human experience.

Marx defined the human essence in terms of active relationships: in his Sixth Thesis on Feuerbach he called it 'the ensemble of the social relations'. As he continued to insist up to the very last of his writings, if we are to talk about actual human beings, rather than abstractions, or some legendary human creature living alone in nature, 'then it is necessary to begin by describing the specific character of this social man, that is, the character of the community in which he lives because its production – the process that enables him to earn his living – already possesses a certain social character'.[18] Or, to put the matter even more succinctly in the much quoted introduction to his 'Towards a Critique of Hegel's *Philosophy of Right*', 'Man is the world of man, the state, society'.[19]

Here is as much initial stress on community as the most avid of contemporary Christian moralists could possibly desire. It might not be irrelevant to ask if in the recent history of Christian moralising some debt of gratitude, as yet unpaid, might not after all be owed to Marx for bringing to light the inherently communal dimensions of morality? However that may be, Christians will not be grateful for the next element in Marx's philosophy: as one of the first of the moderns to see knowledge in terms of praxis, and morality as a consequence predominantly in terms of creativity, he believed the human species to be the creator of its own life and world. This 'mortal god' (though the phrase is Hobbes', not Marx's), was for Marx the only acceptable candidate for the role of creator of a human order, a human world.

It was not that Marx shared or even implied any creation myth of the bringing of order out of chaos, with humans as creators where Yahweh used to be. Rather, for Marx, 'plants, animals, stones, air, light etc ... form part of human life and activity'. And so he concludes, 'Nature is the inorganic body of a man, that is, in so far as it is not itself a human body. That man lives from nature means that nature is his body with which he must maintain a constant interchange so as not to die. That man's physical intellectual life depends on nature merely means that nature depends on itself, for man is part of nature.'[20] The difference between human beings and other animals in their intrinsic relationship with the rest of nature consists in the 'universality' of the human species' relationship, that is to say, this species is confined to no particular ecological niche, but can envisage and relate to a whole world, *qua* world. Hence the rather attractive picture of humanity and natural world forming one whole, all of it called nature, but with humanity exercising the function of freedom and true creativity within it, a kind of parallel to an idea of soul and body, where each was essential to the other's life for as long as both existed. To go beyond this unity of humanity and its body, to seek some other creator, is not only unnecessary for all present purposes of creating our lives and our world, it positively invites that kind of religious alienation which is the epitome of all other alienation, and hence the point at which critique must begin.

So, all other candidates for the role of creator represented basic forms of religious alienations of our power, privileges, and responsibilities. For Hegel, Spirit was the subject of universal history, the latest interpretation of the Christian creator God; Feuerbach had shown this God to be a projection of the human species-being, to be in fact human nature itself in its highest attributes and essential activities; but for Marx even that was too much of an abstraction – the only *real* alternative to these illusory subjects of history was the concreteness of human beings in all the concrete active relationships which now or at any concrete point of time made themselves and their world what these actually were: the creator is human beings in community. Once again, as previously in the case of the communal nature of morality, it would be difficult to find a more thoroughgoing endorsement of the identity of morality with human living in its entirety, but quite specifically with the free agency involved in human living, its ubiquitous power to change, to make new, to create.

As Schaff put it: 'The notion of man's self creation through labor is an utterly radical denial of theocentricism and its related heteronomy.'[21] On a more positive account of the matter a picture of human freedom begins to emerge, and in its composition it places such high emphasis on human creativity that it rivals, if it does not exceed, the finest pictures of human morality ever painted. It is on this picture that both the student and would-be critic of Marx should concentrate, rather than on Marx's critique of religion. For Marx's last word on that subject – about religion withering away – is so like Sartre's 'even if God did exist, that would change nothing',[22] that the onus is really placed on the opposition to, first, envisage a human freedom and creativity at least as impressive as this, and, then, to propose a religious faith which would develop, and not detract from, this. But, if relations between morality and religion are at all similar to those depicted so far, that is in any case the proper kind of procedure: to retrace the steps by which the ubiquitous moral quest reaches a specific religious dimension, and to allow our common allegiance to moral criteria to judge any emergent religious dimension to its very end.

There is no need to rehearse once more the primacy which Marx accorded to what he called 'relations of production', amongst all those active relationships within our cosmic 'body' which constituted the 'ensemble of the social relations', and by which both we and our world are fashioned at any particular stage of our history. Certainly there is a sense in which the provision of the more material supports of life, food, clothing, and shelter, retain a certain priority over all additional creativity, and there are well-defined stages in the development of what Marx called the 'material forces of production', that is, the sources of our subsistence and the methods of making them ours. But that is to say no more than has been said already in this chapter about material constraints upon that creativity in which our freedom and morality consist; although it perhaps does add an element of declining subjection to material necessity as our creative powers increase over the ages.

So, for example, at the more elementary stages of agriculture the active relationships between humans and between them and their world were constrained, and allowed less room for more enriching relationships than were later achieved. Yet the picture is never the deterministic one that doctrinaire communists have wanted to paint. People were always, and always are, the creators in this world; and so they are responsible for the relationships which their use and distribution of the means of production entail, and for the actual damage which is thereby done to themselves and to their world. Note what Marx had to say about private property, the system which allows some to monopolise the means of the production of human living at the expense of others, and in this way enables some to lord it over others to the point of depriving these of their native freedom and, what amounts to the same thing, of the human dignity of full and equal co-operative creativity: 'although private property appears to be the ground and reason for externalised labour, it is rather a consequence of it'.[23] This must certainly be taken to mean, in general and with due allowance for all those real but, one hopes, declining material constraints upon them, that people themselves in the process of sustaining, producing, creating their lives and their world, create also the very economic structures, and the legal and political structures which follow on these, some of which may in turn deprive them all of their full and proper humanity. Nobody, really, is more persuaded than Marx of the co-operative creativity in which the essence of human freedom and dignity consists: people create both the good they enjoy and the evil that can make them its victims across the generations. There are even hints of art as the analogue or instance of morality: 'man also fashions things according to the laws of beauty' – and that can apply surely as much to the most basic provision of food, as to the highest realisation of what is more frequently called fine art.[24] In the most menial tasks from the most primal era humans create, simultaneously, culture and society, and within that complex they create both the good and evil they then enjoy and suffer, but from this evil and suffering they must be their own saviours.

[Marx's] view that true law is freedom, the inner moral consciousness of the truly human and truly self-determined human being, remains at the core of his mature belief in the withering away of the state, and of the communist doctrine that under communism law will wither away and be replaced by the inner moral consciousness of the communist citizen; if law is the expression of freedom, if the criminal must suffer no violence from *without*, then under truly human conditions, law must disappear.[25]

It would be difficult at this point to fail to hear some echoes of so much that has been said in our previous analysis of the anatomy of morals. Law – and it is the law enforced by the state that is meant at the moment – has elements within it or attached to it (extrinsic punishment and threat thereof) which are at best inimical to true human morality; and even morality in the form of those formulated propositions beloved of professional ethicists and called norms, rules, precepts, laws, even this, it has been suggested, is of more use to law-makers than it is to others, who could otherwise see in it only ancillary clarifications of more concrete pictures of good human creativity. For Marx, of course, the prospective achievement of the highest human morality – the 'law' of perfect freedom – is not the only reason for wishing the withering away of the law as we now know it. Where people have created dehumanising relationships, as they undoubtedly have in present political economies, the current laws simply serve to maintain the injustice, the oppression of people by people which characterises these relationships, and so for those reasons also the law as the imposition of rulers upon ruled, must wither away.

Marx, of course, was more than well aware of the claims made by, and on behalf of, the new liberal democracies, particularly France and the United States of America, to the effect that in them was to be found, epitomised at last, the fullest measure of human freedom and self-determination. But all that Marx could see when he looked closely at those models held up for his admiration, was a conflict between what he called the 'political community' with the 'general interest' which it sought to secure, and the 'civil community' which was still a jungle of competing interests of 'private individuals' – echoes here already of those efforts to draw distinctions between private and public morality in which the legal theorists of these democratic states still sometimes persist? Certainly, in the very act of governing themselves through their freely elected representatives, the peoples of these new democracies created some communal values. They abolished, at the level of the state, both religion and private property. That is to say, by separating church and state, and by seeing to it that the government as such could not be an owner of private property, the communal human being does in fact realise the abolition of twin factors in the self-alienation from which he has hitherto suffered – well, scarcely *twin* factors, for to Marx religious alienation or projection in churches is merely the shadowy *doppelganger* of real, i.e. social, alienation by monopoly of capital.

In these new liberal democracies, then, members of a particular nation-community declare themselves free from religion and private property, but they do this only in their political *personae*, only through those who represent them in governing themselves: in society, as in religious imagery and practice, they see and realise their true freedom and dignity only through intermediaries. In the other part of their now split beings, that is, on behalf of themselves as private persons rather than as social beings, in their civil *personae* they pursue and legalise private property, each one free to amass as much wealth as possible, as much as possible of the means and fruits of production, provided only that certain 'Queensbury Rules' are observed, but quite irrespective of the misfortunes that may befall others. In addition (but this is no accidental addition in Marx's view of religion), each one is entitled in law, within the same broad rules of engagement, to practice the religion of his or her choice. Religion remains the expression of human alienation and, it is often forgotten of Marx, of the protest against the resulting oppression; not least in the pictures it paints of a kingdom of God wherein those without money could eat and drink with the best, where no man need instruct or would lord it over another, where the perfect law of freedom would suffice – all interestingly similar to Marx's own vision.[26]

The modern liberal democratic state is at best a step on the way towards a truly human society in which our full freedom and the final dignity of our creative self-determination could be realised. That is Marx's assessment. For in the modern state we still act as 'political' animals, seeing and in part realising some of our highest values, but only through intermediaries, through representative institutions fashioned by us, yes, but still projected beyond our individual lives and still largely alien to these. And in the meantime we still legislate for just those features of our lives that we had created to their own diminishment. We must therefore create a civil society in which there would be no state as such, no politics, no mere representation of the best which in turn sanctioned the worst, but full creative co-operative creativity, full human freedom and dignity.

It is commonplace to remark that Marx himself was not quite as forthcoming as one could wish on the concrete details of the new society which was to succeed the withering away of the state and of the law as we now know these. In his 'Critique of the Gotha Programme', Marx did fill in some of the details of a society in which the very 'conditions of production' and not just the 'means of consumption' were distributed into the co-operative ownership of the active producers, the workers, the creators themselves. In his notes on Bakunin's *Statism and Anarchy*, in which he explained to some degree the transitory nature of the 'dictatorship of the proletariat', he explained also why Bakunin's suspicions are unfounded when the latter suspects that a whole people cannot govern themselves without creating a state in which the distinction between rulers and ruled will be a real distinction in something like its present political sense. And he suggests that the mystical 'will of the people' which can claim to be incarnate in the most despotic of rulers will be replaced by the 'real will of the cooperative'; that the maintenance of cohesion of community and of common purpose and action can be achieved by forms of 'administrative functions' rather than state governmental functions, and that those who exercise the former functions need no more cease to be genuine members of a co-operative of equals than 'a manufacturer today ceases to be a capitalist when he becomes a member of the municipal council'.[27]

It is even more commonplace most recently to remark that the theory did not work anyway; Communism has collapsed in the West, and it would appear to have little future elsewhere. A cynic, or a surviving Marxist, might retort that the real mistake made by Marxists was to actually attempt to bring about the ideal human society here and in the near future; they should have followed the example of the Christians in postponing the ideal as far away as possible in time and space, even if they could not quite postpone it to another life and another world. But there are less cynical explanations of this recent and well-documented failure. The great Sartre, who saw in Marx one of those 'moments' in the modern world – the others were the 'moments' of Descartes and Locke, and of Kant and Hegel – in which philosophy becomes creative to the point of being a totalisation of knowledge, a regulative idea, a community of language, a vision of the world, offered the following explanation of the practical failure of this practical philosophy:

Marxism stopped. Precisely because this philosophy wants to change the world, because its aim is 'philosophy-becoming-the-world', because it is and wants to be *practical*, there arose within it a veritable schism which placed theory on the one side and *praxis* on the other. From the moment the USSR, encircled and alone, undertook its gigantic effort at industrialization, Marxism found itself unable to bear the shock of these new struggles, the practical necessities and the mistakes which are always inseparable from them. At this period of withdrawal (for the USSR) and of ebb-tide (for the revolutionary proletariats), the ideology itself was subordinated to a double need: security (that is, unity) and the construction of socialism *inside* the USSR. Concrete thought must be born from *praxis* and must turn back upon it in order to clarify it, not by chance and without rules, but – as in all sciences and techniques – in conformity with principles. Now the Party leaders, bent on pushing the integration of the group to the limit, feared that the free process of truth, with all the discussions and all the conflicts which it involves, would break the unity of combat; they reserved for themselves the right to define the line and to interpret the event.[28]

Thus was a practical philosophy, designed to elicit and promote a heady sense of the freedom and responsibility of human creativity, turned into a coercive ideology.

If human visions were judged solely by human failure to make them fully real in act, few would be worth remembering. Its competitors should not congratulate themselves too quickly on the present demise of Marxist communism in the West. Marx's vision still remains the most impressive and comprehensive humanist moral vision so far extant. There have been, of course, other humanist visions. At the first Catholic–

Humanist Conference in the United States of America held in New York in 1973, Charles Frankel offered an atheistic humanist's philosophy of the state and its power.[29] Like most of the liberal agnostic or atheistic kinds of humanism, and very unlike the Marxist kind, Frankel's philosophy saw no need to look beyond the state structures of modern representative democracies. His definition of humanism itself is minimalist in the extreme: 'humanists agree that it is possible to discuss moral and political questions, and to arrive at answers to them as well grounded as can be reached by any other approach, without appealing to the existence of a supernatural God'. A notable absence of any appeal to God is thus both necessary and sufficient to render humanist any proffered political philosophy.

An appeal to God is quite unnecessary for one who tries to describe as well as well may be, the moral basis for the authority of the state, the bounds of such authority, and 'the rules by which state-behaviour should be judged'. Frankel observes that there is no 'wholesale' justification of authority in any of the manifold forms in which it is operative in everyday existence for all of us. And that goes for the state as much as for any other 'authority.' There is at most a presumption in favour of the authority of the state, there is a '*de facto* authority', 'if one thinks that the values it secures are greater than the values likely to be gained by overthrowing it or disobeying it'. And, if the state has built into its structure legal and effective means of removing those in positions of authority when such values appear to be threatened, there is so much additional reason for maintaining the authority of such a state. What are the values, the 'higher moral principles' which provide the *raison d'être* for the state and for its legislative, judicial, and executive functions? These consist, ensemble, in 'a vision of the possibilities of human life, and of the conditions which men must strive to fulfil if life is to have any flavour'. This is not, of course, a fixed vision. Indeed each civilisation 'may have such a vision ... only partially articulate, but incorporated in its traditions, its most cherished habits, its literature and philosophy, its central memories and institutions'. This vision, these values, are of an order which only a community as comprehensive as a state could properly pursue; they thus provide its *raison d'être*, and at the same time act as criteria for the legitimate conduct of its affairs, and for finding the bounds of such conduct. As ends these higher values and visions are 'broader, more persisting, more centrally integrative'; more particular laws and acts of the state, on the contrary, are 'the means whose validity is established in relation to these ends [and] thus become more deeply obligatory'. The higher moral principles are 'not matters of convention or current fashion. Nevertheless, although they are, in this sense, transcendent principles, they are not vindicated by escaping the human frame and moving to one that is transcendental.' There, surely, in admirably succinct form, is a typical liberal humanist philosophy of state power in the mode of authority and in a purely secularist frame.

But, one might well say, these are political philosophies worked out in the minds of philosophers. What of political philosophies worked out for actual states, philosophies which have in part reflected, in part influenced the development of states still very much with us? Do any of these exhibit a purely secular sense of power? If one were to cast about for examples of a possibly affirmative answer to this question, Hobbes would surely spring quickly to mind. Described by D'Entrèves and by others as 'the first modern theory of the modern state', Hobbes' philosophy is centrally concerned with the nature and locus of sovereignty (*summa potestas*), a topic returned to common currency in this country in the present anguish over increasing political unity in Europe. Sovereignty to Hobbes was the very soul of the state – but it was, of course, an artifact as the state itself is an artifact; no organic theory confers supreme power here on some corporate personality to which individuals are by nature subjected. The artifact is created rather by those pacts and covenants by which people reject the war of all against all, the rule of naked force, the reign of terror which, far from being a distant memory or a legendary construct, still lies in wait beneath the civilised surface of society, sometimes as close to that surface as to distort and disrupt it, and to call up the lines of Yeats from 'The Second Coming':

> And what rough beast, its hour come round at last,
> slouches towards Bethlehem to be born?

This sovereignty, created by these pacts and covenants, and once conferred on the 'sovereign representative' of the people, be that an individual or 'an assembly of men', is absolute (*legibus solutus*) and indivisible. While it exists a living state exists; when it ceases nothing is left but the remains, subject once more to naked force from within and without. But, although this sovereign is absolute, even in the jurisprudential sense that all law is an expression of its will, and its will, and nothing beyond its will, is the necessary and sufficient condition for valid law, it is not arbitrary, not itself an instance of force. This is because it is 'authorised' power, authorised by the people's covenant; and also because it exists in order to provide precisely that basic security of life which gives prospects of life more abundant for all: it has authorised source and rational purpose.

Hobbes' concept of sovereignty has been criticised for failing to accommodate certain features which were later taken to be necessary, or at least desirable, namely, a certain compatibility with the so-called 'division of powers' into legislative, judicial, and executive categories, and with the growth of international law by which sovereign states could be, if only voluntarily, regulated in their mutual relationships. But it is quite another criticism of Hobbes that makes his theory most relevant to this present analysis. This was the criticism mounted by church-men of Hobbes' explicit and, to him, logical conclusion from the unity and absoluteness of state sovereignty: the conclusion that no comparable authority could exist within a sovereign state; no church, for example, which might claim to exercise 'spiritual' government as distinct from 'temporal,' sacred, as we might say, as distinct from secular. This exclusion was fully in accord with another and larger exclusion, which may be expressed positively as Hobbes' nominalism or his positivist conception of law: only that laid down by the will of the authorised sovereign in the state could be deemed law. Thus was excluded any possibility of appeal to law deriving from any other source. Alleged laws of nature, or of God, were then no

laws in fact, however many people might feel themselves subjects in a 'kingdom of fairies, in the dark', and might believe
such things to be laws obligatory upon them.[30]

Hobbes was a philosopher primarily, and not a recognised
authority in jurisprudence. If his portrait of Leviathan is so
austerely secular, at least in this respect, that it excludes any
source of legal obligation other than the sovereign will of the
'mortal god' created by the people for their own temporal ends,
the question may still remain: does British jurisprudence ever
paint a similar portrait? The answer most likely is, yes. But
much more erudition and space than is available here, would
be necessary in order to support that monosyllabic response.

The supporting evidence would take one from Henry VIII's
Caesaro-papism through Cromwell's model of the king-in-
parliament to Sir William Blackstone's jurisprudential theory
in the 1760s. At a time when the traditional limitations on state
sovereignty, to wit, natural and divine law, were themselves
proving weak, Blackstone set out to counter Locke's claim that
the people had the power to remove or alter the legislature
when it acted contrary to their trust. Such 'devolution of power
to the people at large' Blackstone thought subversive of the
very form of government established by these same people; and
so he insisted that, so long as the English constitution lasted,
the power of parliament would be absolute and without
control. The weakening of the sense of the presence of such
moral limitations as natural or divine law seems important for
the success of Blackstone's move, for unless people have something like these to which to appeal in time of rebellion, the
reign of raw force is with us once again. Blackstone did not
quite see this, for he tried to introduce a concept of fundamental law to the English constitution. His efforts were ridi-
culed by Bentham as evidence of the intrusion of Anglican
articles, and it was Bentham and his disciple, Austin, who
really sought to strip the common-law sovereign of its Anglican
and natural law limitations. 'These were, they held, mere
fictions, part of the rhetoric of the Anglican Church and King
ascendancy. That done, both Austin and Bentham were
content to accept Hobbes' absolute precept that law was

merely whatever the sovereign commanded.'[31] The Victorian jurist Dicey considered and promptly rejected the proposition that parliament could pass laws which would be irrevocably binding upon future parliaments; for that too would limit sovereignty. The end result was a jurisprudence for which sovereignty resides, not in the people as a whole, but in an institution (Crown, Lords and Commons), and an orthodoxy of legal textbooks for which the only fundamental law was that parliament was supreme, and there was no constitutional law at all in Britain – only the arbitrary power of parliament.

Before assessing the claims of that kind of jurisprudence to present a purely secular model of sovereign power, and because one of the churches which has been used as an example of power structure, and will shortly be used again, is the established Church of Scotland, it may be well to consider the possible implications of Lord Davidson's view that: 'so far as common law in concerned, it is essential to distinguish England and Scotland. Whereas the bulk of Parliamentary legislation applies to both jurisdictions, there is still a body of statute law which applies to Scotland alone.'[32] Does Scotland then present a picture of state sovereignty as seemingly secular as that painted in English jurisprudence? At first sight it might seem not.

Scotland's version of Hobbes was surely Samuel Rutherford, whose *Lex Rex* appeared in 1644. Sovereignty for Rutherford resides in God, and to such an extent that it is God's will, and God's will alone, which constitutes good and evil: 'Things are just and good because God willeth them and God does not will things, because they are good and just.'[33] There is no need to seek a unitary location for any alleged *summa potestas* in human society, and certainly not in some institution created by a social contract binding upon future generations and allowing little or no room for resistance. Rather has God instituted a moral and political order in which each is free to follow conscience. Ruler or government will have its own role and status in such an order, and its own authority, but there will be no presumption in its favour that it can discern any better than others the just and good which God has willed. 'The creature, be he king or any never so eminent, do will things because they are good and just.'[34] Things are good and just because God willed them so, as was said, but God's constitutive will in matters of morality and law is so transparent in all essentials that it can be discovered by all: 'the Scriptures in all fundamentals are clear and expone themselves and this is true of all laws of men in their fundamentals, which are the law of nature and of nations'.[35] Hence it may be deemed as likely that the people will correct the king as that the king will most wisely direct his people, and in cases where both go astray the remedy must lie with God alone. No human institution could be entrusted with the overarching, sovereign right to arbitrate between them, much less to take charge of both when together they stray from justice.

Leave out of account for the moment the obvious moral objection to the thesis that something, anything indeed, is good or just in the moral meaning of these words simply because God wills it, and we surely have here the very antithesis of Hobbes. The *summa potestas* is sacred, the only real sovereignty belongs to God. Yet the result in purely political terms is thoroughly democratic, since in the discernment of what is just no one has any intrinsic advantage over another. As Anthony Carty puts it: 'The interchange between the institution and the wider society would have to be continuous, as would be dispute over the evident principles of scripture and the law of nature.'[36]

Although Francis Hutcheson's name is confidently inscribed amongst the luminaries of the Scottish Enlightenment of the eighteenth century, that most anglicising of events in Scotland's cultural history, his theory of jurisprudence is demonstrably closer to Rutherford than to any of his English or European counterparts.[37] Nowhere is this more obvious than in the contrast with the views of his fellow Scottish Enlightener, Adam Smith, whose basic theory could be quite easily mistaken for Blackstone's if title-pages went missing. Allegations of divine right of kings or of the inherited rights of king-in-parliament would simply lead Hutcheson, in Carty's words, 'to say that whatever contracts of government are concluded the people remain the arbiters of their interest and can revoke these powers as they see fit'.[38] In Hutcheson's own words, 'The rights of governors, magistrates, or clergy are no otherwise sacred than those of other men ... God has not by any revelation determined the forms of government ... His law requires that government should be settled ... But the form of polity, and the degrees of power to be committed, are left to human prudence.'[39] This, in Hutcheson's view as in Rutherford's, is because rulers, like their subjects, are bound by the laws of God and of nature; no presumption can favour the former's interpretation of these laws over the latter's; indeed, if anything, the latter are more likely to discern and actively seek the common good.

Now there is the clearest difference between these Scottish, indeed characteristically Presbyterian, views of power in human society, and the views of the sovereignty of crown-in-parliament which won the day south of the Scottish border. The difference centres upon the twin themes of the overarching authority of the law of God and of nature, and the diffusion of power amongst rulers and ruled. In the Rutherford–Hutcheson model these elements were as conspicuously present in jurisprudential theory as in the other model they were with persistent determination removed. This should mean that where the Scottish model prevailed even state power was never seen to be purely secular; for the interplay of restricted empowerment of rulers and ruled was, on this model, always predicated upon the discernment and application of what God had made good and just by the sole exercise of the legislative authority of the divine will. Unfortunately, however, it is not only philosophers whose prescriptions fail to correspond with historical realities; theories of jurisprudence can also fail to reflect the concrete realities of the play of power in a particular state. And so it is necessary to attend to the practical details of legislatures and judiciaries and to their specific acts and decisions, in order to be able to say with some confidence that a given civil power is secular or sacred, or to say which of these it seems to take itself to be in its actual exercises. That brings us back to Lord Davidson's position, and to two practical features of that position in particular: the practical influence of Christianity upon the actual laws of the land in Scotland, and the (probably changing) practical implications of the establishment principle.

By an Act of 1567, according to Lord Davidson, the Scottish Parliament abrogated all laws canon, civil or municipal which were not in accord with the Reformed Faith. That might suggest a rather complete influence of Reformed Christianity upon the law of Scotland. Yet when Lord Davidson quotes the *Stair Memorial Encyclopedia* on the sources of law, he finds that 'The Law of the Bible' is given as explicit source in but a restricted number of legal matters: forbidden degrees in relation to incest, the contraction of marriage, divorce, succession, blasphemy, Sunday observance, and witchcraft. Even in these cases he shows how a variety of influences, ranging from desuetude to the simple practical recognition that not all could be expected to live up to the full Christian ideal, could work to limit the influence of biblical principles upon the legislative process. Outside of these restricted areas, it is Lord Davidson's opinion that, although it is possible to discern Christian origins, over the course of time the laws have come to be justified upon purely secular and utilitarian grounds. In part illustrative of this point he quotes Lord Atkin: 'the rule that you are to love your neighbour becomes in law you must not injure your neighbour, and the lawyer's question "who is my neighbour?" receives a restricted reply.'[40]

Of course, as Lord Davidson notes, up until the middle of the nineteenth century there is a body of judicial dicta, some by eminent English judges also, asserting that Christianity was part of the law of the land; and in Scotland confessions of faith of the General Assembly of the Church of Scotland were enacted by the Scots parliament, some of which still stand unappealed. But the first part of that double proposition must surely make us wonder what effect ensued upon actual legislation, given the drift towards secular or utilitarian grounds for laws, and given also the fact that the most obvious legislative results, the laws which discriminated against unwanted claimants to Christianity, to wit, Dissenters and Roman Catholics, had to be repealed (in 1828 and 1829 respectively); and the second part of that double proposition postulates an analysis and interpretation of the establishment principle.

The trouble with analysing the establishment principle in a context which focusses upon the distinction of secular and sacred power, is caused not so much by the problem of sifting through the many acts in which the principle might be said to be contained, defined or changed, but rather by the ambivalence with respect to the present focus of interest which some of the clearest examples of the establishment principle can be seen to entail. Take, for example, the legal disputes which led up to the celebrated Disruption of the Church of Scotland in 1843.

These disputes between church courts and civil courts in Scotland concerned ordination and appointments to parishes, and an increase in the number of parish churches and *quoad sacra* parishes. The upshot of these disputes, in the words of Stewart J. Brown, was that,

according to the judgments of the Court of Sessions and the House of Lords ... the Church of Scotland, as an established church, was a creation of statute law. At the Scottish Reformation of 1560, the old medieval Roman Catholic Church had been swept away and a new national religious Establishment had been created by the state to provide religious instruction and administer the sacraments to the people of Scotland. The state had given the Established Church certain privileges, including the privilege of managing its internal affairs. But the Established Church possessed no independent jurisdiction and no inherent rights. It was not outside the civil law, nor could it encroach on civil rights as defined by the state. There could be only one sovereign power in the state, that of the Crown in Parliament, and this power could not alienate sovereignty by recognising any independent jurisdiction.[41]

By this time there was no longer a Scottish parliament and, as Brown observes, 'for English Whigs, moreover, Parliament was the safeguard of civil and religious liberties, the force that had withstood the efforts of Stuart monarchs to impose absolutist rule or to revive the "tyranny" of the Roman Catholic Church. To them it seemed absurd for Scottish Non-intrusionists to insist that the Established Church must be outside the sovereignty of Parliament in order to secure its liberty.'[42] A certain secularisation of sovereignty could be said to have resulted from the Reform Bill of 1832 in that the suppression of 140 proprietory parliamentary seats, the granting of the vote to much of the urban middle class, and the right of inclusion of Dissenters and Roman Catholics, made it difficult to conceive of a sovereignty that was exercised by a divine right monarchy, a divinely sanctioned social hierarchy, and a specific confession.[43]

This was naturally not the view of the entailment of establishment status that was taken by those churchmen in Scotland who initiated the Disruption; nor is it taken by all Scottish lawyers, even today. The former espoused the doctrine of 'the two kingdoms', one civil under the sovereignty of the crown in parliament, the other spiritual under the sovereignty of Christ. Establishment involved a contract with the state, not subordination to it; and, if the church in pursuance of its spiritual objectives incidentally affected the livelihood or reputation of individuals, their civil rights, that could not be deemed to diminish its intrinsic power in its proper province. Lord Davidson may provide an example of a similar view taken by a modern expert in jurisprudence. He quotes as an expression of the establishment principle the Articles Declaratory of the Constitution of the Church of Scotland, enacted by parliament in 1921. According to Article 6:

This Church acknowledges the divine appointment and authority of the civil magistrate within his sphere, and maintains its historic testimony to the duty of the nation acting in its corporate capacity to render homage to God, to acknowledge the Lord Jesus Christ to be King over the nations, to obey his laws, to reverence his ordinances, to honour his Church, and to promote in all appropriate ways the Kingdom of God. The Church and the State owe mutual duties to each other, and acting within their respective spheres may singly promote each other's welfare. The Church and the State have the right to determine each for itself all questions concerning the extent and the continuance of their mutual relations in the discharge of these duties and the obligations arising therefrom.

Lord Davidson himself points to a weakness in this formula, in that 'it is a mere opinion as to what some third person is bound to do, which he may neglect or refuse to do and which he cannot be compelled to do'.[44] This to a layman seems to mean that no specific law need be deemed to be imposed because of its Christian or ecclesiastical origin. Yet Lord Davidson believes that the very enactment of this Article implies state acceptance of duties to the church broadly defined in the terms used in its first sentence. That first sentence expressed *church* acknowledgment and *church* testimony to the divine origin of civil authority and of its religious duties; and so it would perhaps be a fair assessment of Lord Davidson's view of the implications of establishment, to say that the state in a manner of speaking engages the kirk to preach to the nation an idealist rather than a materialist philosophy of life, and that the resulting influence upon the legislation on which the corporate body of the state embarks through its institutions, would be both generally beneficent and reasonably specific, even if it were to be an influence that was thought to operate directly upon the populace at large, and only more indirectly upon their legislators (who are in any case now located in London).

It would be difficult to say that this Scottish excursus ended in a view of state power that is very much less secular than its English counterpart. Even the 'politics of suspicion' which derive from Rutherford's and Hutcheson's refusal to see any sovereignty located on earth can be translated these days into a purely secular, post-modern theory of power in human society, a theory of rapidly revolving governments as frequently and fully answerable as possible to the people's changing perceptions of their common good; with the only remaining idea of sovereignty confined, as Rutherford wanted, to God (and this only in the private opinions of remaining religious groups), whence it would no longer exercise any statutory influence upon the practice of civil power.

Hence the presumption in favour of the actual existence of powers operative at the societal level, which are purely secular in nature and function, is by now quite overwhelming. In the case of those modern democratic governments with which we are most familiar, neither the source of their power nor the content of their laws and practices seems to require the support of religious objects or beliefs. Remaining state references to God, religion, and churches, look more like the flotsam of sunken vessels than the necessary rigging of a still seaworthy ship; or else they look like little more than the necessary dealings with large private corporations within a state which, despite the fact that some of them are religious in purpose, are like other corporations both in needing to be regulated and in exercising a certain 'lobbying' influence, directly or indirectly, upon legislative bodies.

Now why, it might well be asked, should the distinction between secular and sacred, and the impression that purely and persistently secular powers exist at a certain part of the range of social structuring, why should this appear to be clearer in the case of governments when it is so unclear in the case of that plethora of moral craftspersons considered in a previous part of this chapter? Partly, no doubt, because so much recent political theory and practice, since the end of the *ancien régime*, has explicitly addressed the distinction of sacred and secular and, very frequently, the issue of their separation, if not also the suppression of the sacred. Yet some of the considerations urged in earlier parts of this chapter in order to prevent too premature a distinction between powers secular and powers sacred are also relevant here, where governments rather than individuals or groups are in question.

At the American Catholic–Humanist Dialogue, to which reference has already been made, the Catholic counterpart to Frankel's paper was Daniel C. Maguire's 'Catholic Conscience and the State'.[45] In Maguire's view,

Both church and state must somehow manifest the sacred and reflect absolute value. They must evoke from their faithful a devotion so great that they will go even to the point of death for the institution and its causes. This may seem poetic imagery but it is very practical truth. As A. D. Lindsay writes in his *The Essentials of Democracy*, 'There can be no stable government unless men are prepared to die for it. If government itself is not recognised as absolute – and that is no longer possible – it must stand for, be the instrument of something absolute.' Neither church nor state can be a mere corporation of utility. Men will not die for utility.

Add to this what Goethe's Mephistopheles called 'the cruel thirst for worship' which infects most people in the presence of the greatest power they know, and the prospect of state power seeming more sacred than secular returns with a vengeance; and it attaches itself to a wider range of examples than those totalitarian states erected in the name of modern humanisms of the fascist or communist kinds which spring most readily to mind.

So here, also, in the case of states and their governments, as previously in the case of the more diffuse company of ethical 'powers', the task of distinguishing secular from sacred reaches a point of apparently innate uncertainty. Tillich talked about the divine in terms of that which engaged our ultimate concern, but allowed the possibility that people can make into objects of ultimate concern things (my country right or wrong) or goals (control of resources) which do not deserve that status, and as a result he was prepared to describe as quasi-religious the ensuing commitments, beliefs, and practices. That is one way, certainly, of trying to plot a graph at some point of which powers secular begin to be and to act very like powers sacred; powers, that is, that deal out life and death, and to whom, or to the absolutes they make present, the sacrifice of human life itself is due.[46]

CHURCHES AND POWER SACRED

What then, finally, of Christian churches? If it is difficult to find amongst other moral powers clear-cut distinctions between secular and sacred, is it possible to find in churches at least some undiluted examples of powers sacred? In order to answer this question with any degree of accuracy it would be necessary to survey the range of pronouncements which a particular church makes in matters of morals, as well as actions it might take which have a bearing on the ethical interests of society at large. Take the Roman Catholic Church for instance. It talks about reaching 'authority' (*magisterium*) in matters of faith and morals; but it would probably be necessary to expand that twofold distinction to at least a threefold one.

There are, first, church pronouncements (or other forms of communication) which have as their subject matter what is known or believed about God or about God's plans. These make up what believers call 'the faith' and they do not concern us directly here.[47] There are, second, what one might call the 'rules of the club', the rules and regulations which govern the membership of any private association, where 'private' is now used to distinguish such associations from the *res publica*, the state. These rules are voluntarily adopted upon joining the association, and for serious breaches of them individuals might well be asked, or even forced, to leave. These are at most of indirect interest in this context. It might well be that the 'rules of the club' are subject to the overarching regulation of laws governing just dealings in society at large: for example, the 'club' might wish to remove a member who made his or her living out of a job within the club, but in so doing it would have to respect due process in dismissal proceedings, and perhaps to pay such redundancy moneys as the society at large deemed just. But for the rest, the 'rules of the club', rules and regulations concerning admission, meetings, conduct of the associations' distinctive business, offices and officers, and so on, are matters of private agreement, not matters of moral interest to people at large.

There are, thirdly and finally, the rules, portraits and ideals which are designed for the well-being of free creative persons in this world. These are properly moral matters and it is with respect to these that our question can be properly specified. Do churches act with power in these matters, and are we then dealing with secular or sacred power? That Christian churches do seek to act with power in such moral matters is rather obvious to the most neutral observer; but will the answer to the 'secular or sacred?' question prove any the less elusive in this final category than it has in the categories already considered? Perhaps the only way to answer that question is to take some concrete examples of Christian churches in their public moralising mode. The Roman Catholic Church (in Ireland) and the Church of Scotland can continue to supply the spectrum of images along which other churches could with little enough difficulty be aligned.

The forging of the Roman Catholic Church into a truly effective influence in Irish society owes most to one man, Archbishop Paul Cullen, who arrived in Armagh in 1850 and was transferred to the See of Dublin in 1852. With the full blessing and the resources of the Vatican behind him, he reformed the Irish clergy and religious and drew people to the practice of a very Romanised Catholicism with awesome enthusiasm and remarkable success. He moved against his fellow archbishops in significant ways. With the Archbishop of Cashel it was a matter of mainly pastoral reform, but with the archbishops of Tuam and Dublin Cullen's opposition to their policies revealed a very significant choice of interest in education over interest in politics. John McHale of Tuam rather favoured the direct involvement of the clergy in secular politics, in particular in the Tenant League, a land reform movement; Daniel Murray of Dublin favoured co-operation with the new Queen's Colleges, the state system for third-level education, of which only the Queen's University of Belfast still retains the name. But Cullen opposed clerical involvement in the native political movement – he found the home-rulers too Fenian and too Protestant – and he fell out with the Liberals when Gladstone refused him his desired Catholic University; he then single-mindedly concentrated his quest for clerical power and influence upon the provisions being made for the education of the Irish people.[48]

The English have long learned the good imperial practice of trying some social experiment first in an outer region before bringing it to the home counties. When it goes wrong, as in the recent case of the Poll Tax in Scotland, the home counties *could* benefit from the lesson; when it goes right the peripheries benefit first, a due reward for first undergoing the risk. A national school system was first tried in Ireland in the 1830s. It worked, and it was this system which the local Catholic clergy came to control. Then religious orders, some of them, the Christian Brothers for instance, founded for this very purpose, provided for the Irish people in the impoverished state in which the withdrawing English left them early in this century, the truly Christian service of a secondary education also, something they could not otherwise have afforded. The university system alone retained some independence of the clergy, though local bishops exercised as much influence as they could upon its colleges, and the Archbishop of Dublin until a few decades ago forbade Catholics, under pain of excommunication, to enter Trinity College without special permission from himself. Because the newly born Irish Free State in the 1920s preserved in its constitutional framework the usual separation of church and state characteristic of new democracies in the West, the nature and extent of the Catholic Church's influence upon Irish affairs is to be understood to this day primarily in terms of its claim to secure the education of the vast majority of the Irish people as Roman Catholics.[49] That claim naturally carries over into, is already part and parcel of, the claim to instruct all of the Irish people who are members of the Catholic Church, in matters of Catholic morality. It would come as no surprise to find the Irish Catholic Church involved – and let this be our set of concrete examples – when the Irish State in recent times proposed legislation, or changes in legislation, in matters of family morality: divorce, abortion, and contraception.

Now the main thing to notice about the matters just mentioned is this: from the point of view of our present question they are all in substance secular matters. That is to say, since, according to the more reliable authorities, the other world will have neither marriage nor giving in marriage and hence, at least in the Roman Catholic view, sexual activity will neither be required nor permitted, the matters just mentioned belong to the *saecula*, the ages of history, the secular era. The marriage of Christians may be a symbol of sacred things – the union of Christ and his church, for instance – but its *raison d'être*, its tenancy of time, its substance, is not the less secular for that. Any claim to the exercise of sacred power in these matters would have to be based, therefore, not on their substance, but on some special divine revelation alleged in their regard. The problems connected with claims to special divine revelation or moral precepts have been aired already in a previous chapter.[50] But let us take here three concrete examples of Roman

Catholic teaching on the morality of sex and marriage – contraception, divorce, abortion – and see if the substance of the teaching can reveal its source and basis.

The papal prohibition of the use of 'artificial' methods of contraception, in the Encyclical *Humanae Vitae* of 1968, could scarcely be based on texts of Scripture; it was in fact argued from natural law. Paul VI argued in *Humanae Vitae* that each act of intercourse is dual purpose: it unites the couple, and has a natural potential to procreate life. He claimed that God established 'an inseparable connection' between these two purposes, so that anyone who deliberately deprived the act of its natural potential to procreate, and used it only to express married union, thereby defied God's will. Yet he positively recommended use of the so-called safe period for purposes of avoiding conception in the course of family planning. Now nothing either in the 'sources of revelation' or in 'natural law' shows God establishing an inseparable connection between union and potential for procreation in every act of marital intercourse. As a matter of fact, the very existence of an infertile period proves that such an inseparable connection for every act of intercourse does not exist. For God has not forbidden marital intercourse during this period; and to speak of the act retaining a natural potential to procreate human life at a time when such procreation is biologically impossible, is a forcing of language in order to secure a conclusion which, without such forcing, could never stand up.

The papal argument was fatally flawed, as an unprecedented 'revolt' amongst Catholic theologians most amply illustrated, making the power with which Rome has since tried to impose that precept more like a form of attempted force than a genuine exercise of authority. In this piece of moral legislation, then, Rome simply got it wrong; and it would be foolish of anyone to try to say, in face of such a bad law, that the power behind it was sacred.

The case of divorce is more complex. The Roman Catholic Church claims that 'a marriage which is ratified and consummated cannot be dissolved by any human power or by any cause other than death' (canon 1141), whereas 'a non-consummated marriage between baptised persons or between a baptised party and an unbaptised party can be dissolved by the Roman Pontiff for a just reason' (canon 1142); and there are conditions under which the marriages of the non-baptised are dissolved, which need not concern us further here. This means of course that, contrary to popular impressions, the Roman Catholic Church does allow divorce, in the strict sense of a process involving the dissolution of an existing marriage bond, and not just a declaration of the nullity of a putative marriage. There would appear to be two major restrictions upon the prospects of divorce, however, and both call for some brief comment. First, if a valid marriage between two baptised persons (an adequate gloss on 'ratified') is consummated (by an act of natural intercourse), that marriage cannot be dissolved. Second, the Roman Pontiff is the one to whom the power to dissolve marriages, the power to grant divorces, is attributed in cases where it is allowed that this can be done.

Once again it would be extremely difficult to draw from the Scriptures a clear ruling upon the morality of divorce. Any prospect of unanimity in the two main New Testament texts where Jesus is made to discuss the issue (Matthew 9: 3–10; Mark 10: 2–12) is ruined by Matthew's insertion of the *me epi porneia*, 'except for unchastity' clause; and the Pauline text which contains the most obscure phrase 'This is a great mystery, and I take it to mean Christ and his Church', is all about the wife being subject to her husband 'in everything' (as the Church is to Christ?), and the husband loving his wife like his own body (as Christ does the Church?); and nothing further can be easily read out of this pedagogic use of imagery, either about the sacramentality of matrimony, or about divorce (Ephesians 5: 21–3).

In fact, if some prohibition of divorce could be read into these texts – by eisegesis rather than exegesis – it would certainly be a general one, and as such it would undermine rather than support the practice and theory of the Roman Catholic Church, which allows the possibility of divorce for specified reasons in all but one class of marriage. That church, is short, implicitly invokes 'the hardness of your hearts' in certain specified forms as justifying divorce, and thus implies that it itself does not take Jesus to have ruled out divorce legislation entirely, however much he stressed the ideal of fidelity unto death for all types of marriage.[51] Further, even when one fully accepts the Roman Catholic view that the marriages of baptised Christians is a sacrament, the simple fact of its sacramental character does not rule out divorce and remarriage, for some sacraments can be conferred more than once, and in the case of the dissolution of the non-consummated marriage of the baptised, it must be presumed that this has happened. Which leads to the really fascinating question of the role of the 'consummation' now that it appears to carry the burden of alleged indissolubility.

It is possible that only a celibate, and one who was a virgin to boot, could read such significance into a single act of natural intercourse, especially one which, in orthodox Roman Catholic expectation, might well represent one's first performance. In 1978 the International Theological Commission of the Roman Catholic Church published some 'propositions' on this matter and did raise the question of a thorough examination of this notion of the consummation of marriage,[52] but little or nothing has since emerged to render less incomprehensible the continuing claim that this class of marriage is absolutely indissoluble by God's will or by divine law. We would appear to be once again in the presence of an institution, marriage, which is secular in substance, the prospects of the annulment of which are governed by precepts which reveal no real traces of sacred origin; all in all a thoroughly secular exercise of legislative power.

This impression is strengthened rather than weakened by the apparent claim that where marriages can be and are dissolved this must be done by the Roman Catholic powers that be, and not by any other legislature or judiciary; a factor which in the Republic of Ireland gives rise to the farcical, were it not such a potentially tragic, situation in which people are divorced or have their marriages declared null by the church, and remarry, though the state, which does not permit divorce, must regard their first marriages to be still valid. The real extent and significance of this church's claim to power in this matter becomes obvious when one realises that the power is said to extend to marriages of the unbaptised (even consummated marriages of the unbaptised), despite the fact that the Genesis text which Jesus quoted applied to just such marriages – Christian marriage not having been as yet instituted – and despite the fact that these are so thoroughly secular that they are in no way sacramental.[53] Now this claim of Rome to be the judicial and executive power over marriages of Christian and non-Christian alike, as well as the legislative power, is clearly a hangover from the theocratic days of the Holy Roman Empire; it is Caesaro-papism in its purest form, and in the modern era it could succeed in establishing itself only in a country the majority of the citizens of which had been well educated to accept it.

The Roman Catholic Church leaders, then, are wrong to represent the introduction of divorce legislation as being contrary to the teaching of Jesus and the law of God, or to seem to represent divorce as immoral in itself. Their church's own practice does not bear out such alleged convictions. It is even disingenuous of them to say that they do not wish to tell people how to vote on a government proposal to introduce divorce legislation, that they only wish to inform people's consciences before they decide themselves how to vote; for people must vote for legislation (which is a form of morality) according to their consciences, and church leaders are in this case misinforming people's consciences.[54]

Abortion, to take the third of the legal and moral issues on which church and state in Ireland have recently encountered each other, is a most complex moral problem. A reasonable end to the quest for reasonable legislation on this issue depends on such elusives as, first, the detection of the moment of origin of a new and truly human life (a common assumption being that other forms of life, even conscious and sensitive life, can be freely taken for human use and benefit); second, the related matters of the threat to a mother's life which may be posed by pregnancy (whether one must count in this respect the expected length and quality of the mother's life, and her mental health also, or just the physical continuance of that life), and of the 'innocence' of the foetus. The usual ambiance of hypocrisy surrounds the discussion of this moral issue also in 'First World' countries, in which the very high material quality of life is relentlessly pursued by all at the cost of the stunting of human life and the deaths of millions elsewhere on the earth. Not much evidence of anguished moralising at the political or ecclesiastical level here, as to whether it is right that so many should die for the quality of life of the already over privileged.

The traditional teaching of the Roman Catholic Church allowed abortion – i.e. the removal of a foetus from the womb when such removal would be fatal for it, or the termination of its life – only as the indirect and unwanted side-effect of a justifiable operation to save a woman's life. If, for example, a cancerous womb threatened a pregnant woman's life, it could be removed or operated on even though it contained a live foetus not yet viable on its own. These cases the Catholic hierarchy seeks to gather under the rubric of the so-called 'act of two effects', where the one effect, the saving of the mother's life, is direct and intended, the other, the threat to the life of the foetus, an unfortunate and unwanted side-effect of the action taken. (The second effect can hardly be said to be unintentional; a known effect of an action intentionally taken itself falls under the intentionality of that act.) Now this seems to some to be a clear case of casuistry. But it would surely be more promising to call it a piece of case law, and to seek to develop its logic with a view to arriving at a more comprehensive morality of abortion.

Put it this way. It might be a mistake to give priority in this piece of moralising to the language of direct and indirect (and the language of intentional and unintentional does not really work). That could simply obscure what is really at issue, namely, the fact that tragic cases do occur in which the right to life of foetus and mother come into conflict; one can be saved only at the expense of threatening or positively ending the other. In cases where it might appear that it can manage to apply the language of direct and indirect, the Catholic hierarchy allows the mother's life to be saved at the expense of the foetus. But there are cases in which people are faced with exactly the same clash of rights, the same anguished choice between saving the mother and threatening or destroying the foetus, or refusing to threaten the life of the foetus and thereby putting the mother's life at serious risk; and in these cases the distinction between direct and indirect is difficult if not impossible to maintain with any honesty. The treatment of a pregnant woman for breast cancer attacks the foetus in the womb just as directly as it attacks the malignant cells at which it is aimed. The 'morning after pill' is directly abortifacient when offered to victims of rape or incest. And in the classic case of ectopic pregnancy the pretence that one is directly removing 'an obstruction' or 'a sack', but only indirectly removing a foetus, marks the point at which such language has become self-delusory. Church leaders who continue to insist on such language in instructing the faithful are either deluding themselves into thinking that they are not really allowing abortion at all, or they are restricting without adequate reason the cases in which it could be argued that the mother's life may be protected at the expense of the life of a foetus. In either case, adherence to this language in Ireland has the effect of misleading the faithful in matters of morals.

Once again, since church leaders can claim no special divine revelation on this complex issue, they co-operate, from the viewpoint of a modern secular society, as one authority amongst others in seeking answers to the double question: what is the morality of abortion? And what of this ought to be passed into the law of the land? Whatever authority the institutional church might claim over its voluntary membership (and it might well urge them towards ideals which could not be enforced by law upon all); whatever distinctive aids it might claim in the general human task of creative morality (and that must be considered fully in the second half of this book), it cannot claim the power to pre-decide issues of morality or law for society at large, much less to dictate the details of legislation to the state.

The conclusion just drawn has been based upon the examples just analysed, but it cannot be confined to these examples. It stems from the nature of morality and from the relationships of morality and law, which these examples and others like them serve only to illustrate. And it applies to all forms of attempted ecclesiastical dictation of state legislation. The Roman Catholic Church in Ireland has frequently affirmed through its highest office-bearers that it desires 'a clear distinction between Church and State and that the Constitution was for the people to decide and the laws for the legislators'.[55] It has even more frequently claimed the right and the duty to form the consciences of its members on matters of moral import. Both positions are beyond criticism, provided only that the latter properly acknowledges the rights of the members' moral consciences, and the fact that in many such moral matters lay people have more of the necessary insight and experience than priests. But when the same church mobilises the vast Catholic majority in the Republic of Ireland to see through a particular constitutional amendment, as happened in the case of abortion in 1983, or to prevent the passing of legislation on divorce, as happened in 1987, there are some grounds for the accusation that it seeks to impose its own moral judgments on the state by abuse of the voting power of a majority. It has been said already that democracy does not guarantee the rejection of power as force, in favour of power as authority; majority rule can show a force as naked as any despot could exercise. In instances like these the exercise of ecclesiastical power may be in all respects as secular as the most ardent secularist could wish to see – a power to impose precepts which are ethically wrong, such as a ban on contraceptives, or which are too restrictive, such as the attempted prohibition on all divorce legislation and all abortion legislation; and a power exercised by the unjustifiable manipulation of an educational system and a majority vote.[56]

In the case of the Church of Scotland interaction with the state's legislative and judicial functions can once again provide the samples by which to test the sacred or secular nature of the moral power it sought, and seeks, to wield. The case is different from the preceding, in that we now deal with an established church, and not with one which had to learn to live with the modern practice of separation of church and state. And yet, in

the decades immediately preceding Cullen's efforts to forge the
Roman Catholic Church in Ireland into a reformed and
effective instrument in Irish life, the Church of Scotland in the
course of the Disruption of 1843 seemed to be seeking to secure
the autonomy of its spiritual authority against the pretensions
of British sovereignty.

The Disruption, it was noted, was brought on basically by a
row about patronage, a property right held in virtually every
parish in Scotland by which its possessors – the crown, the
landed aristocracy, a burgh council, a university – could
present a licensed candidate for ministry to a parish living. In
1834 the kirk sought to restrict this patronage by giving
increased weight to certain parishioners in the appointment of
ministers. In a second measure in 1834 the kirk, through its
highest court, the General Assembly, adopted a measure
known as the Chapel Act, by which the number of parish
churches would be increased to meet demographic needs. But
it was the litigation concerning patronage that led most
directly to the final clash of church and state when the House of
Lords in 1839 not only decided in favour of the original form of
patronage but offered, through Lord Brougham, its judgment
that the church's courts were subordinate to civil courts,
making the church essentially a department of state. In the
view of the Evangelical Party which at this stage controlled the
General Assembly, as the state had civil authority in its own
province under the sovereignty of crown-in-parliament, the
church had a distinct and separate spiritual authority in its
province under the headship of Christ; and establishment was
a pact freely entered into by these authorities. It was allowed
that, in the exercise of its spiritual jurisdiction, the kirk might
indeed affect such 'civil rights' as a person's livelihood or
reputation, but that prospect was not felt to be sufficient to
qualify the kirk's autonomy of spiritual power in its own
spiritual affairs. It seemed on the face of it a classic distinction
between secular and sacred, even though it was still within the
terms of establishment. All the more so then in 1843, when, in a
truly fine act of disinterested allegiance to principle, over one
third of the ministers left the well-endowed established

church;[57] (this is the 'Disruption'), it seemed as if one could look to a persistent example of the exercise of spiritual power.

However, it must be obvious by now, these matters are never quite as simple as the highest-sounding and best-intentioned declarations would make them seem. As in the case of the Roman Catholic Church, one of the fastest routes to the conclusion that a power is not in practice as sacred as it claims to be, is the analysis of instances of its exercise in which in moral and legal matters it misleads, either by making mistakes in the content of moral rules it seeks to impose, or by attempting to force into state legislation too much of the always time-conditioned morality it has espoused; or both. When this analysis is done in the case of the kirk, it could again appear that whatever might be said of other aspects of its nature and functions, as a *moral power* in society it may not seem very sacred at all.

It should scarcely be necessary to say that the choice of instances in which ecclesiastical moralising went wrong is meant neither to detract from the great and diffuse moral influence for good which churches and religions have always wielded in human society, nor so to pick on some churches that others might be left to feel superior. It is not the superficial humanist game of seeking to discredit religion that is being played here. Rather are the current examples designed to show the fragility of simple assumptions on the part of churches that they have divine guidance on concrete moral matters. They are also designed to show that, if Christians in particular do not analyse more critically and carefully the real, positive factors which their distinctive faith might bring to the common human quest, the aforesaid simple assumptions can do double damage: inflict further moral ineptitude on human society, and deprive it simultaneously of what might prove a promising direction. Certainly, nothing shows better than their occasional moral ineptitude when they seek to act as powers in society, the extent to which churches also are on all fours with the more admittedly secular moral powers which engage in the perennial task of seeking to create, according to their lights, the moral values by which human life can be enhanced, and occasionally also of seeking to define or influence the formal legislation by which a necessary minimum of value must be imposed.

The positive quest for the nature and traces of the sacred allegedly detected by and in the Christian 'way' must await a chapter on the Christian experience of power. It is sufficient for the moment to continue to illustrate the difficulty of distinguishing secular and sacred in this matter, and to do that at this point by questioning the sufficiency of simple official claims and concrete church efforts to act as spiritual powers in moral affairs. The two examples of kirk moralising which must suffice for present purposes, come from the present century, though somewhat earlier than our Irish examples; from the period of depression which followed the early euphoria of the end of the First World War.

The Church of Scotland's Commission on War in 1918 declared the aim of that church to be 'to make Scotland a Christian country in fact as well as name, to realise the vision of our forefathers, and to build on Scottish fields a true city of God'.[58] For this purpose the General Assembly of the church set up a permanent Church and Nation Committee in 1919. No longer acquiescent to the *laissez-faire* doctrine that the pursuit of private interests would secure the common good, the church argued rather reasonably that, since all had suffered in the war, all classes should now enjoy a more equitable distribution of the blessings of a new-born civilisation. But the shared hope of a bright new dawn soon foundered on economic recession, the government soon committed itself to the restoration of *laissez-faire* capitalism, the Scottish working class turned to Labour in such numbers that the Labour Party became the main opposition party in Scotland, and the leaders of the Presbyterian churches in the 1920s faced the choice of sticking with the original vision of equity despite the dark socialist suspicions that greeted the rise of Labour, or receding to a more comfortable alliance with the propertied classes. A Dr John Whyte became something of a *primus inter pares* amongst these leaders. Already a co-convener of the Church and Nation Committee in 1919, he saw his task in the 1920s as the unification of the Presbyterian churches on which, he thought, general social harmony in Scotland could be made to follow. On the concrete social and economic issues which could scarcely be expected to await church reunification, there was first the tendency to retreat into silence on the earlier social commitments, and concentrate on religious duties and 'personal' morality. But the general strike which followed the miners' lock-out in 1926, rendered such silence difficult to sustain, and the real thoughts of many hearts were revealed.

Whyte co-operated with the moderator of the United Free Church in a public statement which focussed on the evils of the general strike, claimed that the churches had no competence in such economic and political issues, and called for prayers for the healing of the nation's wounds. This same moderator it was who saw the ending of the general strike in defeat, as 'a victory for God'. But the miners soldiered on alone. When a deputation from the miners managed to address the church assemblies, both churches continued to take refuge in their alleged incompetence in social and political affairs. And when the Church of Scotland, led by Whyte in this matter also, pressed its willingness to act as mediator, it could hardly have been surprised when the Coal Owners' Association reminded it that the laws of economics, on which it had declared itself incompetent, had to be allowed to hold sway, without any 'meddlement' from the church. Neither could the United Free Church have been too surprised that an evangelising campaign aimed at the mining communities of Fife, where it thought the 'fighting line' which the socialist enemy battered was to be seen, foundered on angry questions put to it about economic laws, the nature of God, and human responsibility. The miners were forced to surrender in 1926, and to return to reprisals and to greater hardship than even they had hitherto experienced, a far cry indeed from the visions of a more equitable society which churchmen had taken to so avidly less than a decade before.

Meanwhile, as Stewart J. Brown observes, church leaders did intervene in political matters in Scotland: 'In 1926, while professing to have no competency to pronounce on the political and economic aspects of the General Strike Presbyterian leaders were pressing for legislation directed against the Scots–Irish Catholic community, as a means, in part, of upholding the existing social order.'[59]

Catholics in Scotland during the First World War had answered the call of their archbishops in Glasgow and Edinburgh to volunteer for military service; they had suffered their fair share of death and mutilation, and might have expected a fair share in the new social order to which the established church committed itself when the war was won. Instead the Church and Nation Committee, which was set up to seek the new order, and church leaders such as John Whyte, initiated and carried through against them a campaign which for sheer racist prejudice had few equals in this unfortunate century, and these few are easily named. The fact that Roman Catholics of Irish descent in the west of Scotland played such a prominent role in the rise of the Labour Party connects this issue with the previous one, and it may go some way towards explaining, though it could never in the least excuse, a campaign in which the most prominent ministers in the two main Scottish Presbyterian churches were the leaders and enthusiastic promoters, rather than the reluctantly led.

The campaign sought to make of this ethnic group the scapegoat for the social problems of post-war Scotland, and simultaneously to revive the church's leadership in uniting the Scottish people against them. This was done in two main ways: by using the church's organisation to collect statistics which were meant to be damaging and which turned out to be, in all important respects, misleading (a special committee of the Church and Nation Committee was set up and given this task); and, above all, by using the so-called 'scientific racism' of Victorian Britain against those representatives of an allegedly inferior 'Irish' or 'Celtic' race.[60]

When on 5 November 1926 a deputation from a Joint Committee of the Scottish (Presbyterian) Churches gained an interview with the Secretary of State for Scotland, John Whyte said of the question of Irish immigration that 'they desired to discuss it entirely as a racial and not as a religious question'.[61]

But not even the religious claim that we were all children of our heavenly Father could deter this ecclesiastical racism for, as the report to the General Assembly of 1922 put it, 'God placed the people of this world in families, and history, which is the narrative of His providence, tells us that when kingdoms are divided against themselves they cannot stand. The nations that are homogeneous in Faith and ideals, that have maintained unity of race, have ever been more prosperous, and to them the Almighty has committed the highest tasks.'[62]

There is scarcely much need to comment on that volatile mixture of racial ideology and pseudo-religion, or to point to other examples of it from which the world has rightly turned in revulsion. But there is some need to indicate how long the campaign continued – for it was no flash in the pan. In July of 1928 a deputation from the Scottish churches met the Home Secretary in London, and clearly hoped that anti-Irish legislation would coincide with the church union which was expected the following year. When the union of the Church of Scotland and the United Free Church did take place in 1929, despite the lack of co-operation from the Home Secretary, the new moderator, John Whyte (again!) proclaimed it a priority of the united church to combat the menace of Irish Catholicism. The 1931 General Assembly decided to approach employers to persuade them to give jobs only to 'those of the Scottish race'. An argument raised in the General Assembly of 1933 recognised some parallels between the Jewish question in Germany and the Irish question in Scotland. But the last shout in this campaign was heard as late as 1938 when the then convener of the Church and Nation Committee was still pamphleteering on behalf of keeping Scotland for the 'Scottish race'. The following year Catholics and Protestants from Scotland were once more dying in roughly proportionate numbers, killed by an enemy which proved more extremely and effectively racist than John Whyte and his colleagues had ever sought to be, and which, while showing how relatively mild Scottish Presbyterian racism was, showed also how morally irresponsible was its rhetoric, and how very dangerous such rhetoric must always appear.

The point of citing these examples of actual churches' public
moralising and of their attempts at times to influence state
legislation, has not been to lower these churches in human
esteem, or to lower them relatively to other churches, for it is
doubtful if any church could fail to supply us with comparable
examples. Nor has it been to detract from the high moral
influence which churches on the whole do wield in society. But
the problem has been to identify and distinguish powers
secular and powers sacred. This proved difficult in the case of
moral authority in human society at large, so many are its
forms, so much is human creative imagination at the origin and
of the essence of it. It seemed at first blush that it would be
easier with public bodies such as states and churches, the
former so anxious at times to secure their autonomous secula-
rity, the latter almost always anxious to assert their sacred
source. Yet in the case of both, suspicions could be raised from
their practices which ran counter to their own most confident
assertions of principle. In the case of states, they did sometimes
seem to deal in absolutes, and then the religious dimension, if
only in the distorted form of idolatry, did appear to cloud the
purity of their secular pretensions.

In the case of churches, when they too deal in practice with
moral and legislative issues, they often appear to be on all fours
with other human seekers after truth, and never more so than
when their mistakes become obvious, especially to those who
enjoy the enormous advantage of hindsight. For if churches do
badly, or at least not well at times, in the quest for moral ideal
or legal rectitude, it would be naive to continue with the
simple, general and uncritical claims that divine authority was
theirs, but unfortunately not on just those questions at issue, or
that the Irish Catholic Church did not have this authority on
the rights of contraception, whereas it was on the wrongs of
racism that the Church of Scotland did not have it. In the case
of churches then also, the line between secular and sacred
power is not so simply drawn.

CONCLUSION

When one surveys the scene in human society on which so many sets of moral authorities and their protégés, so many revolving sets of masters and apprentices, are at work, the very variety of it all threatens from the outset any ease distinction between powers secular and sacred. But the problematic does not stem solely from this variety. For at first sight the whole scene looks thoroughly secular: people in all walks of life making a living in this world, and doing it with that Eros-driven creativity which is at once the hallmark of moral agency and the true essence of being human. Even ecclesiastical office is, from one point of view, and that not a negligible one, a 'living'.

People in all walks of life do use religious language, imagery, ritual. States do so also – the Declaration of Independence of the United States of America appeals to the law of nature and of nature's God; its Irish counterpart is set out 'in the name of God' – and of course churches do so all the time, even when acting alongside trade unions, for instance, in favour of a very secular piece of social justice. The appeal to God, to God's will, to a divine dimension of truth, is everywhere. But appearances, it has been suggested, can deceive; and claims, explicit much less implicit, seldom suffice to establish without more ado the truth of what is claimed.

In the end the human quest for truth and goodness (or well-being) for all is one and the same process, conducted by each one in co-operation with others, from birth to death. The dignity of arriving at truth and well-being, and at the successive dimensions of that composite state, belongs to each one equally in the essentially co-operative venture which forms and accompanies human community. The subordination of apprentices to masters is an essentially temporary affair. This means, and the nature of morality which is of the essence of human dignity requires, that the input of the master should be of such kind as to enable the apprentice himself or herself to arrive at a similar or higher vision and result, so that the master's formulation always awaits the eventual exercise of the inalienable right of judgment of the apprentice as to the level of truth and goodness really reached. This means, in turn, not only that the only tolerable exercise of power amongst moral agents is of power in the form of authority (with the exception of such threat and application of force as might be necessary to save the communal moral enterprise itself from destruction); but that the judgment concerning a genuinely religious dimension of truth and justice is one which every moral agent may, perhaps must, at some time exercise.

Stated in terms of power exercised as authority, stated in terms of the revolving relationships between masters or 'authorities' on the one hand, and apprentices or subordinates, on the other, the question as to whether or when any particular authority is truly mediating anything that could reasonably be called a divine dimension of truth and goodness, a dimension of truth and goodness in such form that it could be deemed ultimately originating or simply ultimate, or both, is for each individual-in-community to answer from personal experience for himself or herself. And since the scene seems so secular at first sight – inevitably so perhaps since all human quest for truth and goodness begins and persists in the search for food, clothing, shelter, protection, and the very human co-operation which all of this also requires – since a religious dimension appears at some height or depth of that quest not always easily identified, that answer is never easily given.

All that can easily be said in general in favour of an affirmative answer to the religious question is this: the more intensely one enters upon this Eros-driven, creative process of maintaining and promoting what one discerns to be good and beautiful, the more one seems to become aware of an analogous process going on in the natural world; the struggle of order over chaos, life-enhancing beauty over disorderly ugliness and natural evil. One is naturally tempted to think that a similar process has a similar source, a cosmic moral agent, and that natural evolution is that agent's original letter of invitation. Further, in efforts to depict this cosmic agent one projects onto it the highest features of ordering functions or functionaries that one knows, with footnotes concerning its total superiority to these; it is Lord of the Seasons, Shepherd, King. And one then retrojects its authority back onto the most advanced ideals and rules at which one has yet arrived: the king's truth, wisdom, justice is from God, and on it depends not merely the order of society, but the sustaining fruitfulness of the earth.

But the world of nature is a deeply ambivalent analogue of the human ethical *élan vital*. Nature red in tooth and claw, the worm in the brain, and what seems to us at least as the constant display of power as force in the huge indifference shown by natural disasters; none of this fits easily into a vision of a cosmos that results from the Eros of a truly moral cosmic source. The natural world has its dark side, its powers of chaos. Primal religion represents this as the adversarial element, the satanic force, sometimes personified, its origin and destiny variously assessed. The effect of this dark apprehension upon the prospects of a religious dimension to the inevitable moral quest is seldom, except in the case of the more superficial forms of modern humanism, a summary end to such a prospect. Its effect is rather to increase the hope quotient in human faith at the expense of the quotient of presumed knowledge.

To believe in divine creation and providence is at least as much a matter of hope as a matter of knowledge. But that is to say no more than most religions say anyway; that the divine 'in itself' is to be encountered at the end of the journey rather than at the beginning. Nor does this change of balance in favour of hope over knowledge decrease the stature of common human faith at its religious height or depth. For people can live without much knowledge, and with very little certainty, but they cannot live at all without hope. In fact, human faith's inclination towards hope as it reaches the religious dimension chimes in well with the experience of Eros as a power that seems to pull us ever onward and upward, rather than push us forward inch by inch from behind; upward to heights of possibility for ourselves and our world that only a very false humanism would tend in the name of the same moral quest to delimit in advance.

Such is the only general account that can be given of the

process by which the common moral quest reaches a religious dimension, and is thereafter infused with a higher and deeper (religious) level of belief and hope. The process can occur in duly differentiated fashion in the case of any of the revolving sets of masters and apprentices who work with nature or society, or both. The process yields in every passing age what is called primal religion, that basic sense of, and perhaps adherence to, religious awareness and imagery, to which all historic religions (or 'world religions') must address themselves and adapt themselves, under threat of otherwise remaining, not merely irrelevant, but unintelligible. These historic religions are characterised by founders or re-fashioners of a more ancient religious tradition – the Buddha who rediscovered an ancient path to an ancient city; the Christ who came, not to destroy the Jewish Torah, but to fulfil it – who claim, or on whose behalf it is claimed, that they were more open to the cosmic moral agent than any others, or any who had gone before. But by the very nature of the case such claims are open to testing, not only by such levels of faith–hope as any group or people has already achieved, but by the common Eros-driven quest that binds together all who live in this world. When we look towards Christianity we expect to see a distinctive, historical version of a dimension of human experience with which we are all naturally familiar, and something therefore which we are all naturally competent to judge (though some, no doubt, more competent than others, because of more refined moral sensitivity). Hence the next chapter is devoted to asking after the distinctiveness of that form of ethical monotheism, as it is called, which is named Christianity. And the final chapter discusses the degree to which the practical exercises of power in Christianity live up to that distinctive vision.

CHAPTER 4

The Christian experience of power

Readers and writers of a book like this would expect a change-over from a broadly philosophical to a theological point of view. And such an expectation need not be disappointed, provided that neither reader nor writer is trapped in the peculiarly modern prejudice which sees theology and philosophy as quite distinct, if not in fact opposed disciplines. For those who understand that theology refers to the 'logos' of 'theos', and that the origins of Western philosophy are found precisely in a growing preference for 'logos' over 'mythos', can well see that theology is a constitutive part of philosophy.[1] Even the philosophical conclusion that there is no god is a piece of theology, if only because it requires as much effort to define the term 'god' as do any of the philosophies that profess to deal with such an entity. Gods have been on the philosophical agenda from the very outset, and even their removal from the agenda can scarcely succeed without critical consideration of the functions they fulfilled in the human prospect, and the reasons as to how these functions can now be fulfilled without them, or the reasons as to why they must be thought to remain unfulfilled. So then, the expected changeover from a broadly philosophical to a theological point of view must really take the form of a move to the more intentionally theological reaches of philosophy.

But this chapter has the adjective 'Christian' in its title. Are we to understand that Christian theology is a form, or even a province of philosophy? Yes, Christianity, like other religions, is first and foremost a way of life. The fact that civilisations existed which had no specific word for 'religion' illustrates in its own manner the extent to which religions are ways of life; broad, general configurations of human living, each particular example of which can be multiform and evolutionary while still preserving the distinctiveness of at least a family resemblance. The word religion, when it does come to be used, merely indicates that life is now looked at in relationship to some ultimate source or goal, some relevant totality from which it may take direction, and some level of its meaning. Philosophy in its theological reaches focusses on that ultimate or absolute source, even if only to argue about the propriety of using the term 'god' for a particular candidate for ultimacy or alleged absoluteness. The Christian life itself involves an attempt at a distinctive configuration of reality at its most absolute or ultimate, and when that attempted configuration is explained and defended as best it can be, by the use of 'logos' or reasoning, the end result is as accurately called Christian philosophy as Christian theology.

People who are inclined to resist this kind of conclusion fall into one of two categories: those would-be philosophers who are so desperate for the end of any religion or religious influence that they cannot tolerate even a question about, much less a quest for, anything absolute or ultimate; and those would-be theologians who take a particular view of divine revelation, the view that God's words, or equivalent signs, that God's mind is unequivocably available, without intermediary, to human beings. But those who study these matters with any care at all, quickly come to realise that neither Christianity nor any other religion claims to put people in such direct contact with the divine while they sojourn in this empirical world. On the contrary, Christianity, like Judaism and the religion of Israel before it, would put the enquirer directly in touch with some things, persons, events, which are very much part and parcel of this empirical world or of its history, and would claim that through these intermediaries something of the truly divine presence, power, rule or guidance is palpable such that, if one is but faithful to it, one may reach the ultimate goal of life in some blissful possession, some union, some great home-coming at the end. Revelation refers to the lights which these allegedly privileged encounters can throw on the whole of existence, and in particular on the nature of the ultimate in existence. Philosophy which is, as its name connotes, the love of wisdom seeks the comprehensive knowledge which such alleged insights promise into the nature of the whole of existence and its ultimate reaches. Christian philosophy analyses, explains, and attempts to promote the Christian version of the revelatory intermediaries, and of the truth of all existence which they are alleged to reveal. Philosophy in general, in its theological reaches, will analyse and critically compare a number of the specific experiences and events on which different religions or competing humanisms focus in their attempts to have revealed the truth and meaning of all life and existence.

Philosophy at large is related to theology, much as morality is to religion, and as that relationship was briefly outlined in earlier chapters. Morality is a creative way of interacting with the real world, driven by Eros, and it is thus the original way of coming to know the reality of which moral agents are so much a part. In its creative and questing *élan* it may well come upon heights or depths of reality which might be thought to merit the adjective 'divine', and then again it might not, or its claim to do so might well be disputed. Religion also, in origin and essence, is a total way of life – only a superficial view of it in a self-styled rationalist age confines it to a compartment of life, and there it is usually thought to be, if not false or fanciful, at best private and irrelevant to all important public affairs. Religion, however, it has already been noted, puts one directly in touch, not with the divine being itself, however that is imagined or conceived, but rather with persons and events in the concrete patterns of whose lives and existence it claims to find the clues to the nature of the highest reality, and thus to the nature and destiny of reality as a whole. It differs from morality only in its conviction that it has discovered at least something of the pattern of ultimate reality, and in its effort to shape the whole of life according to this pattern, or according to its own evolving grasp of it. In both cases practical wisdom, efficacious wisdom, is sought and found, and life is lived along the discovering way.

Another way of describing the difference between morality and religion, philosophy and theology, is this: the former always seems to talk 'from below', from the midst of life, the centre of the empirical world, the flux of time, saying what can be seen, if only very dimly perceived, as it goes along; the latter always seems to talk 'from above' – 'thus saith the Lord', it says, as if it was sitting at the Lord's right hand already and his words were still ringing in its ears. But that merely reflects the profound conviction of the religious believer that in some person or event here below something of the ultimate is already to be encountered and known, and the words spoken or written are a fairly adequate formula for that. There is still nothing to suggest that this conviction is not open to continuing verification by the concrete experiences of life and existence – for from some such the 'light' came originally – and nothing to suggest that the 'revelation' cannot increase, even if it may not substantially differ, in future developments of the recommended patterns of life and existence. All of this must really be kept in mind when moving to the examination of religious texts and theological arguments.[2]

One more matter needs to be raised about the title of this chapter before plunging into the waters it names. As well as drawing attention to the adjective contained in the title, and then having to say something about the implications of changing from broadly philosophical to specifically theological discourse, it is well to draw attention to the article, which is the definite article. Can one really speak about *the* Christian experience of power?

The short answer, of course is, no. Whatever definition or description one might give of power, and even if one were to confine one's examples to Christian history, it is perfectly obvious that the recorded experience would turn out to be pluriform rather than uniform. Even if one were to take a very rigid view of the criteria on which one could decide what is authentically Christian, if one were to adopt a *Scriptura Sola* stance and insist that only what is authorised in the scriptures is authentically Christian, one could not escape from pluriformity. Nothing is more obvious from the recent history of scripture scholarship than the varieties of religious experience and theological perspective, except perhaps the fact that it cannot all be contained within rather linear formulaic patterns such as 'progressive revelation' or 'development of doctrine'. As a consequence, no one who searches for the authentic Christian experience or view of some matter of importance can avoid the search for a 'canon within the canon', that is to say, for a set of texts or segments of scripture which one is convinced give the best perspective on the rest, and can therefore be used to interpret the rest.

What Christians call the New Testament, after all, is what they believe to be the best perspective, and therefore the best interpretative book, for what they call the Old Testament; although it is quite obvious from the very continuance of Judaism that it is not the only validly religious interpretation of that ancient body of sacred literature. And, since the New Testament itself contains quite a variety of responses to what early Christians believed to be the revelatory event of the life, death, and destiny of Jesus of Nazareth, and these were human responses, however helped by the spirit of God, it follows that even the most Scripture-bound of Christian scholars – particularly these – have used preferred sections of the New Testament in order to interpret the rest. There is nothing to prevent us, or indeed to excuse us, from doing something similar when setting out in search of the Christian experience of power. Of course, we may take the theme of power, and its cognates, and inform ourselves of the manner in which the New Testament has already reinterpreted it, but we cannot complete even that task without making our own selection of 'key' New Testament passages. We can give reasons for our choice, and we will do this almost immediately, but we cannot deny that such a choice always has to be made. It is simply part of the continuing need to try to see in the persons and events focussed by a particular faith, and in the sequence of events which carry the notice of these down to us, as much as possible of the light these are alleged to shed on our human condition, and on the deepest reaches of the reality in which it is lived.

When approaching the sources of the Christian faith, and

first of all the Bible, it would of course be possible to institute a search of that authoritative collection for all references to power or allusions to it, and to try to construct from the results a *vue d'ensemble*. This kind of thing has been attempted by a number of authors, and the results are always informative.[3] But there is another way, which might prove more in line with the understanding of morality and religion already adopted.

Both morality and religion have been identified in their differing but closely aligned ways with life, with human living. Think of life, then, and of human life in particular. It is in essence a kind of a knowing-doing, a continuous activity continuously aware of itself in its context. Sometimes it is more aware of itself and its related surrounds, more knowledgeable; sometimes it is more practical and probing. But it is always a combination of just those two elements which emerge when knowledge is described as primarily a matter of praxis, when morality is presented as the paradigm of all knowing. Life is both a way, a progress (or regress), and a truth (or falsehood). For its least success or its greatest it needs dynamism and direction, an energy and a word, power and knowledge, and its needs these simultaneously. In approaching the sources of Christian faith, then, why not look first to a text which deals directly with the prospect of life or death, and which heightens our awareness of the intertwining of the elements of power and knowledge in the very process of pointing us towards just those persons or events from which it is claimed we can see a little at least into the ultimate depths of reality, which are then presented as the springs of life and death, of being and non-being.

Take a text from somewhere near the 'middle' of the Bible, from which to look back to the Original Testament and forward to the New. Take the Book of Proverbs, chapter 8. This book is accepted by all Christian churches as a fully canonical work; but it should be possible, without causing undue controversy, to illustrate the themes taken here from this text, from other works of the so-called Wisdom Literature of the Bible, even though there may be outstanding disputes between Christian traditions about the canonical status of some of these.

'For he who finds me finds life ... all who hate me love death': so we are told in verse 35 of Proverbs 8. Who or what is thus raised to the status of a matter of life and death? Wisdom, *sophia*, presented in the form of a woman, and a divine woman at that. One should not make too much of the verb in the sentence in which, in verse 22, she begins her monologue, the verse which the Revised Standard Version of the Bible translates: 'The Lord created me at the beginning of his way'; for as the RSV itself notes, the same verb could as easily be translated 'came to possess me', and in the rest of the passage, when the existence of this woman is being placed before any of the creative events outlined in Genesis 1, the verb 'to bring forth' or 'give birth to' is the one that is used in order to describe her origin. And the reason for thinking that she is divine? Whatever the problems of being sure of correct translation of the word rendered 'master workman' in verse 30, it is clear, as the note in the RSV allows,[4] that this passage as a whole merely develops the thought of chapter 3, verse 19 ('The Lord by Wisdom founded the earth'), towards the concept of a divine agent, a 'first-born of all creation' through whom 'all things were made'.

The very choice of these phrases already anticipates a forward look to the New Testament. But much needs to be discussed before taking that forward look, and first perhaps must come the question: is this a real woman, a real person? The RSV is quite anxious to assure us that it is not; we are dealing rather with an 'aspect or activity of God' which is here 'metaphorically endowed with speech', but not with 'a divine being distinct from God'. One can only pause at this point to observe that the immediate creation of the empirical world is here no less clearly attributed to an agent distinct from God, than is the case with the 'Word' at the beginning of the Gospel of John, and that the problem of calling Wisdom on that account a distinct person need be no more, and no less intractable, than that of so designating the 'Word' in later Christian Trinitarian doctrine. The divinity of the being here described is just as clear from her creative activity, as it is in the case of the New Testament 'Word'; and one cannot help wondering if it is not then her gender that creates this reluctance to call her a person as aptly, and ineptly as the Word is called a person?

She is, in any case, a creator, or, as the *Wisdom of Solomon* puts it, 'The fashioner of all things' (7: 22); 'she reaches mightily from one end of the earth to the other and she orders all things well' (8: 1). Plato could well call her a *demiourgos*, and by that he would mean, not some cosmic power lesser than God who did the dirty work of creating material worlds, but God the Creator, or God in the mode of being (to use later orthodox Trinitarian terminology) of creator. After all, Augustine in Book I of his *De Trinitate* derived the full and distinct divinity of the Word from similar statements in the prologue to John's Gospel to the effect that through the Word which was with God in the beginning, all things were made. Now creation, whether the subject is called *sophia* or simply God, essentially involves forming, shaping, ordering, setting up dynamic relationships in which the creator continues to be involved. In this sense, and in this sense only, creation involves bringing things into existence.

The question sometimes forced with pre-emptive triumphalism on those who describe creation, as for example the Genesis story does, in terms of ordering, of fashioning an ordered cosmos as a tissue of vital relationships: but does this mean creating out of pre-existent matter? is in reality a nonsense question. Matter which is entirely without form is unintelligible; it is in fact nothing, no thing. It could not therefore pre-exist things. Hence the matter out of which all things are created comes into existence simultaneously with their forming or fashioning. It is something like prime matter in Aristotle's metaphysic, and it is represented in the mythic manner of creation stories by images of the void, emptiness, entire absence of form. The same may be said of the concept of nothingness: it too comes into existence as a kind of by-product of creation, as a relative entity, the limit 'out of which' they are sustained, and into which they may always slip.

So, too, the question as to whether or not stories of the fashioning of all things, their dynamic ordering throughout their tenure of time, contain the 'doctrine' of 'creation out of nothing'? This question, too often asked of Genesis-type stories which we find repeated of *sophia* in the Wisdom Literature of the Bible, must simply be answered: yes. These stories of fashioning and ordering contain the idea of creation out of nothing in the only form in which 'creation out of nothing' is intelligible.[5]

Sophia, then, is the creator of the heavens and the earth. As Proverbs put it, 'Wisdom has built her house, and set up her seven pillars' (9: 1), and her house is the world. Further, since the concept of creation refers to fashioning, ordering, dynamic relationships, it has less to do with remote origins than it has to do with present conditions and future prospects. For that very good reason *The Wisdom of Solomon* begins in chapter 10 to tell the story of the race from Adam onward as Wisdom's doings; and creation ideas and imagery are the stock-in-trade of the Bible in dealing with all of God's ways with the world from beginning to end. When the New Testament wishes to make its most advanced claims for the salvific implications of the life, death, and destiny of Jesus of Nazareth, the imagery of Wisdom the creator will be back in full force. But that is to anticipate.

It was noted at the outset that Wisdom the creator is a life-force, our encounter with her a matter of life or death for us. It was also noted that life itself characteristically bears the dual aspect of knowing and doing, seeing and being able, word (or wisdom, or light) and spirit (or power, or soul), in any case the perceptive and the dynamic. When naming the life-source itself, it makes little difference whether creatures make their initial choice from one set of terms or from the other. In the original Genesis story, God the creator appears first as word spoken, then as spirit rushing upon or brooding upon the primeval chaos. Wisdom belongs to the first set of terms, and it is sometimes doubled with Word as its equivalent: in *The Wisdom of Solomon* God is the one 'who hast made all things by thy word, and by thy wisdom hast formed man' (9: 1).

But the life-force so named is also and equally spirit or power. In our master canonical text of *Proverbs* 8, for 'Ages ago I was set up' the RSV offers as equivalent 'or "poured out"', with a reference to the pouring out of the spirit in Acts 2: 17.

The Wisdom of Jesus son of Sirach (*Ben Sira*, for short) has 'I came forth from the mouth of the Most High' (24: 3) and that could refer either to a word or to a breath, the master-image behind the symbolism of spirit. But again *The Wisdom of Solomon* is clearest: 'Who has learned thy counsel unless thou hast given Wisdom and sent thy Holy Spirit from on high' (9: 17), 'For in her [Wisdom] there is a spirit that is ... holy ... loving the good ... steadfast ... all-powerful, overseeing all and penetrating through all spirits' (7: 22); 'for she is a breath of the power of God' (7: 25, as well as being a reflection of his light and an image of his goodness).

When one is seeking the source of existence, which for us is the source of life in this world, it would not much matter, then, from which aspect of life, knowledge or power, one named this source. Nor, when one is trying to deal systematically with the different 'modes of being' in which the source of life is thought to be encountered in the world, would it much matter which of these one placed first and which second. One is enabled to talk of two 'modes of being' of God *vis-à-vis* this world at all only on the analogy of life as it is experienced, as this inseparable combination of knowledge and power. The important question on which to focus is this: *where* is this God–Wisdom–Power, or God–Word–Spirit to be encountered, and how? It is an important question since this word and power is a matter of life or death for us.

But perhaps that question is itself put the wrong way round? It has already been pointed out that people, even the most religious people, do not begin from God's side to see and to speak, even though their conviction-preaching might make it seem as if that were the case. Rather, like all the rest of us, they identify something of or in this world, something that seems to them to reveal the vision and force of the ultimate source of life and existence, and this they propose as the access to the nature of, and to some union with, the source of life itself, which is commonly called God. So it is with our text. It seems to speak from God's side; but it is actually intent on pointing to the place in the life and history of this world where the ultimate word–spirit, life-force can be encountered.[6]

Where? The answer to that brute question might well be: in the creation as a whole, for the texts have described the fashioning of the whole world and of all of its history as the way or work of the word–spirit of God. And that is a correct answer in its way. The problem is, though, that the world as a whole seems so ambivalent. It would seem that other powers, other than the life-enhancing one that is sought, are active within it. One does not need to take up the question at this point as to whether these are the result of some primeval fault within the cosmic system itself, or whether some supernatural malevolent powers are for some reason let loose within it. It is enough to know that the powers actually encountered within the world are ambivalent, some constructive for good, others destructive, in order to ask if any more specific directions can be given that might guide us to the locus of a purer, less ambivalent presence and operation of the ultimate source of life. Such specific directions are always given in each and every religious tradition. The original Genesis story, for example, sees in the human species as such something made in God's image, and given god-like dominance over all creation, in recognition, no doubt, of the empirical fact that human beings are the truly moral, that is, creative, beings within creation. This is delegated power and authority no doubt, and the truth of the image depends upon the faithful carrying out of the delegation.[7] But because so much of the human species over so much of its history also is either impotent or evil, the focus falls upon some ideal human being, some representative one, the king, for instance.

Proverbs 8 already contains this further focussing, as Wisdom declares: 'By me kings reign, and rulers decree what is just; by me princes rule, and nobles govern the earth' (14–15). *The Wisdom of Solomon* has Solomon pray to God to 'give me the wisdom that sits by thy throne' (9: 4). This further focussing, of course, is characteristic of a number of primal religions, if not in one form or other of all of them. God's wisdom (or truth, or justice) is found *par excellence* in the king. While that continues to be the case, right relationships, goodness, and life will make progress in human society, peace will reign and the earth itself will contribute to human prospering. In the pre-Christian religion of ancient Ireland the twin themes of the *fir flathemon*, the princely truth of his governing function, and his 'marriage' to the Sovereignty goddess, were the basis of peace and justice amongst the people he ruled and of the fruitfulness of nature in all his kingdom. In the history of the kings of Israel justice in the land depends upon the king's possession of divine wisdom. The woman of Tekoa praised David: 'My Lord has wisdom like the wisdom of the angel of God to know all the things that are on earth' (2 Samuel 14: 20), and 'God gave Solomon wisdom' (1 Kings 4: 29). Of the 'shoot from the stump of Jesse' Isaiah says: 'And the Spirit of the Lord will rest upon him, the spirit of wisdom' (Isaiah 11: 2). And Psalm 72 quite explicitly connects the very fruitfulness of the land with the reign of the one on whom God's justice settles.[8] The king who rules on earth while being himself governed by the wisdom or word or spirit of God within him can then bear the titles given David in the Original Testament: Lord, Christ and Son of God.

But kings and queens also betray our expectations, and havoc ensues in society and in nature itself. Ezekiel castigates the King of Tyre for preferring his own wisdom to that of God, 'because you consider yourself wise as a god' (28: 2–7; an echo here of the Fall of humankind itself in wanting to be like gods, wanting to be 'one of us, knowing good and evil'. 2 Samuel 14: 17 glosses divine wisdom as the ability 'to discern good and evil'). If humankind betrays continually its delegation to morality/creation and looks to the representative human beings, and kings and queens betray in turn, where then are we to look? (Notice in all of this the persistent and passionate conviction that there is a truth-of-things-in-the-making, that it comes from the source from which all things ultimately come, and that no matter how often it is betrayed it is still to be found somewhere within the creation that continues to emerge from that source. This is the basic conviction that underlies all religion, that makes all religions a series of quests, and that constructs the common ground of morality and religion.)

Proverbs 3: 18 says of *sophia*: 'She is a tree of life to those who lay hold on her.' Where can one now go to lay hold on her?

Where is the contemporary garden in which the tree of wisdom grows, and which therefore contains the tree of life? The Wisdom literature at this stage points unerringly to the Jewish faith itself, the Law of Moses. This is made clear in *Ben Sira* 24: 23, 'All this is the book of the Covenant of the Most High God, the law which Moses commanded us.' And it is clearer still when *Baruch* says of Wisdom, 'she is the book of the commandments of God, the law which endures forever. All who hold fast to her will live, and those who forsake her will die' (4: 1).

At this stage, then, we are being directed to an actual religion, to a comprehensive way of life; we are met with the claim that this Jewish life is or contains the word–spirit in practice which is the key to the truth of all reality, to the practical essence of our empirical world, and that it is or contains for that very reason the most substantial clue to, the most definitive revelation of, the nearest encounter with the nature of ultimate reality that we are capable of while we are on the way.

When Philo, a Jewish theologian of Alexandria in the first century of the Christian era, declared that the inner being or nature of God could not be comprehended by human minds, but that something of God could be known through his powers (*dynameis*) and their works (*energeiai*) in the world (both of which he assumed under the title of God's word (*logos*); and when he let it be understood, especially in his *Life of Moses* that he considered the Word of God to be virtually *empsychos* in Moses himself, that is to say, to virtually take the form of Moses' own psyche, soul or spirit, he is merely doing in terms which would be even more familiar to the Greek theologians of his day, what the Wisdom Literature had done, or was doing in the kind of imagery we have just seen used. Change the *empsychos* for *sarx egeneto*, change the 'became ensouled in' to 'became flesh in', then listen to Philo call the Word of God to whom this happened, the first-begotten Son of God, and Philo is parallelling, if not anticipating, what will be said shortly of another Jew called Jesus of Nazareth.[9] But for now it is the Jewish religion which is the way, the praxis which contains the truth of reality to which we are all called as co-creators in the continuing process of creation, and to which we must come if there is to be life and life more abundant, existence rather than non-existence in the end. To the truth of this religion even kings must bow, if they too are not to risk the destruction of both nature and society.

But of course religions also in each of their constitutive parts, in their creeds and codes, their rituals and societal institutions, are human constructions. The fact of their claim to reveal something of the nature of ultimate reality, if only by pointing to the kind of processes in the world which exemplify the word–spirit which springs into the world from the source of reality itself, cannot disguise the fact that their very pointing, their very attempts to formulate and fashion in word and act the very way or truth or life they say they see, remain just that, their own very human attempts to formulate and fashion. All religions, therefore, have a history in which they take themselves to be developing and, they hope, thereby improving the vision by which they ask people to live: *religio*, like *ecclesia*, *semper reformanda*. It could come as little surprise then to find some Jews regarding Jesus of Nazareth as the one who brought out the best in the Jewish faith, while shedding some of the features which had tended to encrust it. And having come to regard him in this way, it was natural that they should then use of his life the very imagery of the divine word–spirit present in creation, the very imagery which had always been used in order to express the conviction that a way, a truth, a life did flow from the ultimate source of all reality, and was more palpable in some particular locus than in any others. To those who first decided to follow Jesus, the word–spirit that came from the ultimate source to fashion creation itself was particularly present in Moses. Yes, but perfectly fulfilled, in Jesus. 'Jesus' is now the definitive, divine answer to the question: where precisely is the ultimate creative word–power to be encountered in space and time?

In some of the very earliest of the Christian canonical documents, the Corinthian correspondence of Paul, there occurs the most elaborate deployment of just the kind of wisdom imagery with which we are now so familiar. In the first two chapters of

his *First Letter to the Corinthians*, and especially in 1: 18–30, Paul
points with great accuracy and determination to a very distinctive event in which he claims the divine wisdom is to be
encountered. This is certainly the same divine wisdom of which
we have all along been talking, for it is that on which life or
death depends, or, as Paul would have it, perishing or being
saved; and it is further described in the terms by now so
familiar to use, word and power. The distinctive event in
which this word–spirit is to be encountered, is not what some
theologians generally and rather barbarously call the Christ-
event, or even, without further specification, the incarnation,
as if, on the grounds that God has somehow assumed a human
nature, we were being pointed to something as general as
human nature once again for our clues to the way and the life
we wished so desperately to find. The specific reference is to the
executed state criminal, Jesus of Nazareth, acknowledged as
the Christ; as Paul puts it, 'I decided to know nothing among
you except Christ Jesus and him crucified' (1 Cor. 2: 2).

There it is then, the final attempt in the Bible as Christians
have it to identify the locus in which that life, that word–spirit
is to be encountered, which corresponds to the essential and
ultimate nature of reality and which, for those who can adopt
it, holds out the promise of the victory over death, whatever the
quality and quantity of that victory may turn out to be. For in
the whole context here Paul redeploys with great skill and
characteristic polemical force the whole panoply of imagery
already linking Wisdom literature with the creation and 'fall'
stories,[10] and with the failure and promise of anointed kings.
With fine play on the intertwining contrasts between death-
dealing folly and life-giving wisdom, between those to whom
the real wisdom seems folly and those who see through the
common prejudices of the age, Paul presents Jesus as the one
'whom God made our wisdom', whose cross is the true word
('the word of the cross'), so that 'Christ crucified' emerges as
'the power of God'. This message, he recognises, is folly to the
Greeks who would have expected him to come to them with the
'plausible words of wisdom' familiar to them from their own
not inconsiderable quests for that elusive life-force; and it is a

stumbling-block to Jews who expect something rather more overwhelming.

Nevertheless, Paul insists that his message puts before them nothing less than a 'demonstration of the spirit and of power'. For those who, when they encounter it, can take this life, can live by this word and this power, it is truly a revelation of the ultimate in reality: 'But it is written, "what no eye has seen, nor ear heard, nor the heart of man conceived, what God has prepared for those who love him", God has revealed to us through the Spirit;' for, he continues in a manner once more reminiscent of the attributes of wisdom, 'no one comprehends the thoughts of God except the Spirit of God' and 'we have received not the spirit of the world, but the Spirit which is from God' (1 Corinthians 2: 9–12). That in any case is his conviction and, he would say, represents his experience. Indeed the promise he makes at the end of this particular context is quite extraordinary, for he promises no less than this: that all of the structures of the world, and not least the structures of authoritative leadership in human societies, instead of dominating, will serve those who live according to this latest version of word–spirit, for all will be 'theirs'. 'For all things are yours, whether Paul or Apollos or Cephas or the world or life or death or the present or the future, all are yours' (1 Corinthians 3: 21).

When Paul adds immediately following on these words, 'and you are Christ's; and Christ is God', it may well be our cue to remind ourselves that we should not be tempted by the odd capitalisation of the 's' in Spirit, for example, to read these texts anachronistically from the perspective of much later Trinitarian theology. It is not the purpose of this language used by Paul, any more than it was the purpose of the same language in the Original Testament, to tell us anything about an 'immanent Trinity' of distinguishable' divine persons', one of whom is the Holy Spirit. The purpose of the language remains the same, the purpose of *naming*; of naming the life, the knowledge-power in process which derives from the ultimate reaches of reality and thus leads to its ultimate goal. Bertrand Russell would use the language to name as the ultimate reaches of reality, omnipotent matter rolling on its relentless way; as a consequence he would name the proper life of humans as a hopeless power of defiance in upholding the values created by them to ennoble their little day; and the ultimate goal as extinction, at least for the human race.[11] He deploys the language of power (equivalent to spirit) in order to characterise at one and the same time the ultimate nature of our world and the best kind of life we can manage in that kind of world. Paul, of course, would not agree with such characterisations, but that need not disguise the fact that they are both doing with this language the same kind of thing.

Paul in short points to a kind of spirit (equivalent to power) in order to characterise a kind of life in the world, which is in him because it came to him from Jesus, and to claim that it in turn characterises the ultimate nature of reality, a power or spirit which is divine, which is a 'character' of God, and with which, unlike Russell's omnipotent matter, we may co-operate for our own well-being. The language of way, life, truth, wisdom, word, power, spirit, is used in order to name the (place of the) life, itself a combination of knowledge and power in action, which people believe best represents the ultimate force-for-being in the world, and hence the inner structures of evolving reality. This is then seen, naturally, as a revelation of the ultimate; it *is* that ultimate, or that much of the ultimate which can appear in our space–time continuum. And so it tells us something about the nature of the ultimate at any particular point of our familiarity with it, and promises to tell us more as we progress in the way. Brief and powerless is man's life, says Russell; matter is omnipotent. Both phrases combine to tell us what the ultimate reality is like as it appears in human life. It is the raw force (power in the form of force) of matter which annihilates mind and moral value as mindlessly as it enabled these to come to be and to evolve.

So the language of word–spirit will always denote a life, one might almost say, a life style, and will draw from that its usable meaning-content; in short, you will look to an actual life-form to find a description of the word–spirit being talked about. This in turn may imply some particular claim-of-status for some person, for example, in which the particular life, the word–spirit, is thought to be crucially or even definitively present or revealed; but even then the claim will look back in circular fashion for its ground, as well as its meaning-content, to that actual instance of the life, the specific word–spirit combination, which that person lives, and to one's assessment of that as holding out the highest hope for the well-being of all. Paul, for instance, when he wants to ground his claim to be a channel of the spirit he says was embodied in the crucified Christ, appeals to the lives of those who had followed his example and altered their lives accordingly in response to his preaching (2 Corinthians 3: 1–3). Their lives, lived in imitation of his, and their assessment of these lives, prove his claim to be an apostle in the only way that can be proved. To Paul, of course, the status of Jesus is higher than his own, for he literally owes his present life and all of its distinctive future hope to Jesus, and not to himself. His life, lived in imitation of Jesus, in Jesus' spirit, and his assessment of it, proves to him, in the only way it can be proved, that Jesus is God's anointed, mediator of the divine spirit and truth which is incarnate in Jesus' life. For both Paul and his converts assess and point to the distinctive life of Jesus, now continuing in them, as the life, the word–spirit that characterises and comes from the ultimate reaches of reality, the ultimate life-source of the universe, the being called God. Whether this assessment is true or false will only be known as well-being overcomes all ills for them, or fails to do so. So Jesus is for him and for his converts both the embodiment and the source of the life, the word–spirit, which all are convinced represents (makes present, that is to say, in this particular form) the ultimate life-source of the universe.

For those who have learned the nature of this kind of language and how to use it properly, the same logic applies to the alleged source as applied to the soi-disant channel. We in our turn should have to find ourselves pointing to a kind of living which can actually be experienced in the world, a distinctive type of word–spirit, in order to be able to claim a continuing status for Jesus as embodiment and source, (after the ultimate source, of course, the *archē anarchos*), of the way, the life, and the truth which, we then claim, holds out the highest hopes for all life and existence. And that, in fact, is how we find the language with which we have become so familiar continuing to be used. There is a word–spirit, Christians claim, that can be encountered in the body of the followers of Jesus, and which is to be identified with that embodied or incarnate in the life, death, and destiny of the man Jesus himself.

These corresponding claims, concerning the distinctive life of those now called Christians, and the status of Jesus, are telescoped in the Pauline symbol of the Christian community in the world as the body of Christ (they are represented in an alternative form in the 'other paraclete' symbolism of the Gospel of John). For the Christian community continuing in the world is the body of Christ precisely because, like any body it is held together and animated by a single spirit, and this in turn is identified with the spirit–word (embodied in) Jesus, now himself designated a 'life-giving spirit' (compare 1 Corinthians 12: 12–13 and 15: 45). The language in its final Christian extension, then, invites us to encounter a distinctive life, word–spirit in a body of people in the world, which it identifies with the life or word–spirit (incarnate in) Jesus, which it believes to be the worldly and historical mode of being of the ultimate life-source, finally named as the begetter of the same Jesus so assessed.[12]

There are, of course, problems connected with this final extension of the language which need not concern us here. For example, Jesus no longer walked the earth when Paul was writing to Corinth, and he certainly does not do so now. That leaves, quite naturally, the question: were Paul or *a fortiori* any person or group later than Paul, to claim that they live by the life of Jesus the Christ – we live now, not we, but Christ lives in us – how could they ever prove to the sceptical that they had not begun to live instead or in fact a life quite different from that which Jesus lived? What is to prevent them pointing to their communal life, and claiming this to be a representation of the life of Jesus, though it might misrepresent Jesus and substitute another spirit for his?

The Acts of the Apostles attempts to answer this question on Paul's behalf with the story of the revelation on the road to

Damascus (9: 1–9), and indeed Paul himself refers to 'a revelation of Jesus Christ' by which his gospel came to him (Galatians 1: 12). Yet he can scarcely be taken to mean by this that he received by some single supernatural intervention on his way to Damascus a comprehensive account of the life of Jesus. He had already seen the kind of life that some people lived while describing it as a following of Jesus; he had seen this with the sharp eyes of an enemy of theirs, and with the close attention which persecutors pay to that which they wish to destroy. The 'revelation' which he himself claims to have received probably refers to that event or occasion, mysterious in origin as such events tend to be, in which he saw all of that in a totally new light, and was turned about, converted. It would not be the last time, and no doubt it was not even the first, that the willingness of Christians to suffer and die for the life they believed eternal, rather than meet violence with violence, proved a veritable revelation to others. And Paul, he tells us in the same chapter of Galatians in which he talks of divine revelation, did spend fifteen days with Cephas, one of the leaders of the Jesus movement, in Jerusalem.

Paul was dependent on tradition, then, on the life passed on from follower to follower, from generation to generation. He was aware that people can become unfaithful or simply mistaken, of course. After all Cephas, whom he consulted, was most impressively consistent in getting the point of Jesus' mission wrong on almost every occasion on which he had an opportunity to make a contribution – even when he got Jesus' title right at Caesarea Philippi, he promptly demonstrated how badly he misunderstood it (Matthew 16: 13–23) – and Paul himself found later that he had to withstand Peter on a point which Paul certainly thought crucial to the proper understanding of the Christian life (Galatians 2: 11–21).

Later followers of Jesus canonised certain writings which they felt in a position to say contained accounts of the kind of life Jesus inaugurated, concrete and accurate pictures of the word–spirit which through Jesus entered the world and began to shape its history. These were joined to the scriptures Jesus himself held sacred, and thus formed for all future Christians a rule of life. However, in addition to exhibiting that pluriformity of versions of this life to which attention has already been drawn, these scriptures also contain reference to the misunderstandings of the earliest followers of Jesus, and no doubt other misunderstandings, or at the very least less than adequate apprehensions, to which no explicit reference is made.

One must remember that one is always dealing, first and foremost, with kinds of living here, and always with kinds of human living, and that nothing is more human than to err. The conviction that something of the ultimate word–spirit was breathed through Jesus into a dying world, and breathes still through the continuing body of Jesus in the world, is perfectly compatible with the persistence of shortcomings and downright failures, just as it is compatible with the prospect of developments of that life not yet even envisaged. Christians are never more absolved than any other people from the duty of discerning the spirits, testing the powers that live in them and shape the world. They have their scriptures and their tradition to use for this purpose, but in the end, even in their efforts to discern the best in these sources which will carry them beyond the present and past the worst, they have to depend on the same criterion as every other human being, the criterion of the quality of life and the hope of the future that emerge from the practical consequences of their conviction that in a particular life the ultimate source of existence breathes.

The other question which cannot be allowed to delay us for long in this context, except in so far as it may throw a little extra light on our current theme, is this: when Christians say that they live now by the life of Jesus, does that require them to believe that Jesus is now alive? A full answer to this question would produce a comprehensive theology of the resurrection, one of the more controversial areas of current Christian theology.[13] Suffice it to say here that, whatever else may be said about them, all of the resurrection texts of the New Testament are concerned with the status of Jesus as the embodiment, and the source after his Father, of the distinctive word–spirit by which his followers are in their various degrees enabled to live. Paul's formula in his letter to the Romans is a fine illustration, where he writes of Jesus 'who was descended from David according to the flesh and designated Son of God in power according to the Spirit of holiness by his resurrection from the dead' (Romans 1: 3–4). There is a clear reference to the power of spirit which his followers detected in Jesus and which they felt was poured into their own persons to form their lives. To that power or spirit, since they believe it to be the active presence of the ultimate, they attribute whatever hope they have of defeating death, however difficult they may find it to picture in any concrete fashion the final details of that defeat. Whatever evidence some of Jesus' early followers may have had, then, that he was seen alive after his death, the conviction of present-day Christians that he is still alive, is simply part and parcel of the hope which participation in the life of Jesus holds out for all of them, the human Jesus included. There is never any real escape from the need to provide the primary pointer to a kind of living, for Christians the distinctive word–spirit in action, the life constantly renewed, failing, recovering, evolving towards a final destiny at present unimaginable. It is this kind of living that opens for all, the human Jesus included, the hope that death, the last enemy, is also defeated.

Now it is all very well to point to the community of Christians in the world, and to dignify it with the titles: body of Christ, continuing incarnation of the word that enlightens and the power that enables. But even Christians must realise that that is not enough. The trouble is not just that this body can seem at first sight to be rather amorphous, its shape and outline distinctly indistinct – that, after all, is only to be expected if the word, as the prologue to John's gospel claims, enlightens every man in the world, and if the spirit breathes where it will. And the trouble is not that the body of card-carrying Christians in the world is itself differentiated into a surprisingly large number of Christian churches – that too is only to be expected if only because Christianity, like all religions, is a life, and when it comes to any place at any time, it does not arrive in a vacuum; it comes to a life/religion already formed and functioning; its spread and survival depend upon the ability of its distinctive word and spirit to mould the current forms of life/religion it finds before it, the institutions, the rituals, the ethos, the very language itself; the kind of process that first took place within its Jewish matrix (which neither its founder nor any of its earliest leaders ever thought it need leave), which then succeeded so magnificently with the religious and philosophical forms of the wider Graeco-Roman world, and which provides such instructive evidence of its vitality in some of the newer African churches at the present time.

No, the real trouble is that the community of Christians in the world has such a history of internecine warfare, and that a depressing amount of this is still going on. The ecumenical movement, now almost half a century old, has made considerable headway in bringing the warring parties around a variety of tables, and in recording agreements over a wide range of issues of importance to Christian living. But there is still too much downright disagreement about, still enough failure even to agree to differ. There is still so much of the scandal of Christians accusing each other of so much infidelity to Jesus, of so much falsehood, that they refuse to sit together at the Eucharistic table. Add to this the real failure to live Christian lives, a failure so abundantly characteristic of every Christian church in every age, and it becomes obvious that it will be difficult to point in a single direction even those who come to Christians to inquire as to the place where the word and spirit may be encountered that holds the best promise of reflecting the ultimate life-source in the universe. It might be best, instead of trying to choose between rival barkers for different Christian churches, to try to choose one of the more fundamental ways or forms in which distinctive life-powers may be met, and spirits discerned.

The play's the thing, then. Instead of trying to decide which version of the Christian religion towards which to point the enquirer in the first instance, choose the form of presentation of that allegedly distinctive life which is most basic in human life, most fundamental, most comprehensive, most effective, most in tune with the dignity of human freedom, most participatory. And that is undoubtedly the drama. In religious jargon it is called the ritual. But it is of course the same thing. Or put it this way: drama is to ritual what morality is to religion; something common to all human living from cradle to grave, something crucial to all advances in living, something which continues, and which simply adds another name and dimension to itself, when it reaches those depths or heights of our common human experience which are designated by the word religious.

Shortly before his untimely death – when cancer, which two decades before had taken one of his limbs, cruelly and unexpectedly revisited, and this time with indecent haste took his life – one of Northern Ireland's most promising and most accomplished playwrights, Stewart Parker, gave and published a lecture in memory of the teacher who taught him the meaning of drama. John Malone had argued passionately and persistently that drama should be at the centre of the educational process, instead of being at the periphery in the occasional slot allotted to the school play, for, as he pointed out, drama consisted of its very nature in 'a rich lived experience in which heart as well as mind, body as well as head are involved'. When Stewart Parker in his turn considered the sad plight of his native land, he saw that 'there is a whole culture to be achieved. The politicians, visionless almost to a man, are withdrawing into their sectarian stockades. It falls to the artists to construct a working model of wholeness by means of which this society can begin to hold up its head in the world.' He felt that 'official versions of reality which strike me as malevolent or deceitful are constantly being promulgated by people in power'. He decided that 'I want my work to offer alternative versions.' And he appealed to Huizinga, amongst others, in support of his own conviction that the most natural and effective way of producing something as necessary as an alternative version of reality was drama, the play.

From Huizinga he took the thesis that 'play is how we test the world and register its realities. Play is how we experiment, imagine, invent, and move forward. Play is above all how we enjoy the earth and celebrate our lives upon it.' And he added on his own behalf:

It is no accident of etymology that this fundamental animal instinct, this self-sufficient force shaping the very evolution of human society, should share its name with those works of fiction which are presented by actors before an audience – the stage play, the screenplay, the radio and television play – these are merely particular and local forms of the play-force, consciously shaped, fashioned by human imagination and usage into a highly sophisticated kind of game, the rules of which have remained surprisingly constant for well over two thousand years.[14]

Or more, he might have said. For such a basic way of testing the world, registering its realities, and recreating these, must be as old as human imagination at least; and this even in its more fictive as distinct from its more natural forms, if such a distinction can be sustained. And it is religious as early, and as late, as the realities thus registered are thought to be ultimate or absolute, or at least a matter of life and death for humans, if not of being and non-being for all.

Religions always place the ritual drama at the centre of their efforts to test the world and to register its realities. The great seasonal festivals of awakening, burgeoning, ripening, dying, which measure each and every year that measures life, were designed to seek out and to celebrate in dramatic mimesis the source of life as it seemed to reveal itself in creation to each particular people. The ritual dramas of these great seasonal festivals were true and proper religious sacraments, each in its own right – or at least they had as much chance of being so as the sacraments of the so-called world religions. Seeking to test the world in depth and to register the deepest sources of being and life, they sought also to solicit the continuance and the increasing efficacy of such powerful ultimates. They were, and are, a kind of prayer rather than the survival of magic. Indeed, because of their dramatic form they involved participation in a battle between malevolent versions of reality, however these were thought to come about, and the benevolent forces normally thought to be original and dominant, and thus they incited and expressed the whole moral creativity of the participants.

When social development evolved representative persons, the king or queen, naturally embodied the power and wisdom which made life in society possible and fruitful; but no dichotomy between society and nature ever really emerged – as even Marx realised, the creation is humanity's extended body, and their destinies are bound together for better or worse. Hence the rituals of enthronement often evoked also the renewal of the ultimate life-source in all of nature, as the death of the monarch could symbolise its decline. The symbolism of the sacral king was applied by his followers to Jesus when it appeared to them that he embodied the power and wisdom of the ultimate source of life and being: he was anointed (though by a woman), and to him were applied the words of the divine enthronement of the kings of old, 'you are my son, this day I have begotten you', 'the Lord said to my lord, sit at my right hand'. Of course he was anointed for death, and his exaltation to the position of power (his becoming son of God in power, his resurrection) was on the cross – the crucified anointed one is the power of God and the wisdom of God.

That already tells us much about the distinctively Christian perception of the nature of the ultimate power and wisdom behind the world, the kind of thing one would hope to discover more fully through participation in the central Christian ritual. For the moment it is only necessary to notice that Christianity, too, has a liturgical year: two great festivals rather than four; one in the depth of winter when the advent of the significant new life is celebrated (the general symbolism of light pointing to hope in the Christian Christmas is so reminiscent of the ancient symbolism of Newgrange in Ireland when at the rising of the sun at the winter solstice a ray of light penetrates the inner chamber of the megalithic tumulus, the beginnings of light in the depth of darkness, of life in death), and one in the springtime of the year when the death and resurrection of Jesus are ritually dramatised. (Of course, if Christian harvest festivals were added, though of much lower liturgical profile in all Christian churches, three of the four seasonal rituals could be found replicated in Christianity')

The very idea of a representative human being carries within itself the seed of the democratic idea; an ideal human being cannot but be at some state an ideal *for* human beings. So, for example, as the sovereignty of kings and emperors came to be seen as the sovereignty of the people entrusted to them, the time came when the people began to reclaim the exercise of that sovereignty for themselves, albeit still in representative form: representative monarchy gave way to representative democracy. The coming of Christianity was undoubtedly a watershed for this process in Western civilisation. The explicit conviction that the divine word and power embodied once in the individual, Jesus of Nazareth, continued to ensoul and enliven and inspire what Christians then called his body in the world, like an extension of the incarnation in Jesus himself, carried the clearest implications for the democratisation of human society – however much we may see these later betrayed by certain borrowed practices of church government. The fact that Jesus himself did not hold any office, was neither a king nor a priest, added to his own preference for the form of the servant, led to his 'body' being seen as a body of all ordinary people, differentiated in their basic equality only by their charisms, the variety of services they could render to each other.

It is to the central ritual of this body that one must look, if one is to discover the dramatic participation – if only that of a spectator – which allows one to see in its inimitable manner the shape and form of the ultimate power and wisdom that, according to Christians, rules the world, or forms the kingdom of God. That central ritual is undoubtedly what Christians call the Eucharist. There is neither space nor need here to argue the number of Christian sacraments: suffice it to say that baptism, the sacrament of initiation for Christians, is precisely the initiation to the Eucharistic community, and that, even in Roman Catholic theory, all other sacraments are ordered towards the Eucharist as to their perfection and end. It can therefore do all that all of them can do.[15]

There is a prayer that is used in the Roman Catholic Mass to lead into the Eucharistic Prayer proper, and it looks as if a full commentary upon it could comprehend the whole theology of the Christian Eucharist, and perhaps the whole theology of Christianity: 'Blessed be you, Lord God of all creation, through your goodness we have this bread to offer, which earth has given and human hands have made; it will become for us the bread of life.' You could begin Christian theology with nothing more than a crust of bread, and, with the proper dramatic combination of word and action, carry yourself through that whole range of experience which would otherwise take the whole Bible to depict, from the first grand entrance of word and spirit in the creation story of Genesis to their final form in the symbolism with which Paul assimilates the crucified Christ. In other words, an adequate and adequately perceptive account of a dramatic communal action with a piece of bread – taken, thanked for, broken, given – could provide a complete Christian theology.

The bread is the staff of life, and the symbol of life, and the earth gives it and human hands make it; and for it and the life, and the giving and the making, we bless or give thanks (from which the whole ritual is named, after the Greek verb *eucharein*, to give thanks). This elemental posture of gratitude for life and all the natural supports of life (in Latin, *gratias agere*), means that we take life and the world that gives and sustains it to be grace (in Latin *gratia*, a gift freely given). To test the world like this, and to register its inner reality as grace, is certainly one way of depicting the essence of Christianity, though no doubt not the only one. For it infers for the world a meaning and a power. To relate to all life and existence, life and all the supports of life, as gift is to see that kind of meaning in it; and despite the fact that in much of our human experience a gift freely given too often meets only a response of envy and resentment and even greater greed, the native power of gift-giving or grace is to make the recipient generous in turn. Grace, in that elementary sense of giving and receiving freely, has an innate power to bring the best out of people, however frequently it may encounter the human proclivity for making the best into the worst. To test the world and to register its inner, its deepest and highest, reality as the word/power of grace is itself a theology of creation: it names the ultimate source of existence and of burgeoning life as *bonum diffusivum sui*, goodness-of-its-nature-poured-out, or words to that effect, however well its ultimate nature may still be hidden from us.

Now if the word is grace, and if the power works as we seem to register it in the opening moves and words of the drama – taking the crust of bread and giving thanks for that which earth has given and human hands have made – we shall find ourselves enabled to make the next move, which is to break the crust and to give some of it to someone. Kings were once the ones who fed their people, as on the truth and justice with which they reigned depended the fruitfulness of the very earth. Jesus, on the night on which he was betrayed, took bread and blessed God for it and broke it, knowing the symbol that bread is, the symbol of life itself. Those who test the world like this and register its reality as grace, existence and life poured out freely over and over, are enlightened and empowered to pour out their own lives in turn, even if on extreme occasions that may mean to them the final pouring out that is death. Jesus lived for others to the point of dying for others, and he drew others into the drama of sensing life as grace poured out. His life, and even more so his death, was for others the incarnation of the word and power of grace, and the channel of that word and power into their own lives.

The Eucharist is the *anamnesis* of the ritual in which he tested the world and registered its reality, and committed himself to its continuous co-creation in line with its source and inner nature, and with the hope of its final perfection in something like the supreme fulfilment of self-giving love. It is therefore the ritual drama in which the Word and spirit which was incarnate in Christ, and above all in the crucified Christ, shapes the lives of those who would be his followers so that they become the body of Christ in the world. The Eucharist interprets the cross and enables those who participate in the drama to encounter the power that would enable them, in turn, to give their lives like that; the cross, in turn, interprets the creation (that is why Paul can apply the wisdom–creation symbolism to the dying Jesus), for the creation is the process by which things are and live, and cease to be and die in order that others may be and live. There is more than a hint of a distinctive life, a way, an ethic, which is religious because it believes that the ultimate source of reality is just such a kind of word–power, an existence or life, which may be encountered more immediately at the end of life or existence pursued along this way, according to this ethic.

You could do the same kind and quantity of theology with half a glass of wine, or with a crust of bread and half a glass of wine. The point is that it is in the drama of taking and thanking for, breaking/pouring out and giving, that the distinctive world-power is encountered which Christians believe reveals and characterises the ultimate power of being and life in the whole of creation, which therefore characterises at its most general and best the creation itself, and which, further still, inspires and informs that human co-creation in which human morality and dignity consists, promising the best future for all. Of course, when one says that the drama, the ritual, is the paradigmatic form for registering the deepest realities of the world, one is not claiming that it is fool-proof. Human beings can turn that too into an instrument of deceit and destruction, as Paul once reminded the Corinthians, and as we shall have occasion to note again from the example of more recent communities. But it is the available form for encountering Jesus as life-giving spirit and God as spirit; and, in its traditional pattern in all Christian churches, it is the most comprehensive form in which this encounter can take place.

CHAPTER 5

The anatomy of church

Communities are not mere agglommerates of discrete individuals. They are, rather, by demands of nature and the needs of survival, structured entities. The most basic structures are provided by role-playing, and the most basic roles, of father and mother for instance, are biologically determined. Other roles may be determined by such elemental features as size and strength, but, as the human species in particular gains a mastery in understanding and imagination over the physical and biological factors that would otherwise determine the whole of its existence, it gains also a certain creative freedom with respect to the structuring of the communities on which its survival depends. It can then begin to institutionalise certain leadership roles: that is to say, offices in the community are named, job descriptions are attached, rights and duties are defined, and means of selection and succession agreed (or imposed, as the case may be).

It is not at all easy to pin-point the year, or even the decade, in which the Christian community became a religious community, and a religion, sufficiently distinguished from its Jewish home and matrix to be capable of notice and description as such, as Christianity rather than (a version of) Judaism. In his recent Cunningham Lectures at the University of Edinburgh, Etienne Trocmé argued that a perceptible cutting of the umbilical cord must be located in the second half of the second century of the so-called Christian era, and possibly later rather than earlier in that period. He used the generally accepted analysis of religion into the constitutive parts of cult, creed, code, and constitution, and argued that in none of these parts –

not in its meals or immersions, not in its authoritative scriptures and dogmas, not in its ethos and its offices – did it display such differences from its Jewish matrix as to advertise itself as a new and different faith or religion.

His arguments would be widely accepted by historians of early Christianity, and they have their counterpart in the apparent assumption of all of those we meet in the Christian scriptures – once we can talk of Christian scriptures, that is, once a canon of these begins to be established in the period mentioned – that they are still part of the faith of Israel, renewed no doubt (at least no doubt in their minds), but for that very reason by no means displaced. Here is something of a paradox: that a set of 'gospels' and letters, the addition of which to the sacred scriptures of the Jews in a move which claimed equal sacredness for them, formed part of the process of creating a new religion, contains within itself no awareness that a new religion is being formed.

Even before the beginning of what would prove to be the final breakaway, structures were emerging in the communities of Jesus-followers which took the forms both of formalised offices and of a variety of less institutionalised roles. The distinction here is not an easy one to maintain, and the more institutionalised any society becomes, the more thoroughly are all the important roles and the sub-groups who exercise these regulated by the most highly institutionalised offices in that society, unless these groups can successfully and demonstrably regulate their own activities and members to the manifest satisfaction of the community at large. Nevertheless one can see in these proto-Christian communities roles which, as in all communities, are called into existence by the very nature of the community itself. The community we now see forming is predicated on the coming of what Jesus called the rule of God (in his distinctive version of it); hence apostles emerged to carry the good news of it; teachers, prophets, healers emerged (for this rule of God was healing, salvific); lists were provided by Paul of those who played such roles in the conviction that they had the 'charisms', the gifts or graces which the playing of these roles required for the advancement of the community.

In addition one can also detect the emergence of more institutionalised offices, for all communities need 'officers of good order'. The Acts of the Apostles describe an early fulfilment of such a need (chapter 6). It would appear that the early communities borrowed the names and forms of such offices from surrounding societies. There was the office of elder or presbyter, based on the kind of group leadership of elders in tribal or village society at the time, and offices of a supervisory nature, such as those named 'episcopoi' and 'diakonoi', more broadly characteristic of a variety of institutional structures of supervision in the Hellenised and Romanised society shared by the early followers of Jesus. Although these titles or their linguistic derivatives were later homologated to name special priestly functions when Christianity did develop the idea and practice, absent in its origins, of cultic priesthood different in kind and not just in degree from the priesthood of the whole Christian people – deacon, priest, bishop – they did not carry any such connotation at the outset. Deacons, presbyters, and 'episcopoi' might in time, and as a matter of course, preside over the Eucharistic meal, since they were officers of good order of the communities and this meal was the constitutive celebration of these communities, but other kinds of leader also presided at the Eucharist, and the presidency carried no implications of a cultic priesthood such as the Jewish and other contemporary religions enjoyed. The founder did not provide, and early Christians simply did not have, priests in that sense of the word. Rather did these institutional offices of good order develop according to their own peculiar logic, and their frequently uneasy relationship with the more 'charismatic' leadership roles on which this, like every other community, depends.[1]

Once one sees that the institutional offices of the Christian community in the world did not have their constitutional forms dictated from heaven, or even prescribed by Jesus of Nazareth, one can feel rather more free to form a balanced assessment of the profits and losses incurred in the very process of borrowing the institutional forms of these offices from surrounding cultures. In the profit column one can certainly enter the contribution to the necessary enculturation of the new Christian word–spirit; and such enculturation is always necessary if the new religious life-giving spirit is to enter the warp and woof of people's lives. Enculturation in this instance means embodying the new faith for a people in the language, ritual, ethos, and institutions that shape their communal lives, and in terms of which they can comprehend and receive, if they will, whatever is put to them. The faith of Jesus found its first enculturation in his own Jewish culture; the break with Judaism entailed its separate enculturation in the broader culture of the Graeco-Roman Empire, and the borrowing of these institutional offices of good order was an essential and important part of that extremely successful process. As a single instance of the beneficent effect which the Christian borrowing of an institutional form may have upon the office borrowed, one could mention the designation of the highest executive officers of civic government as ministers, that is, servants of the civic community's needs. Such influence can come about either by the power of good example which the institutional officers of good order in the Christian community exercise upon their civic counterparts or by the occupation of such civic offices by convinced Christians; although it would be quite unlikely to come about in the latter manner if it did not also operate in the former.

But all cultural borrowing is an essentially ambivalent affair. The characteristic ideas, images, rituals, mores, and institutions of a people are not such shape-free and elastic entities as would enable one to use them simply as containers of the cargo of faith one wished to deliver, in the simple confidence that they would instantly shape themselves to the distinctive outlines of that faith and cause it no further inconvenience. Such is the impression one sometimes gets when listening to Christians describing how their early theologians borrowed the 'philosophical' concepts of the Roman world in order to present their faith to Roman citizens in theological, doctrinal, or credal form; as if these philosophical frameworks did not already have their own theological content and shape. In all borrowing you are as likely to assimilate as much of the vision and directional force, as much of the word and spirit, already embodied in that which you borrow, as you are to reshape the borrowed by the power and form of your new word and spirit.

The early followers of Jesus had trouble deciding how much they were, or should be, carrying forward from current forms of Judaism, and two of their more prominent leaders, Peter and Paul, continued to disagree on the subject. That kind of problem did not quite subside when Christians faced a wider world. The problem does not lie simply in the fact that you assimilate much of the characteristic forms of that which you borrow. Much of that form may be assimilable to your faith – after all, you did say that the word that has come to you in a new and, to you, definitive way was in the world already and you should not be surprised that it has taken some acceptable shapes in civic and religious life around you. But much may also not be assimilable – after all you would not be out there preaching the word newly come to you if you did not think that it had been previously betrayed to some extent, or at least less fully formulated in the course of its pre-existence in the world. The real danger of borrowing may then be specified: it is the danger of assimilating those shapes and forms which are incompatible with the word–spirit you wish to spread, and which then threaten to diminish or even to destroy that word or spirit. The question that really needs to be answered, therefore, with respect to the offices of good order, the institutional forms borrowed by the early Christian community is this: is there something to be entered in the loss column as a result of this borrowing? Was there, is there still, something in the characteristic shapes and forms of these institutional structures which was assimilated in the borrowing, but which was really not assimilable to the distinctive word and spirit of Christianity without operating to the latter's detriment?

A full and adequate answer to that question could only follow in the wake of a fairly comprehensive account of what has been called Christendom or, much more unkindly, Caesaro-papism. The reference is to that set of social structures, ecclesiastical and civil, and the relationships between them, which developed over the areas of the Roman Empire, east and west, once Constantine in the early fourth century of the Christian era had virtually made Christianity the established religion of the empire. It would be impossible for a variety of reasons to provide here an account of this complex process, even if it does represent the single most thoroughgoing enculturation that Christianity the religion has as yet achieved; so thoroughgoing that it represents to this day a scarcely diminished threat to the necessary enculturation of Christianity in all other areas of the world. All that one can hope to do here is to evoke some of the salient features of Christendom, and to use these to hint at the kind of answer to our question which a fuller analysis would be likely to support.

Reference has already been made to the famous doctrine of the two swords, immortalised in the Bull *Unam Sanctam* of Boniface VIII in CE 1302; the spiritual sword and the temporal sword, corresponding to spiritual and temporal power, both under the control of the church, but the latter wielded on behalf of the church by the civil ruler. It was easy for the Bull to draw from this image the implication that the ecclesiastical power could judge the practice and performance of the 'earthly' power, and that could mean no less than the licence to interfere directly in the legislative, judicial, and executive functions of the empire or, later, the state. Despite the fact that William of Ockham in the same fourteenth century mounted a determined attack upon the claims of the medieval church, and particularly of the papacy, to such universal spiritual and secular power – in this he could be said to have tried to envisage better conditions for the emergence of European nation states[2] – the sixteenth century, the age of the Protestant Reformation, saw Robert Bellarmine, one of the principal protagonists of what would henceforth have to be known as the Roman Catholic Church, continue to insist that popes and kings, clergy and laity, form one commonwealth. The two powers continued to be seen in union; in fact the image of the two swords originally in one scabbard by now yields pride of place to the image of the two powers united as soul is united to body, with the spiritual power naturally represented by the directive soul.

Christendom, of course, did come to an end, despite the preference of Roman Catholicism for the *ancien régime*, when the autonomous nation states did finally emerge in Europe, but the image of a church structured, and with its structures understood, very much as Christendom had been structured and understood, survives in Roman Catholicism to this day. The image of the ensouled body was taken up again by Pius X in his encyclical *Mystici Corporis* of 1943, and, in case anybody should get the idea that the church was now to be seen as some sort of 'invisible' entity, a mystical union of inner spirits or minds, with none of the massive and obtrusive structures of other formed societies of human beings, the encyclical is frequent in its insistence that the church is a perfect society, 'possessing all juridical and social elements'. Describing Christ as someone who was king, as well as teacher and priest – although in the proper meanings of these words in the social context he was neither the first nor the last – the encyclical insists that he instituted a church as a kingdom which is social and visible, and which is endowed by him with an *imperium* (as well as a *magisterium*, and a *ministerium*); and the *imperium* consists of those legislative, judicial, and executive powers that feature in both the old empire and the new states. Little wonder, on this understanding of itself, that the Roman Catholic Church insisted, in the era of the nation state, on having its own sovereign statelet, though one which is currently reduced to the size of the Vatican in Rome.

Now it is not at all surprising that a church which thought itself authorised to regulate the exercise of power in civic offices and institutions, should come to think of the exercise of power by its own offices and institutions after the model of those it regulated, and in *all* the salient features of that model. Nor is it surprising that it should have continued the use of such a model of the exercise of power long after it had had to withdraw within its own boundaries, as it were, and cease to claim the authority to regulate directly the exercise of civic powers. But before asking after some possibly detrimental effects of such modelling upon the institutional practices of a Christian church, look briefly at some significant moments in the development of church–state institutional relationships in the case of some Protestant churches.

It has already been remarked that when Henry VIII declared himself head of the church in England, he was doing no more than taking over the two-swords symbolism of sovereign power in the world, and simply disputing the identity of the controller of the swords. It would be doubtful if one could successfully charge him with inverting the natural superiority of spiritual over temporal power, for, apart from the fact that the last chapter but one revealed considerable difficulty in any attempt to distinguish powers secular from powers sacred in actual instances of governing institutions in human societies, there really is nothing in the sources of the Christian religion to tell us that sovereign power, *imperium*, even in matters spiritual, should be exercised by clergy rather than laity, popes rather than kings. In the event, however, the Henrician formula did undoubtedly solidify the impression already gained from the medieval church that the exercise of institutional power could be similar in all respects in church and state.

As for other churches stemming from the Protestant Reformation of the sixteenth century, there are undoubtedly significant differences on the point of interest here between Lutheran and Calvinist theory and practice. Luther's work was later cited in favour of religious toleration, whereas Calvin seemed to have envisaged a more direct use of the secular powers for the establishment of the external conditions of Christian as well as civic virtue; and that once again would inevitably lead to a rather direct regulation of the exercise of civic powers by proponents of Christian principle, and to a certain assimilation of the detailed means of exercising power in society as between the offices of church and state.[3] The event known as the Disruption of the Church of Scotland, and some of its implications, have already been noted. The event itself concerned the freedom of the church rather than its influence over the exercise of state powers. Yet its general background consisted of such legal initiatives as an Act of the Scottish Parliament of 1567 which abrogated all laws canon, civil, or municipal which were not in accord with the Christian faith, and a deliverance of the presiding judge in the last blasphemy trial to be held in Scotland, in 1843, to the effect that 'the Bible and the Christian religion were part of the law of the land, and that whatever vilified them was an infringement of the law'.

Christian claims to regulate the exercise of civic *imperium* are quite varied in form and strength. They can scarcely ever be altogether absent where some form of church establishment is still in force; but even where these claims are thought to be quite obsolete (and establishment reduced to a matter of ceremony rather than substance), churches can still attempt to abuse the democratic process by manipulating a majority in order to regulate the exercise of a modern state's legislative power. There is some evidence that the Roman Catholic Church in Ireland indulged in such abuse over the last decade, as there is ample evidence that establishment of Protestant churches in these islands at an earlier stage damaged very considerably the civic status of Roman Catholics. Critics of these ecclesiastical regulatory claims and practices usually concentrate on the implicit disenfranchisement, or the reduction of the civil rights of those who do not belong to the churches in question, but are citizens of the states or subjects of the civic government. And that is quite right and proper, for such offences against civil rights are not tolerable. But the effect of these varied involvements of ecclesiastical with civil offices which is of most immediate interest for us is quite different: it is the effect upon the image and praxis of Christian ecclesiastical institutional office of this long and varied involvement, and in particular the possibility of detrimental effect upon the very image of the Christian religion.

Well, then, did the kind and manner of the close involvement of ecclesiastical structures with civil structures which we have glimpsed entail the borrowing of some features of the latter's praxis which, even if these features could be shown to be justified in the case of civil structures, prove detrimental to the moral and religious fibre of Christianity itself? One could well recall at this point the celebrated Hart–Devlin debate. At issue there, as the relevant section of chapter 2 above argued, was not so much the question as to whether state law and moral value or duty should coincide as to content. All state law, it was argued, must have moral content, for nothing that was immoral could be imposed by law; although it did not at all follow that anything like the whole of morality should be imposed by state law. What was really at issue in the Hart–Devlin debate, as chapter 2 argued, was the question as to whether a law enforced, as state laws tend to be, could still be deemed a moral entity, a moral precept, precisely in view of the fact and manner of its enforcement or, in other terms, in view of the manner in which enforcement acts as a solvent of moral substance. Now, although it is the case that most modern governments operate with a distinction of legislative, judicial, and executive powers, these are connected in such a way that the decisions of the legislature and the judiciary can be enforced by the executive arm of government. The enforcement usually takes the form of the restriction of the will and freedom of the individual, or the application of other forms of punishment, like pain or deprivation, or both. Force and its subjective counterpart, fear, can then act to deprive resultant human behaviour of its moral dignity and status. This clearly occurs in the case of those who break the law and are apprehended; but force and fear may also operate to reduce the moral stature of agents when these become their major motivations in keeping the laws thus enforced.

The major instance of enforcement by the civil government is to be seen in the case of the criminal law. Moralists may find it off-putting that legal theorists appear reluctant to define criminal, as distinct from civil, law, by reference to the kinds of behaviour or actions regulated. In that circular manner which seems characteristic of legal theorising – is this a means of keeping the discussion of law out of reach of all except lawyers? – criminal law is defined as that which deals with crimes or offences, and these in turn are defined as wrongful acts which are capable of being followed by criminal proceedings. Nevertheless this is the range of state law enforced by prosecution, conviction of wrong-doing, and punishment applied by the co-operative penal institutions of the state.

The rest is reckoned as civil law. Abjuring the language of

crime and punishment, the talk here is all about a wrongful act
that gives rise to civil proceedings – the circularity again! – in
which a plaintiff sues or brings an action against a defendant.
The judgment in such cases may require the transfer of money
or other property; it may be an injunction to do something or
to refrain, or to perform a contract entered into; in family law
it may be to dissolve a marriage, to decide on subsequent
financial arrangments and on the custody of children; and so
on. The language of crime and punishment, the harbinger of
force and trigger of fear, is noticeably absent here. But that
must not be taken to mean that the element of enforcement is
altogether absent from this larger area of the government of a
society, in which it exercises its much larger and more positive
remit or moral authority, in seeking to provide for each and all
a just share of the means of livelihood, as well as health,
education, and other means of human advancement. For
whether individual citizens invoke the civil legal proceedings
to right alleged wrongs, or the institutions of state invoke them
to see to it that its citizens do not abuse the larger provisions
made for all, the judgment of the relevant court can be followed by enforcement, and by forms of enforcement quite
similar to those used in the execution of the criminal law, if the
judgements handed down by the civil proceedings are not
accepted and obeyed.

It has been argued already that the enforcement of law in
civil society, despite its innate tendency to diminish, even if it
does not always eradicate, the moral substance of human
behaviour, by encouraging the acquiescence of fear as a
replacement for free, rational decision, is justified on the
grounds that only by this means can the basic securities of life
in society be guaranteed, and on these all possibility of truly
human social and moral existence and progress depends.
Clearly the criminal law is of its nature designed to provide
such elementary security of life and morals – despite the
unwillingness of lawyers to define crime according to the
nature of particular actions. And the additional enforcement
by penal process of judgments given in civil law, where these
are ignored or contravened, has or can be given a similar

justification. Further, as has been noted, not everyone faced
with criminal law need be motivated by the fear induced by
the penalties attached; and even the penalties themselves can
be applied so as not to diminish any further the freedom and
dignity of those convicted, and perhaps even to rehabilitate
these essential human qualities.

The question now is, have Christian churches adopted such
practices and features of the exercise of civil government, and
are these equally justifiable in their cases, or do they represent,
on the contrary, the damaging side of the borrowing that has so
obviously taken place? There is plenty of prima facie evidence
for the contention that Christian churches have borrowed, as a
result of the close involvements with civil government which
have been indicated, just these enforcement features which of
their nature operate to the detriment of morality. The Roman
Catholic *Code of Canon Law* has Book VI devoted to sanctions in
the church. The first part of that book is entitled 'Offences and
Punishments in General', and its first canon reads: 'The church
has its own inherent right to constrain with penal sanctions
Christ's faithful who commit offences' (canon 1311). Cox's
Practice and Procedure in the Church of Scotland which devotes
chapter 15 to the subject of disciplines, declares that 'the
subjects of discipline are those who hold office in the Church,
communicants, and baptised persons who are adherents', and
that 'discipline consists in the administration of the appropriate censures of the Church to those whose conduct shall
have given occasion for it'. Its censures are named as admoni-
tion, rebuke, suspension, deposition from office, and excommunication. The Roman Catholic list is somewhat similar,
although there are also sinister references to 'other expiatory
penalties which deprive a member of Christ's faithful of some
spiritual or temporal good' (canon 1312).

It would be possible, one might suppose, to see in these penal
codes no more than efforts at enforcement of what have already
been described as 'rules of the club' types of precept, and to
claim as a consequence that there are no implications for the
dissolution of morality. Churches are purely voluntary organisations, like tennis clubs in this respect, and if they decide to

rebuke, admonish, strip members of office, and eventually eject
members on certain well-stated criteria, it would be strange to
regard such behaviour as being to the detriment of human
morality, provided that the normal requirements of fairness
and justice were observed. So it might be argued, and so it
might be agreed. But it would also be wise to observe that the
tennis-club analogy is not quite as strong as it seems. Churches
on their own understanding of themselves are not quite as
voluntary, in the sense of optional organisations, as are tennis
clubs and such-like. They are, rather, in the moral business by
definition, because they are in the business of enlightening and
empowering for human life itself and in view of its most
definitive prospects. That is not to say that they cannot have
something equivalent to 'rules of the club', sets of regulations
which make no pretence of being universally applicable to the
human race, but which represent regulations for the orderly
administration of a particular ecclesiastical community at a
particular time and place. It does mean that in the process of
applying even these rules, and judging and dealing with the
people who come under them, churches must still be true to the
distinctive moral spirit and word which it is their very *raison
d'être* to promote. On this account the question can legitimately
be asked if Christian churches in particular are ever entitled to
use models of enforcement, by threat and fear of judicially
applied punishment, after the manner of that area of civil
legislation in which this is justified, even in the case of their
'rules of the club'.

It is a much more serious matter if Christian churches were
to be found to be using the model of penal enforcement beyond
the limits of the 'rules of the club', in that much broader range
of truly moral precepts, stories and values which, on being
proposed as truly moral, would inevitably be thought to be
proposed for general human observation. Yet there is every
reason to believe that traditional teaching in all of the mainstream Christian churches, and perhaps even more so in some
of the smaller ones, did invoke the model of penal enforcement
in favour of what all of these Christians took to be morality.
The model is most clearly and explicitly invoked in most

traditional Christian doctrines of hell. It matters little if a doctrine included the gruesome detail of eternal physical torture or whether, shorn of such picturesque details of flesh at once sizzling and putrid, a more fastidious modern mind painted a picture of eternal deprivation of blessed divine intimacy. The simple fact that God was envisaged, and, where this doctrine is in vogue, still is envisaged in the role of judge and executioner, condemning the guilty and applying the terrible penalty of their guilt, means that the penal enforcement model is fully intact in Christian morality. The same model may be much more implicit, though no less really present, even if the lurid details of divine punishment are omitted, in certain theocratic, deontological theories of ethics proposed by Christians: where morality, for instance, is simply defined as the will of God, whether revealed in nature or in some special divine revelations, and where God appears as the omnipotent one whose will cannot be evaded or gainsaid.

There are no doubt many other places and contexts in which the penal enforcement model of human morality, although it is the natural enemy of human morality, is at least implicit in Christian doctrine, and it would be tedious to search all of them out. A very few examples must suffice. Many models in soteriology, for instance, would seem to harbour this anti-moral model somewhere close to their hearts. The death of Jesus, in particular, has been interpreted in terms of the payment of a penalty due for sin. The very term 'redemption' contains the idea of a ransom paid, and if the metaphor intended here is taken literally, as doctrine tends to take metaphors, then the idea of penalty imagined here as some kind of hefty fine, takes its place at the centre of the doctrine. It is then developed and refined according to medieval and feudal categories of 'honour price' or *eiric* as the ancient Irish called it, in which the penalty to be paid, the fine, was measured according to the dignity and status, of the one offended or injured. An offended God required an infinite penalty, which only a God could pay; and so the mercy of God was secured as well as his justice when he sent his own son to make recompense. But the whole literal reading of the meta-

phor is shot through with the substance of the penal enforcement model for all that can be said about God's love and
mercy, and the consequences for the perception of Christian
morality are none the less serious.

It would be idle to suggest that the damage done to the very
nature of human morality, in having it pictured as something
enforced by fear of punishment, could be ameliorated by the
addition of the information that the innocent had been
punished in place of the guilty. That would simply add to the
impression that morality is something imposed by fear of
penalty, the temptation to the irresponsibility of hoping that
some innocent person might be punished in one's stead. It
would certainly do nothing to heal the damage done to the
very nature of morality by the central presence of the penal
enforcement model.[4] The very presence of that model simply
ruins in advance every well-intentioned effort to express the
Christian's and, according to the Christian, everyone's deep
indebtedness to Jesus.

There are other instances of traditional Christian doctrine
that reveal or conceal this same mentality. One of the most
obvious ones is no doubt the traditional and more recently
Roman Catholic doctrine of the sacrament of the forgiviness of
sins, with its incumbent symbolism of the tribunal, confession,
penance. But there is no need to add further examples; the
perceptive analyst will find the suspect model wherever some of
its characteristic qualities appear. It is sufficient here to note
that the tenacity and ubiquity of this model is not to be
explained by any attempt of religious leaders as such to impose
it on those who would otherwise not have wanted it. On the
contrary, spokespersons for many a society have welcomed the
presence of religion in that society, or regretted its decline,
precisely because of the value they placed on the presence of
the penal enforcement model in its religious mode. The
common expression that people would go to the dogs, morally
speaking, without religion's restraining presence finds a much
older and more elegant expression amongst the pre-Socratics.
The clear impression that one gets from Critias' *Sisyphus*, for
example, is that the idea of a God who could act as moral

policeman, prepared to apprehend and punish in the end, was a very good idea indeed, especially for those who were confident that so much of their evil-doing could evade the eyes of human policemen – as indeed, no doubt, it could. Critias would lead one to believe, and it may have been his intention to do so, that if God did not exist, it would be wise of the intelligent statesman to invent him for this very role.

It is well to note, since there has been so much talk of penalty, and the suspect model itself is called the penal enforcement model, that the same detrimental effect upon the very substance of morality can be produced by promise of reward, provided that, in the case of the reward for observance of moral duty as in the case of the penalty for breach of it, what is promised/threatened is additional or extrinsic to any good or evil that accrues naturally to the agent from the very performance of the deed in question. This means, in effect, that traditional doctrines of heaven can be as detrimental to one's moral fibre as doctrines of hell, for they can induce a kind of long-sighted selfishness, the kind that so many smugly religious people can so often exemplify. Fear is no doubt the most destructive of human emotions, but self-interest and greed is not very far behind. Pictures of heaven have always lagged behind those of hell, if only in their relative failure to sustain much interest, but the principle is the same, that the promise (in this case) of an outcome to be applied and which is extrinsic to the natural outcome of the act or behaviour contemplated, substitutes for properly moral intent an emotion which of its nature acts to the detriment of morality. Too many humanist critics of Christianity have pointed out how long-sighted desire for the rewards of heaven have evacuated earth of its values, and how loving one's neighbour for the sake of loving God effectively sucks the substance out of the love of neighbour, for the neighbour becomes a means to an end. There is no need to amplify such well-directed criticism here. But the distinction between intrinsic and extrinsic rewards and punishments for moral action might merit a few extra comments, since this subtle but important distinction can help detect the presence of the penal enforcement model and, one must now add, of the rewarding self-interest model.

It goes without saying that there are natural consequences of all our actions, and that they are in broad generalities either life enhancing for ourselves and for others, or life diminishing. It is part of the very practice of morality to take these into account, in so far as they can be known to us or controlled by us. The judgment we pass on them, whether they are good or bad, is part of the judgment on the goodness or badness of the activity or behaviour contemplated. Consideration of them is thus part of the overall intentionality of our moral behaviour, and as such does not detract in the least from its moral status. If someone were to point out to us the consequence of our actions, even if that were to be done where the actions were deemed evil in the most striking imagery, in order to bring home to us the fullest appreciation of these natural consequences, that would have to be deemed an effort to facilitate our own moral deliberation. On such careful deliberation the highest moral status of human action, good or evil, depends. Malice aforethought makes a crime more blameworthy, as careful consideration makes a virtuous act more praiseworthy.

It may sometimes be difficult to decide whether someone is trying to frighten us or to incite our inborn greed or, on the other hand, trying to inform our consciences so that we may make the best moral decision; but it is essential to take a decision, and the best way to do so is to ascertain whether the good or evil to follow is part of the natural consequences of action or, on the contrary, something additional to that to be adduced by an agent acting as policeman, judge, and executioner. One could describe various kinds of 'hell' as natural consequences of certain types of moral behaviour, and various types of 'heaven' too, and one might even feel entitled to project some of these into a life beyond death as we know it, but it is doubtful if one could describe any of these as automatically eternal without slipping into the extrinsic application of reward and punishment again (to the detriment of morality), since moral relationships, and particularly the relationship of unconditional grace which Jesus envisaged, would appear to be incompatible with such decreed or automatic eternity. This does not take away from the total seriousness of morality and the possibility of total human failure which follows from that; it simply refuses the extrinsic decreeing of such things.

There is scarcely any doubt that the penal enforcement model has been both widespread and insidious in Christian teaching; not merely in Christian teaching about ethics and law, but, in implicit form at least, in a great many other areas of Christian doctrine. This is, no doubt, a long hangover from the early theocracies, when kings were sons of God and channels, or sources, of divine decrees, divine judgments and their execution. Whether one talks of channels or sources in this context is often thought to depend on whether one thinks the king the natural or adopted son of God, whether one takes the title metaphorically or literally. So people say that Jesus is called the son of God literally, and perhaps some ancient kings of Egypt, for instance, were erroneously so called also, whereas David was called the son of God metaphorically as a result of a kind of adoption (Psalm 2. 7: You are my son, today I have begotten you), for unlike Jesus he was not a natural son of God. It is not necessary to dispute the fact that there are good polemical and even theological reasons for shaping such distinctions; nevertheless one may be permitted to observe that the same distinctions may make very little practical difference, if any difference at all, in the resulting and intermeshing areas of ethics and politics.

To the subjects of these kings and of their decrees, their judgments on observance or non-observance, and their execution of consequent penalties and (if any) rewards, such theological and polemical distinctions must have remained largely irrelevant, if not also unintelligible. Nor was there much change in their condition in the Christian era and in the Christian realms. Even if only Jesus could now carry the title 'son of God', the doctrine of the divine right of kings in the secular realm and the doctrine of the pope as the vicar of Christ on earth, carried much the same implications for the apparent divine origin of the legislative, judicial, and executive power of one man as had been carried under the old 'divine' monarchies. From this point of view the doctrine of the two swords formulated, though by no means invented, by Boniface VIII, had an equally detrimental effect upon the image of political power in church and state. Which brings us full circle to the point made earlier: such intimate connections, such reciprocal relationships between divine and human powers is inclined to infect the divine with all the salient features of the human. This could be expanded into a general thesis in the philosophy of religion: people create their images of gods from the features of the powers over life and death that they know in nature or society, and the gods then endorse these features at the highest metaphysical level, however politically and ethically undeveloped these may be.[5] This in turn was what made Marx point to religious faith as the *vis inertiae* of history, and he was right to do so, however much he may be accused of ignoring the corresponding prophetic element in some religious traditions.

Theocracies cast a long shadow, and there is some evidence that religion in its governmental structures has lagged behind modern secular governments in the matter of the extent to which the penal enforcement model operates in the moral functioning of a religion like Christianity. Some effort has been made to define the acceptable minimum range of the application of penal enforcement in civic legislation, but it is very arguable that the Roman Catholic Papacy, amongst other religious authorities, still uses this model over a far greater and quite unacceptable range of moral ruling.

Now it is one thing to make a case that Christian churches, when compared to modern democratic states, indulge in excessive use of the penal enforcement model, and that they do so because they lag behind secular developments of moral and political sentiment. It would be quite another thing to maintain that they should make no use of this model at all. For, although it may very well be that their involvement with secular powers in the past was such as to infect them with overuse of threat of penalty and the consequent transformation of power into force, it is difficult to envisage a point at which churches would have no involvement whatever with secular powers. At the very least they have always in the past been

modelled on some of the structures that were also available to
secular government, and such similarity of structure is likely to
continue. This surely means not only that issues of mutual
example are likely to arise from the activation of similar structures of government in church and state, but that, since both
are human societies of the same general kind in the same
spatio-temporal continuum, the basic argument for a restricted
use of force and fear in the case of states might also be valid in
the case of churches. Is it?

It is possible to answer here only for Christianity, and not,
for instance, for Islam, or for any other religion. And in the
case of Christianity it seems possible to argue that all use of
force and fear is quite incompatible with its nature, that the
model of force by the use or even the threat of punishment
should never be invoked at all. The argument can be mounted
on both general and specific grounds. The general grounds are
found in the reason/power or word/spirit symbolism which is
in evidence throughout the Bible, and which was used to
elucidate the kind of life and hope made possible in all parts
and aspects of the community of Jesus-followers in the world.
The more specific grounds are found, naturally enough, in the
more distinctive paradigms for living that derive from the
ministry of Jesus himself.

In general, it is surely very noticeable that in the symbolism
of life- or indeed existence-giving word or spirit, there is a
persistent predominance of word-symbolism over spirit-
symbolism. This would appear to be of some significance for in
the symbolising of life, its nature, source, and prospects, 'word'
and its cognates (wisdom, truth, and justice in the most expan-
sive sense of the order that replaces chaos) symbolise that
which enables one to know, to see for oneself, hence to decide,
to choose, to reach moral status; 'spirit' and its cognates
(power, right hand), on the other hand, symbolise that which
enables one to do, that which sets one in motion. Now it is not
that there is anything essentially or inevitably non-rational
about spirit or power so used; it is not that it is to be thought to
induce blind or unknowing activity in those on whom it is
operative. Spirit, power names something which is as crucial to

staying alive as is seeing and knowing, something therefore which is discriminatory in its own way. But left to themselves and without any reference to their more specifically cognitive partners, these terms might well suggest something that looks more like a force than an authority, to use our by now familiar terms.

It is therefore of some significance that, in the particular trajectory through the Bible which we followed, spirit/power is constantly contextualised by word/wisdom, if not usually dominated by the latter. The life that comes to us from the source of all existence is thus depicted as one that we live knowingly, not one through which we are propelled without our conscious consent. That does not mean that there were not kings in the Original Testament, that they did not rule by force, and often by use of more force than the minimum required by more modern political theory would allow. But the theme was even then present, that Yahweh's king could rule only by wisdom, truth, righteousness, so that it was really Yahweh's wisdom that ruled the people. And there already were the seeds of a growing realisation that power should take the form of authority, and not of force. To the point of ruling out all use of force in human society? The Original Testament would scarcely allow one to reach that conclusion. Could it be reached by way of the specific paradigms of Jesus' ministry in the New?

In nothing short of a book-length discussion of the life, death, and destiny of Jesus would it be possible even to attempt a definitive answer to that question. In an interdisciplinary investigation such as that presently being conducted one can hope for little more than summary suggestions concerning the relevant parts of the disciplines to be brought together for elucidation of the topic in question. At this point one must be satisfied with some hints as to how the life and faith of Jesus could be read, in order to answer the question about a specific kind of living in Christian community which that faith envisages and inspires and, more specifically still, about a possible place for power exercised as force in that community. There are a number of different ways in which one could go about construing these hints.

One could, for instance, trawl through the New Testament, collect all those sayings and incidents in which Jesus seemed to be addressing the matter of the use of force in one form or another, and offer the results as a kind of pastiche. Jesus telling people to turn the other cheek, to give to those who take from them by force, to love one's enemies, to pray for one's persecutors, to forgive seventy times seven times those who wrong us; Jesus opening his table to outcasts and sinners, gathering into his inner circle on an equal footing the zealot as well as the tax-collector, declaring and behaving as if all were to be forgiven by the creative act of love, none to be judged and sentenced; Jesus explicitly forbidding the use of force in order to liberate him from unjust arrest and detention, declaring even in these circumstances that those who live by such force will die by it; Jesus, though he never decides on the forms of governmental structures which his community of followers will eventually need, being most explicit that those who would be leaders in that community must act always as servants of all the others and never in any way attempt to lord it over them, and himself giving the example of being their slave to the ultimate point of consistency of dying a death reserved for slaves and other non-citizens; and so on, and so on. Of course, in using such a method one would also have to come to grips with what might look like counter-examples: Jesus clearing the temple of money-changers, giving Peter the keys of the kingdom, for binding and loosing. But that is quite normal in this kind of exegesis of the Bible, and there is little doubt in this case that one could be successful in showing that the use of force to deter or chastise, or to induce conformity, is incompatible with the life and faith of Jesus.

An alternative approach – alternative, that is to say, to the pastiche – would be to seek some master image which could encapsulate the whole life, death, and destiny of Jesus and all that it envisages and inspires. Jesus himself used the image of the kingdom of God for that purpose, but since it was an image already at the disposal of other would-be leaders of a new Israel, only a full account of Jesus' own life, death, and destiny can give to it for us the concrete meaning he intended. And so we are thrown back again into the search for a master image that might give a key to the living faith of Jesus. The image of unconditional grace has been suggested: the vision and inspiration of seeing life and all of the supports of life as gift freely given; the ensuing ability to give life and all that supports and enhances life as freely and unconditionally as it has been received. That, certainly, is a compelling image for all that is dramatised and enacted, envisioned and intended in the Eucharist.[6] The vision and inspiration that coincides with the radical and encompassing sense of life as grace enlightens and empowers people to imagine and create an ever better life, and also to overcome the forces of destruction which one could otherwise only join and increase, but never beat.

The early followers of Jesus drew this kind of conclusion when they refused to join armies; they believed that there was a greater power than power in the form of force, and that this greater power could overcome even the force of arms. But armed force and criminal law with penal law attached or coincident have this in common, that they both try to coerce human conduct by threat or use of restraint and, if necessary, injury and even death. Warfare is used for this purpose against large organised groups from without the state's boundaries, or sometimes, in the case of civil conflict, from within; the penal system is used for individual offenders who are thought to threaten the very basic securities of life and the necessities of life within the community. It is arguable, therefore, that the lived and living faith of Jesus, the vision and power by which his followers are supposed to live, is one that eschews all access to power in the form of force, and allows only for what we have termed power in the form of authority. To depict the resultant ethic of Jesus in this manner is to restrict it to one of its results, and a negative one at that; the only excuse that can be offered is that it is a result most apposite in an inquiry into the relationship of power to Christian ethics.

Two sets of remarks to close this section. First, is this refusal of force distinctive of a Christian ethic? That question can only be answered after some reflection on the whole question of a distinctive Christian ethic. For it is obvious that Christians

have borrowed a great deal of their current ethic in every age
from surrounding cultures. It is clear also that even where
there is no obvious borrowing, there are similarities with other
ethical systems – think of Jain rejection of violence of all kinds,
for instance. And, most importantly of all, it is clear Christian
conviction from the beginning that the word/power, the ethic
that came into the world with Jesus, was in the world before
Jesus and outside the range of direct influence of himself and
his followers – *the light that enlightens* everyone who comes into
the world, depending on how one translates John 1: 9.

The most that Christians could claim, as one can see from
the creation imagery already described at the origin of all
Christology and Soteriology, is that with Jesus the definitive
form of the original word–spirit emerges into history; but even
that claim would have to be modified by the realisation that
Christians have seldom managed to live up to the stature of
Jesus, so that what passes for Christian ethic at any one point of
time and space, may be corrupt indeed, and in some instances
the truer light may be preserved by some non-Christians who
proved truer to it in its more general source. The best that
Christians can say or do about the so-called distinctiveness of
Christian ethic, therefore, is to try as best they can to discern
the true word and spirit which was incarnate in Jesus and is
always struggling to form his body in the world, to compare
this for all positive purposes with other ethical systems, religious or non-religious, as willing to be criticised in this process as
they are to claim superiority, and to hope that the best vision
and inspiration they can thus achieve and put into practice will
prove in the end-results to be the source word and spirit of all of
creation, so that it will recommend itself to all, and in this way
reveal its occasional distinctiveness to be an essentially self-
destructive property.

Second, it is well to recall the point, made many times at the
beginning of this book, about the lack of alignment between
forms of power and forms of structure of government: power in
the form of force can characterise democracies, power in the
form of authority monarchies. The corresponding point which
can surely be made at this stage of the analysis of the anatomy

of a Christian church is this: the characteristic form of power in the form of authority which one glimpses through the real presence of Jesus in his continuing body could equally inform and inspire any of the available structures for the government of human societies. Churches are human societies, and as such they need structures of government as effective as any other human societies; but Christian churches with their claim to unique insight into the original nature of the source-power, the creative word–spirit of the universe, as something enlightening and enabling, but never enforcing, must surely see themselves as capable of adopting any of the available structures of government that human societies evolve in the course of history, and making them into authority structures enabling their subjects to reach full moral stature, and never in any degree reducing that stature by recourse to force. Only in the eschaton may this example be fully effective in society at large, and only then if the example given by ecclesiastical communities has been unambiguous. It is far from being unambiguous at this time.

Of Christian churches and secular states

How, from the point of view of power and ethics, does the Christian religion relate to political societies, and how should it relate to these? It might be thought that the social sciences would offer a purchase on the kind of material which would best help to answer this question. But this is not the case; partly because one still meets amongst the social scientists too many who are still trapped in the kind of kindergarten materialism which dominated the earlier decades of this century; partly because quantitative research in the social sciences, and especially in political science, so greatly outweighs qualitative research. A recent ESRC seminar on 'Religion and Scottish politics' at the University of Edinburgh concentrated almost exclusively on political manifestations, or non-manifestations of sectarian divisions in the south-west of Scotland. Both the conference itself and the kind of research on which it was based illustrated very clearly that it is the kind of programmes which churches or sects push most energetically onto the political agenda that is taken to satisfy the needs of the word 'religion' for the social scientists, while the question of the possible religious reaches of political secularism itself in some of its manifestations goes unanalysed. So that the suspicion does emerge that the social sciences still need to measure up to some of their subject matter. Nothing is more obvious in the contemporary world-scene than the fact that religion misunderstood can do a great deal of damage, that it is almost equally misunderstood by its fanatical promoters and by its scientific despisers, and that the misunderstanding does as little credit to the latter's science as to the former's religious faith.

However that may be, this conclusion must confine itself to some remarks about Christian churches, and to the task of drawing some implications from the preceding philosophical and theological analyses.

First, it goes without saying that there is a great variety to be seen in both the institutional structures and the practical ways in which Christianity the religion relates to modern states: from establishment (in any of its many forms) to constitutional recognition by the state (again in many forms, from anonymous recognition of freedom of religions to a special recognition accorded to one religion); from Christian democratic parties which operate directly on the political scene, to other forms of public association (trade unions, youth movements) which are aligned to a Christian church and which wield more indirect, though no less real, political influence; from the voting power of a church small in numbers (like a small ethnic minority), to the voting power of a Christian community the size of which gives it a massive majority in the population of a state.

The point made in the earlier chapters about the non-alignment of the kind of political structure with the kind of power exercised, applies here also to the concrete kind of constitutional structures and practical ways in which a religion may relate to a state. Institutional or practical form need not align itself automatically with quality of power exercised, with the placing of that power on the range of forms that stretches from force to authority. The Papal government of the Roman Catholic Church represents the most absolute of imperial forms, and that church has been established in some sovereign states and has signed concordats with others. That does not necessarily mean that the power exercised by that church in its relationship with, say, a democracy in these circumstances must necessarily take the form of the force of dictation. The power of example, after all, is perhaps the most effective form of influence known in moral matters. Picture, then, a papacy which was the very model of power exercised exclusively in the form of authority; a pope constantly consulting the faithful, leading them only where they would willingly go, a true and total servant of all the servants of God. A church led by such a leader could be the most powerful influence upon any democracy with which it happened to be associated in any of the practical ways mentioned above, for it would foster by its example the very qualities which are at the heart of any democracy, the freedom and equal dignity of all the people, served rather than lorded over by their 'ministers'.

There is, of course, a drawback to this particular example of non-alignment of forms of institutional structure and forms of power exercised. It emerges most clearly when something goes wrong with papal leadership; when, for example, the majority of Roman Catholics disagree with their pope on substantial areas of the morality of sex and marriage, or when those who are at the forefront and literally in the firing-line in the Christian struggle for justice in Latin America, find themselves continuously undermined by Vatican intervention, what means do they have of turning what is increasingly seen as the exercise of force upon their consciences into an exercise of true authority once again? They do not have any means of removing an incumbent from papal office, and they are made the more painfully aware of their impotence when their pope uses his powers of local appointment to place bishops in dioceses around the world with little or no attention to the voices of the faithful in the choice of these bishops, and often against their wishes. This kind of drawback affects all Christian churches which are highly clerical or hierarchical in their disposal of governmental power, all churches which are not truly democratic. And it raises the question as to whether churches should not return more frequently to the process of creating the governmental structures of their Christian communities, a process in which they may have last engaged quite a long time ago. For, just as the exercise of power in the form of authority, a process which coincides with the genesis of moral value, is most effective through the influence of example, so it is clear that a Christian church structured as a representative democracy could exercise the most effective influence upon modern representative democracies.

So, how should the Christian religion act in and towards

political society? The answer to that question can only be found to the extent that Christians rediscover, over and over again, the true and undiluted nature of the power that, their very existence proclaims, manifests itself *par excellence* in Jesus and in his faithful followers; and rediscovers simultaneously the truly creative nature and communitarian structure of all morality.

Perhaps the single factor most likely to prevent such persistent rediscovery is what might be called 'the revelation complex'. This complex affects many religions, but more particularly those in possession of bodies of authoritative texts. It was illustrated earlier in this book by reference to the so-called propositional view of revelation. It reduces people to feeling that certain well-defined patterns of human behaviour and of societal structure are the revealed will of God rather than time-conditioned creations of human kind, albeit as a result of particular empowerment or inspiration believed to be of divine origin.

The revelation complex – a good sociological analysis of which can be found in Peter Berger's *A Rumour of Angels* – can result in direct damage to both the creative essence and the communitarian structure of morality. Just as a modern sociologist can think a moral stance religious simply because some church officials or groups endorse it, so the church itself can take it to be God's will because it has long forgotten when it was first produced, or by whom; and the church can then contrive to impose it, or seek to do so, despite the fact that the creativity of morality itself in an evolving world would suggest that a new creation of moral behaviour patterns should now take over from an older human creation of now obsolete patterns. A complete embargo on sex outside marriage might have made much sense in an age in which by social convention marriage could coincide roughly with the onset of puberty. Now that social convention, in combination with economic and other forces, requires an average space of ten years or more between puberty and marriage, such a complete embargo simply no longer represents a responsible moral formula for adolescent sexuality. A church's attitude to contraception before the more advanced artificial means became available can come to be thought the will of God more because its status as church teaching has outlasted any convincing memory of the cultural circumstances in which it was first borrowed or created, than because of any cogent argument that would link it with an alleged incidence of divine revelation. And when this kind of mentality combines the last two cases into a temptation to positively resist programmes involving the recommendation of the use of condoms in order to prevent the spread of Aids, there may be a well-founded suspicion that the revelation complex has run a little wild, and that the moral authority of a Christian church is being brought into disrepute by some of its own officers.

Damage to the communitarian structure of morality is implicit in the examples just given, for by the communitarian structure of morality is meant that structure of ethics which is visible in the coincidence of the genesis of moral value and the phenomenon of power exercised as authority or, more briefly put, in the coincidence of the genesis of moral value and the formation of community. From infancy we arrive at our own apprehension of moral values under the tutelage of others, and thus is our community with them fashioned and forever refashioned. Yet we have just seen examples in which values (or anti-values, mistaken obligations) are imposed rather than elicited, in which under the influence of the revelation complex, a true community of free and responsible people is hindered rather than advanced. But the revelation complex can do greater and more immediate damage still to the essentially communitarian structure of the creation of a moral universe, and the consequent furtherance of the cause of religious faith itself: when it affects the Christian perception of the very institutions themselves which Christians adopted and adapted over the centuries.

Consider these institutions to have been designed by God rather than created and adapted by time-conditioned people, and some truly incalculable damage can be detected as a result. It has been argued in the body of this book that the central ritual, the religious drama, the Eucharist is the place *par excellence* in which the spirit (of) Jesus is encountered and can shape people into the body of Christ in the world; a creative community which in turn creates the world according to the word incarnate in Jesus. It follows that the communities which gather round the table of the Lord represent the primary forms of Christian community in the world, and this by Jesus' own institution. Eucharistic fellowship represents the primary form of the essentially communitarian nature of the creative enterprise of Christian ethics in the world. Yet we find that 'officers of good order' actually place obstacles in the way of what they quaintly call intercommunion between members of different Christian churches, that is, they positively prevent Christians from different churches from sitting together round the table of the Lord, and they do this on occasion because of remaining objections to the institutions of government in other Christian churches. Needless to say, the existence of different Christian churches is not in itself a problem for the Christian faith. On the contrary, it can illustrate the rich variety of forms which this incarnate power and word can create in the different and changing circumstances of time and place and in all the main manifestations of communitarian life: cult, code, creed, and constitution.

But when the revelation complex persuades a church to think that its governmental structures were laid down by God, then it may well come to regard itself on these grounds as the one true church, and then the damage begins to be done. The most blatant case of this in recent times has been the conduct of the Roman Catholic Church, particularly in its discussions with the Anglican Communion (ARCIC). Despite the fact that sufficient agreement has long been achieved on both the general understanding of the faith and the particular understanding of the Eucharist, Rome still refuses to allow intercommunion with Anglicans, because agreement has still not been reached on church government. In one sense people should have expected little else from Rome. After all, the Decree on Ecumenism from the Second Vatican Council never really envisaged the outcome of the ecumenical movement as anything other than the return of other Christian bodies to the papal fold, which already enjoys 'that unity which Christ bestowed on his church from the beginning'.

But the point of interest in this context is this: allegiance to a form of government, evolved by Christians themselves in the course of their history, is thought more important for the creative community of the Christian faith in the world than its form as a Eucharistic community; and that is surely a most grievous distortion of the true essence of Christianity. At this point the impression is clearly given that the power or spirit which Christianity continues to breathe into the world is more in the *suprema potestas* of the governing institution than in the celebrating and serving community which takes life and all its supports as gifts, and breaks them open to the world. This in turn gives rise to suspicions that an impression of power as force rather than authority is lurking somewhere in the undergrowth of many Christian minds. And the resulting damage continues. For Christians who focus upon institutional forms of ministry rather than on the community-fashioning spirit will be heard saying, sometimes with the encouragement of their leaders in office, that other Christian churches do not have real Eucharistic ministers, and so their Eucharists are not real Eucharists. Once again the damage to the primarily Eucharistic nature of Christian community increases; and again, usually, under the false impression conveyed by the revelation complex, that Jesus actually legislated either for officers of good order or for forms of Eucharistic presidency, when history makes abundantly clear that he did neither.

One could continue to illustrate the damage done by the revelation complex when it touches directly the issue of the communitarian structures of the Christian faith and persuades people that they must stay apart and question each other's Christianity on grounds of institutional difference, however substantial their agreements on basic Christian belief, Christian living, and Christian ritual. But space runs out; so one or two final illustrations must suffice. First, one that is of interest in these islands. It is the demand for separate schools for children of differing Christian churches. People who continue to deny that this has little or no adverse effects upon already divided and estranged communities in places like Northern Ireland and, to a lesser extent, the west of Scotland, deserve very little patience at this point of time. It is only too massively obvious to the least intelligent observer that when churches which have so much of the true essence of Christianity in common, treat the remaining differences between them as failures in each other's Christianity, rather than as the mutual enrichment which naturally arises from varieties of created forms; when they proceed on grounds of such mutual criticism to segregate in the schools the children of the broader community; they do in fact contribute quite substantially to the destruction of the broader community. And they do this, unfortunately, in times and places when the healing power of the Christian faith, and most of all of its central ritual of breaking one's bread for the other, is most needed.

There are yet other ways in which the revelation complex in matters of church government can damage first Christian community and then the broader community which it is in the world to serve. Take, for example, the false assumption that decisions about hierarchical priestly structures in the church were revealed by God through Jesus. Notice how this has led both to opposition within the Church of England to the ordination of women, and to the wish of many of those who mounted such oppositions to transfer to the Roman Catholic Church. Consider how this results in damage to Christian community, and, as further discrimination against women, damage to the broader human community. In addition, the very last thing we need in the Roman Catholic Church is an influx of failed Anglican opponents of women priests. Rome is only too capable on its own of inflicting the kind of communitarian damage which one can only illustrate here. And these illustrations must now suffice, as an effort to persuade people, if persuasion were needed, that the extent of this kind of damage really is incalculable.

In general, when specific institutions and defined rules of faith and morals take priority over the mutually supportive factors of community and creativity in which the genesis of moral value and the phenomenon of power exercised as authority coincide, the Christian faith is impeded and damage is done. This has been described above as the result of the revelation complex; which does not mean that Christians cannot use the image of revelation, but that they have least reason, perhaps of all world religions, to think of divine revelation in definitional form. For they believe that the definitive divine revelation took the form, not of dogmas or commandments, nor indeed of books or any kind of word-sequences, but of the life of a man. A fully human life, lived out in the messy particularities of history, is in question here; and so the word and power it is believed to incarnate can be carried forward and made fully effective in this world only through the medium of other human lives lived out in the still messy particularities of history. Human life from its very inception in this world is in the business of generating moral value by use of intersubjective structures, eliciting the necessary aid of chosen authoritative others towards its own free creativity. The point at which the evolving universe crossed the threshold of intersubjective creativity may have been – if there is no superhuman moral agent active in the universe – the point at which the universe became a moral entity, the point at which the adjective 'moral' could at last be applied to states of affairs, any and all states of affairs in the universe in so far as they were now maintained, modified, brought about or merely accepted by free creatures. That point must forever remain a mystery as to the precise nature of the occurrence, and perhaps also as to its date and location.

Similarly, the point at which the experience of communal creativity, and the consequent experience of the world as at least to that degree a moral entity, gave rise to the suspicion that the world in its entirety and from the outset may be a moral entity, a comprehensive state of evolving affairs brought about by some utterly originating moral agent; the point, in short, at which religion enters the history of the universe, is also mysterious as to date and location, but not quite so mysterious as to the nature of that event. For we can all reconstruct the origin of religious faith out of that general moral creativity which, as Sartre insisted, is close to the essence of being human. It consists in small part in the apparent analogy of our own creativity with that of an evolutionary process which seems also to strive for well-being for all, and of the hint which that may give of a creative moral agency, and a moral universe in existence from its ultimate origin and source. But it consists in far greater part in the hope engendered by communal creativity, that well-being will triumph for all over all obstacles and limitations, for that entails the hope that our human creativity is really a co-operation with an original creator, that morality really has a religious dimension. Hope in God is the stronger part of belief in God; hope itself a far greater blessing than bare faith. Looked at in this way religious faith is humanist through and through, and atheistic humanists, usually of quite materialist persuasion, who dogmatically truncate the possible extent of human hope, do less than justice to the humanist cause they so stridently seek to monopolise.

The creative community of Christian believers emerges out of our common human history, inspired and directed, it claims, by the life of a human being who was like all of us in all things, except that he did no evil. In this man's life the members of this community believe they see both the original and definitive form of that power and meaning, that spirit and word, that characterises the source of all that exists and will exist, and they seek to propagate that word and spirit in all the essential creativity of common human living. Hence they present themselves as communal creators alongside others of what will then be ever new moral states of affairs, directed by a spirit of self-sacrificing love, a conviction of unconditioned grace, which they believe to be distinctive in descriptional terms, but available to all in all of this universe, for it characterises the ultimate source of the universe itself. They are aware that they live amongst other communities of creators who work with different specific inspirations and perceptions; as they are also aware that they very frequently, in word, deed, and omission, betray their own. But at least they lay no claim to pre-defined rule as they structure their communal existence, engage in their rituals, tell their stories, and strive for that elusive final well-being in every walk of life. Their endemic commitment to selfless love and to the reception as a grace of everything that comes to them, enables them to test everything simply from the point of view of its possible contribution to the greatest well-being of all; irrespective of whether it comes from themselves or from another religion or from a self-styled secular community. Their work on the successive and varied forms which their own communal structures, rituals, stories, and rules may take is judged by the twin criteria of its alliance with the spirit and word incarnate in Jesus and its prospect of contributing to the well-being of all.

And the so-called secular states of modern civilisation? It is a good deal more difficult to describe how they should relate to Christianity than to describe how Christianity should relate to them. Their varied claims to *summa potestas* face them also with the need to choose between power exercised as authority and power exercised as force. And that should remind them that the *imperium* through which the *summa potestas* is exercised reveals in many circumstances such influence in matters of life and death, that it becomes less than fanciful to talk of secular religion or of substitute absolutes. At the very least it must be acknowledged that the human spirit is so driven by the hope of a final well-being that, if it cannot hope in the co-operation of some divine creator, it may well attempt to act like one itself. The temptation of absolute power is there for all who cannot hope in its benign form and existence.

For the rest, the problems of a modern state with organised religion are little different from the problems such a state may have with a plurality of nations or ethnic groups within its jurisdiction: the government of the state is a moral authority in matters in which the groups also are, or contain, moral authorities, and on which they will have differing programmes. It is not possible to segregate certain areas of human life and say: on these matters the secular government is the authority and no others are authorities on these matters. Neither can any solution to this problem be provided by concentrating solely on the formal legislation in which governments engage, for the government of society is an effective moral authority on a far greater range of matters than can be comprised within the limits of these laws which can be enforced in order to secure the minimum safety and stability of society itself. Everything else, from the details of overall economic policy to decisions as to the values for which human life may be sacrificed, falls within the moral responsibility of that authority known as the government of so-called secular society.

As a representative body parliament wields its authority on behalf of all the people, the electorate. But that does not mean that it should take as its policy the lowest common denominator from the plurality of positions represented in a modern pluralist state; much less that it should pass into law or adopt as government policy the positions adopted by the most populous or the strongest body, be that a religious or ethnic body, a class, or a vocational or other special interest body. It has its own distinctive and inalienable 'mastership' role to play in that creation of the world which is the moral enterprise itself. Since its power is exercised mostly in the form of authority, it will seek to lead the people, already organised into other bodies, towards concrete ideals which they themselves will come to appreciate and to adopt freely: otherwise its membership and make-up will be replaced by the people. Even decisions of parliament concerning criminal law, the law which the executive branch of government enforces by threat and application of punishment, can be brought partly within the range of power exercised as authority, in that the people have a democratic right to judge a parliament's legislative record or its promises in respect of such legislation also.

In the end civil government acts as a most comprehensive moral 'master' in society in all that it is and does; and it must deal on its own authority with every aspect of human existence – sex and marriage, work and play, the profane and the sacred. This may bring it into conflict with some churches or some religions in certain aspects of their rules and behaviour – the Hindu rite of suttee, for instance, was resisted by the British Raj – but since these will be cases of two thoroughgoing moral authorities in conflict, no simple resolution can be found by calling one power secular and the other one sacred. For both of them the well-being of all, the moral good, must be the dominant criterion, and people's perception of this will eventually

decide which has truth on its side. For the rest, civil government must act towards the leadership and members of other
bodies in the state, ethnic as well as religious, as these should
act towards each other: allowing the greatest possible diversity
in moral creativity in all aspects of human living which is
compatible with the free and equal access of all to the highest
level of common good achievable at any particular time and
place. For the communal creativity of the race, the moral
enterprise, being what it is – of the essence of the human – there
is no telling when it may reach the religious dimension. It
would be as wrong for one power, in the name of the secular, to
rule against this dimension, as for another, in the name of the
sacred, to seek to monopolise it.

Notes

I THE ANATOMY OF POWER

1 Steven Lukes, *Power*, Oxford: Blackwell 1986.
2 I omit here the words 'though not all such affecting is power and not all power is such affecting', because I think the examples given are more specious than substantive.
3 Lukes, *Power*, p. 4.
4 Lukes, *Power*, p. 17.
5 A. P. D'Entrèves, *The Notion of the State*, Oxford: Clarendon 1967.
6 See, for example, Janet Martin Soskice, 'God of Power and Might', *The Month* (November 1988), 934–8, for a succinct expression of this kind of move, which is otherwise fairly commonly made.
7 The annual conference of the Royal Institute of Philosophy in 1991 was treated to an endearing attempt by John Haldane to substitute for the consolation which Boethius found in belief in, and ultimate union with, the God who exercised such minute providence for the triumph of good, a kind of contemplative thought, similar to the experience of some artists' work, based on the Aristotelian–Thomistic view that the forms of things are not in the mind of God, but are realised in the very acts of our 'higher powers' upon empirical entities, and to see in the latter sufficient reason and support for our occasional and fleeting sense that 'all is well' ('De Consolatione Philosophiae', in M. McGhee, ed., *Philosophy, Religion and the Spiritual Life*, Cambridge University Press 1992, pp. 31–45). One supposes that that is the best that can be done by secularists for whom a personal God does not register on the credibility scale; but one must be left wondering at a reading of Boethius which relinquishes so much of his central attempt to secure the conviction of total and minute providence in place of impressions of the force of fate, and one cannot but feel how little consolation this alternative can offer to those oppressed by a sense

that in a godless world at least as much is force and a source of fear, as might be deemed 'well' or about to become well.

8 For a clear and biographical account of the development of Foucault's basic tenets, though one which errs a little on the uncritical side, see Didier Eribon, *Michel Foucault*, London: Faber, 1992.

9 B. de Jouvenel, *Power: The Natural History of its Growth*, London: Hutchinson 1948, p. 27.

10 See, for example, Thomas Aquinas, *Summa Theologiae*, q.42, art.2, ad3.

11 de Jouvenel, *Power*, 'Theories of Sovereignty', pp. 34ff.

12 D' Entrèves, *The Notion of the State*, p. 135.

13 *Ibid.*, p. 111.

14 *The Code of Canon Law: Codex Iuris Canonici*. English trans., London: Collins 1983.

15 For an account of the 'myth of origins' on which this claim for pope and college of bishops is modelled, see J. P. Mackey, *Modern Theology*, Oxford University Press 1987, pp. 130ff.

16 The relationship of law to morality is to be treated in an extended account of the Devlin–Hart debate in chapter 2.

17 In a contribution to a collection entitled *Morals, Law and Authority*, Dublin: Gill and Macmillan 1969, which I edited, I did make a distinction between matters of faith and matters of morality, in order to argue a case similar to the one argued here. I now doubt the necessity of the distinction for this purpose.

18 Use is made here of S. W. Carruthers' critical edition of *The Westminster Confession of Faith*, Manchester: Aikman 1937.

19 J. T. Cox, *Practice and Procedure in the Church of Scotland*, 6th ed. D. F. M. MacDonald, Church of Scotland Publications 1976, p. 8.

20 Although the lay/clerical distinction is not always resented with too much right by Presbyterians, as might be evident from the chapters on ministry in J. D. G. Dunn and J. P. Mackey, *New Testament Theology in Dialogue*, London: SCM Press 1987. Cox, *Practice and Procedure*, has an interesting reference on p. 427 to a Jesuit priest being admitted to a Presbyterian parish 'by reordination'.

21 Cox, *Practice and Procedure*, pp. 15, 385ff.

22 *Ibid.*, p. 568, from the Preamble, Questions and Formula used for Admission to Office in the Church.

23 *Ibid.*, p. 569.

24 For the misleading features of the scripture-tradition debate see G. Tavard's chapters in J. E. Kelly, ed., *Perspectives on Scripture and*

Tradition, Notre Dame (Indiana): Fides 1976; also J. P. Mackey, *Tradition and Change in the Church*, Dublin and Chicago: Gill and Macmillan, Pflaum 1968.

25 For an attempt to chronicle this movement see J. P. Mackey, 'New Thinking on Revelation', *Herder Correspondence*, 6 (1969), 298–308; *The Problems of Religious Faith*, Dublin and Chicago: Helicon and Herald 1972, Part III; 'The Theology of Faith', *Horizons*, 2 (1975), 207–38, 'The Faith of the Historical Jesus', *Horizons*, 3 (1976), 155–74.

26 Compare canon 750 of the *Code of Canon Law* with the first chapter of the *Westminster Confession of Faith*.

27 Karl Barth is by far the best exponent of this view of the scriptures, and he is surely as adamant an adherent of the *Sola Scriptura* principle as any Protestant could desire. See his *Church Dogmatics*, Edinburgh: T. and T. Clark 1956, 1, 2, ch. 3, 'Holy Scripture'.

2 THE ANATOMY OF MORALS

1 There is scarcely any need to spend time discussing nomenclature here. The Greek *ethē* referred to customs, as did the Latin *mores*. To this day the anglicised 'ethos' refers to the customary behaviour patterns of a particular group of people (the ethos of the English aristocracy) as indeed does the anglicised 'mores' and 'morals' (the mores of the Trobriander islanders, the morals of an alley cat). The suggestion is sometimes made that the derivative 'morality' should be used as a technical term for the actual behaviour patterns which a designated body of people in fact takes to be normative (Christian morality), whereas the derivative 'ethics' should be reserved for the technical term for critical, philosophical reflections upon 'morality' or 'moralities' (the ethics course in philosophy). However, a very little perusal of the relevant literature would reveal the fact that 'ethics' and 'morality' are used interchangeably, as are their cognate adjectives and adverbs, and a very little reflection would conclude that there is little hope of imposing some instant regularity of usage. The best one can do in such circumstances is to try to make each context clarify the use made of each of these terms.

2 B. Williams, *Ethics and the Limits of Philosophy*, Harvard University Press 1985.

3 Williams, *Ethics and the Limits*; see the title to chapter 10.

4 'Virtue Christianly Considered', references here are to a seminar paper delivered by Stanley Hauerwas to the Faculty of Divinity, University of Edinburgh, November 1991.

5 There is a case to be made, though it need not detain us here, that atheistic and agnostic lives may be equally religious, especially, but not solely, if they are seen to include substitute absolutes. These absolutes must be discussed later.

6 In this matter they praise John Milbank's *Theology and Social Theory: Beyond Secular Reason*, Oxford: Blackwell 1990, and they criticise Alisdair MacIntyre. MacIntyre must be considered at more length shortly.

7 D. Bonhoeffer, *Ethics*, London: SCM Press 1978, p. 3. Bonhoeffer's ethical language here is so reminiscent of Barth's exclusivist remarks in the latter's treatment of the Christian's knowledge of God, that this is worth quoting: 'The God of the Christian Confession is, in distinction from all gods, not a found or invented God or one at last and at the end discovered by man ... But we Christians speak of Him who completely takes the place of everything that elsewhere is usually called "God", and therefore suppresses and excludes it all, and claims to be alone the truth.' K. Barth, *Dogmatics in Outlines*, London: SCM Press 1949, p. 36.

8 When I asked Stanley Hauerwas on the occasion of his 'Virtue Christianly Considered' seminar at Edinburgh, how he would envisage someone choosing Christianity over other total life styles, he answered: 'without criteria'; for, he went on to claim, if Christianity were subjected to moral criteria, these would then contain a higher truth than the Christian faith itself, and that he felt a Christian could not accept. At this point of the argument we are back with Bonhoeffer in his earlier and least compromising mood. Besides, if we were to envisage putting Christianity to some prospective convert while denying that person any opportunity of the exercise of individual, rational will in pursuit of moral value – as it was put in chapter 1 – we should surely be risking the prospect of force in some form or other?

9 To the logical embarrassment of those Christian theologians whose only way of identifying a Third Person, the Holy Spirit, is as the Love uniting the Father and the Son.

10 See Iris Murdoch, *The Sovereignty of the Good*, London: Routledge and Kegan Paul 1970, chapter entitled 'On "God" and "Good".'

11 Quoted by Michael McGhee in 'Facing Truths' in M. McGhee (ed.), *Philosophy, Religion and the Spiritual Life*, pp. 239–40. I refer to McGhee's article because I would wish for the support of his subsequent decision to retain a role for 'ought' language in moral discourse, and his view that this is not incompatible with Kant.

12 H. L. A. Hart, *Law, Liberty and Morality*, Oxford University Press 1963, pp. 1–4.

13 Patrick Devlin, *The Enforcement of Morals*, Oxford University Press 1965, see p. 10 and passim.

14 *Ibid.*, p. 16.

15 *Ibid.*, pp. ix–x, 87ff., 224ff.

16 Hart, *Law, Liberty and Morality*, p. 70.

17 Devlin, *The Enforcement of Morals*, pp. 132ff.

18 Hart, *Law, Liberty and Morality*, pp. 57ff.

19 *Ibid.*, p. 4.

20 It is not possible to enter here into the thickets of an ethic of penal systems. Suffice it to say that the spirit of the investigation just conducted could see legal penalty justified in both the fear induced and the physical restraints involved, only by its preventive or deterrent role, but this could scarcely be stretched towards a retributive theory of punishment, and it would probably require a rehabilitatory element as a necessary adjunct, since deprival of moral choice could be compensated for only by an effort to procure a person's moral rehabilitation. For an excellent article on the way in which prisons should operate to enhance rather than stunt moral growth, see Kimmet Edgar, 'Quaker Peace and Prison Values', *Theology* (March/April 1992), 102–9.

21 We should have to envisage a scene such as that depicted in Samuel Beckett's *Malone Dies*, except that our poor dying man would want to die in the instant of having completed, and complied with, the final tally of all he *ought* to have had and done.

22 I. Kant, *Fundamental Principles of the Metaphysic of Ethics*, London: Longmans and Green 1945, p. 74.

23 Murdoch, *The Sovereignty of the Good*, p. 58.

24 *Ibid.*, p. 60.

25 Plato, *Republic*, 508d–509b.

26 One could trawl a rich catch of support for this epistemology from modern philosophical literature: from Heidegger's description of concrete human existence in this world, *Dasein*, as *geworfene Entwurf*, something that is as much a project as it is 'thrown into the world'; Merleau-Ponty's phenomenological explorations of the role of the body in human perception of its world and its goals; Simone Weil's words on work and art and suffering in the pursuit of morality; and so on. For a slightly more extended account, along the lines of this chapter, see J. P. Mackey, 'Moral Values as Religious Absolutes', in McGhee, ed., *Philosophy, Religion and the Spiritual Life*, pp. 145–60.

27 It is fundamental in Aristotle also, but Aristotle cashes such terms in his own down-to-earth manner, cashing this one in

terms of biology and ethics and the layered and detailed teleologies so characteristic of his thought.

28 Murdoch, *The Sovereignty of the Good*, p. 53.

29 Hence the attempts to find some support for belief in human freedom from Heisenberg's indeterminacy principle, can never supply more than the remotest beginnings of a genuine appreciation of the nature of freedom.

30 'Order out of chaos' provides what is probably the only version of the idea of *creatio ex nihilo* that can be given any conceptual or imaginative content at all, where the 'chaos' is thought to be formless matter, which could not conceivably exist on its own.

31 Even Sartre, who rejected the idea of human nature that pre-exists human free activity, had room for some structure in human existence, for he was prepared to talk about and to describe 'the human condition'.

32 See, for example, S. E. Fowl and L. G. Jones, *Reading in Communion*, London: SPCK 1991, especially chapter 1.

33 A. MacIntyre, *After Virtue*, London: Duckworth 1981; also his contribution to Robert Bellah et al., *Habits of the Heart*, London: Hutchinson 1985.

34 Published as *Three Rival Versions of Moral Enquiry*, University of Notre Dame Press 1990. The third version, that of the 'genealogist' which is not considered here, is linked to Nietzsche and sees the succession of moral systems as masks for the advance of raw power.

35 MacIntyre, *Three Rival Versions*, p. 66.

36 *Ibid.*, p. 175.

37 *Ibid.*, p. 138.

38 *Ibid.*, p. 141.

39 Colwyn Trevarthen, 'An infant's motives for speaking and thinking in a culture', in A. H. Wold (ed.), *The Dialogical Alternative*, Oxford University Press 1992, first page.

40 C. Trevarthen and K. Logotheti, 'Child and Culture: genesis of cooperative knowing', in A. Gellatly et al., eds., *Cognition and Social Worlds*, Oxford: Clarendon Press, p. 38.

41 C. Trevarthen, 'Infancy, mind in', in R. L. Gregory, ed., *The Oxford Companion to Mind*, Oxford University Press 1987, p. 363.

42 C. Trevarthen and K. Logotheti, 'First Symbols and the Nature of Human Knowledge', in J. Montangero et al., eds., *Symbolism and Knowledge*, Geneva: Jean Piaget Archives 1987, p. 63.

43 J. Piaget, *Play, Dreams and Imitation in Childhood*, London: Routledge and Kegan Paul 1962, pp. 206, 211.

44 C. Trevarthen, 'Signs Before Speech', in T. A. Seboek,

J. Umiker-Sebeok, eds., *The Semiotic Web*, Berlin: Mouton de Gruyter 1990, p. 689.

45 C. Trevarthen and K. Logotheti, 'Children in Society, and Society in Children', in S. Howell, R. Willis, eds., *Societies At Peace*, London: Routledge 1989, p. 174.

46 C. Trevarthen, 'Instincts for human understanding and for cultural cooperation: their development in infancy', in M. von Cranach et al., eds., *Human Ethology: Claims and Limits of a New Discipline*, Cambridge University Press 1979, p. 530.

47 A recent conference called by Trevarthen at the University of Edinburgh to discuss 'Educating for Cooperative Self-Reliance: From Child to Citizen', saw the philosophers of education present unwilling to discuss the genesis of moral values, one of them more than merely hinting that they were just *there*, at least from the time of the Greeks; despite the fact that one will frequently know what something is and how it functions only by discovering how it is generated. The social scientists seemed equally loath to discuss the issue of genesis; and, despite the fact that some of us thought that Trevarthen's work was actually describing the genesis of morals, and he did agree that this was so, Professor Barry Barnes preached solemnly against the prospect of moralists hijacking Trevarthen's work for homiletic purposes. One social psychologist used the chair to express her discomfort with some speakers' references to religion and, invoking the truly scientific methodology of asking for a show of hands from those similarly discomfited, probably saved us from any suggestion that moral values simply dropped from heaven. But this failure of the conference to address, or to realise who was addressing, the question of the genesis of morals, together with the assumption, seemingly shared by all those mentioned above, that the most commonly heard expressions of moral values, namely, moral precepts, constitute their primary form, made it very difficult for educationists, or for anyone at the conference, to explain satisfactorily how values could be transmitted in education without inducing conformity rather than co-operative self-reliance, on the one hand, or risking the spectre of relativism, on the other. Competitive individualism and unemotional rationalism were roundly denounced, but in the absence of a true account of the genesis of morals, or the recognition of one that lay under all our noses, the passion with which these bogey-men were denounced had to play quite an overcompensatory role.

48 Professor Barnes, at the conference mentioned in the previous note, gave a scintillating display of the intrinsic impossibility of

making any moral rule fit wholly and exactly a concrete piece of contemplated human behaviour, and he showed how the inevitable intrusion of human decision in the form of the moral interpretation of the contemplated behaviour had its exact counterpart in the apparently purest of scientific research in the interpretation of 'results' – a correspondence which could be taken to support the contention that knowing-how, which always involves doing and hence human (moral) behaviour, is at the origin of all human knowing.

3 POWERS SECULAR AND POWERS SACRED

1 Nor should Christians be tempted to grab over-eagerly at the word 'yet' in that sentence. They are already too prone to postpone the actual salvation of the world, which they say has already in some sense taken place, to some future fulfilment, sometimes safely beyond the range of all worldly verification, in another world and life.

2 G. Watson, *Greek Philosophy and the Christian Notion of God*, Dublin: Columba Press 1993, chapter 2.

3 H. Diels, *Die Fragmente der Vorsokratiker*, Berlin 1935, Heraclitus B 62.

4 Quoted in W. Jaeger, *The Theology of the Early Greek Philosophers*, Oxford University Press 1947, pp. 34–5. There is an interesting contemporary confirmation of this approach in E. Levinas' view that prior to being 'for itself' each being is already 'for the other' – see his *Otherwise Than Being or Beyond Essence*, The Hague: Nijhof 1987.

5 See J. P. Mackey, 'Moral Values as Religious Absolutes', in Michael McGhee, ed., *Philosophy, Religion and the Spiritual Life*, where the idea is canvassed that morality itself, i.e. the totality of states of affairs brought about by moral agents, is in a sense absolute, but this would include amongst moral agents God as well as humans.

6 This is an ordering of things to 'an internal finality', as Kant would put it, not to an ulterior purpose.

7 See E. A. Dowey, *The Knowledge of God in Calvin's Theology*, Columbia University Press 1965, p. 81; also T. H. L. Parker's 'or, rather, originally', in *The Doctrine of the Knowledge of God, A Study in the Theology of John Calvin*, Edinburgh: Oliver and Boyd 1952, pp. 26–7.

8 Bertrand Russell, 'A Free Man's Worship', in *Mysticism and Logic*, Penguin Books 1953.

9 A good English translation and introduction by V. E. Watts, Penguin Books 1969.

10 See G. Watson, 'Pagan Philosophy and Christian Ethics', in J. P. Mackey, ed., *Morals, Law and Authority*, Dublin: Gill and Macmillan 1969.

11 One can hardly make faith in God itself a matter of strict moral obligation on humans alone. If God hides so well even in self-revelation, God must take some responsibility for human failure to believe!

12 In this connection one could consult with benefit recent scholarship on the subject of primal religions. The stress now falls not upon the temporal priority of these religions, but upon the way in which they illustrate foundational imagery of persistent relevance to the human project. In some sense taking the place of natural theology, the study of the primal imagination can reveal how people come upon religious categories in the course of the most elementary of human pursuits, and how these in turn are necessary for the very intelligibility of the more advanced claims of 'world religions'. To sample this material see Andrew Walls, 'Primal Religious Traditions in Today's World', in F. Whaling, ed., *Religion in Today's World*, Edinburgh: T. and T. Clark 1987.

13 Simone Weil, *Lectures on Philosophy*, Cambridge University Press 1978, p. 186.

14 Art seems to be very well 'in' with philosophers these days. Two of the papers to the 1991 Conference of the Royal Institute of Philosophy made much of it in relation to religious claims: John Haldane's 'De Consolatione Philosophiae', and Anthony O'Hear's 'The real or the Real? Chardin or Rothko?' The former saw it as the source of an alternative vision, the latter as a more ambivalent witness to religious claims. See both papers in McGhee, ed., *Philosophy, Religion and the Spiritual Life*.

15 See D. Daiches et al., eds., *A Hotbed of Genius*, Edinburgh University Press 1986, p. 18.

16 See Jaeger, *The Theology of the Early Greek Philosophers*, for a reminder of the simultaneous origin of science, philosophy, and theology.

17 See the essays and references in J. P. Mackey, ed., *Religious Imagination*, Edinburgh University Press 1986. See Patrick Grant's characterisation of literature in particular 'by its power of disclosure, showing us once more and anew the latent, value-impregnated union of ourselves with things and with others' (p. 217–18), and for his comparable treatment of religious language: *Literature and Personal Values*, New York: St Martin's Press 1992.

18 David McLellan, *Karl Marx: Selected Writings*, Oxford University Press 1977, p. 581, from 'Comments on Adolph Wagner'.

19 *Ibid.*, p. 63. It is necessary to note here that the decision to summarise Marx by initial reference to human nature or the human essence already amounts to a rejection of certain prominent 'schools' of interpretation, in particular the orthodox communist tradition of erstwhile Soviet officialdom which would replace human nature by universally operable laws of material nature; and neo-structuralists like Louis Althusser who would replace the human essence with a scientific account of social relations so as to produce a notion of history as a process without a subject. This decision also involves the use of Marx's early writings, or at least the refusal to reject them out of hand as the romantic ideas of uncritical youth. For the case that the predominance of society did not, for Marx, dehumanise the individual, see Adam Schaff, *Marxism and the Human Individual*, New York: McGraw-Hill 1970.

20 McLellan, *Karl Marx*, p. 81.

21 Schaff, *Marxism*, p. 73.

22 J. P. Sartre, *Existentialism and Humanism*, London: Methuen 1966, p. 56; for a fuller treatment of this point of God's irrelevance to humanism see J. P. Mackey, *The Christian Experience of God as Trinity*, London: SCM Press 1983, chapter 1.

23 McLellan, *Karl Marx*, p. 85. It has not been possible to include here a full description of Marx's sense of the alienation of humanity – alienation being his chief term for dehumanisation; a slightly fuller account is given in J. P. Mackey, *Modern Theology*, chapter 2.

24 McLellan, *Karl Marx*, p. 82.

25 Eugene Kamenka, *The Ethical Foundations of Marxism*, New York: Praeger 1962, pp. 34, 36. It is perhaps necessary to note that the reader need not at all accept Kamenka's impression of the determinism of the later Marx, nor Marx's alleged failure to come to terms with evil-doing.

26 For a succinct critique of the new liberal democracies, see Marx, 'Bruno Bauer: Die Judenfrage', in T. B. Bottomore, ed., *Karl Marx: Early Writings*, New York: McGraw-Hill 1964, esp. pp. 11–14.

27 McLellan, *Karl Marx*, p. 563.

28 J. P. Sartre, *The Problem of Methods*, London: Methuen 1963, pp. 21–2; for a fuller account of political and economic factors which were seen to threaten Marxist communism before the recent collapse, see Herbert Marcuse, *Soviet Marxism: A Critical*

Analysis, New York: Herder and Herder 1971, esp. pp. 28, 70, 128, 166–9.

29 A participant in that Catholic–Humanist Dialogue, on the Catholic side, I make bold to summarise for my present purposes some of the relevant papers.

30 For a fuller account of Hobbes' views on sovereignty, and for further references, see D'Entrèves, *The Notion of the State*, chapter 6, and Hobbes' own *Leviathan*. One may not be convinced by D'Entrèves' suggestion that the novelty of Hobbes' exclusion of the rival sovereignty of a church is drastically reduced by the precedence of Henry VIII's move; the accordance, noted above, between this exclusion and the exclusion of all other alleged laws of nature or of God would seem to carry Hobbes' political philosophy far beyond anything envisaged in 'Tudor theory'.

31 These words and the summary in which they are embedded are taken from an admirably succinct account of the manner in which British ideas of sovereignty grew to such a degree as to cause problems in insular minds faced with what must seem to them undue haste towards a political union of European States. The account is by Jonathan Clark, in the *Times Literary Supplement* 29 November 1991. For a more extensive treatment of this matter, see A. Carty, 'English Constitutional Law in a Post-Modernist Perspective', in P. Fitzpatrick, ed., *Dangerous Supplements: Resistance and Renewal in Jurisprudence*, London: Pluto 1991, pp. 182–206.

32 This view and others from Lord Davidson, who currently heads the Scottish Law Commission, are contained in a paper, 'The Extraction of Christian Principles from the Basis of Law in Britain', read at Edinburgh in February 1992, and used by courtesy of its author.

33 S. Rutherford, *Les Rex*, Harrisonburg Va: Sprinkle Publications 1982 (reissue of 1644 edition), p. 138.

34 *Ibid.*

35 *Ibid.*, p. 117.

36 This quote is taken from a paper read by Anthony Carty to the Mair Institute at Edinburgh; a paper to which I am otherwise indebted for much of my assessment of Rutherford and Hutcheson.

37 Daiches, ed., *A Hotbed of Genius*, is typical of the failure of the more general surveys of the Scottish Enlightenment to see beyond the more obvious anglicising elements and presumptions.

38 Taken from Carty's paper, cited in note 36.

39 F. Hutcheson, *A System of Moral Philosophy*, London 1755, Bk III, chapter 7, pp. 268–9.

40 From Lord Davidson's paper, cited in note 32.
41 Stewart J. Brown, 'The Ten Years' Conflict and the Disruption of 1843', in S. J. Brown and M. Fry, eds., *Scotland in the Age of the Disruption*, Edinburgh University Press 1993, pp. 19–20. This article provides a full and excellent account of the details of the legal struggles which led to the Disruption.
42 Brown, 'The Ten Years' Conflict', pp. 25–6.
43 *Ibid.*, pp. 3–4.
44 From Lord Davidson's paper, cited in note 32.
45 A paper to the Catholic–Humanist Dialogue of 1973; see note 29.
46 See, for example, Paul Tillich, *Christianity and the Encounter of World Religions*, New York and London 1963. Another, perhaps more controversial means of detecting 'idolatry' in secular political concerns is to argue that any goal for which people are urged to kill or to die is elevated thereby to the rank of a moral absolute and as such may be thought to partake of divine or quasi-divine status; see Mackey, *Modern Theology*, pp. 179ff.
47 Indirectly perhaps, in so far as they might fall under a general moral obligation to seek the truth in all things.
48 See Emmet Larkin, 'The Devotional Revolution in Ireland 1850–1875', *The American Historical Review*, 77 (1972), 625–52.
49 This claim, in strict compliance with the church's own conciliar deliverances, has to be pursued through the parents' rights as citizens to their chosen form of education for their children, rather than by direct clerical interference in political decision-making.
50 These issues are more fully analysed and argued in chapter 3 of Patrick Hannon's *Church, State, Morality and Law*, Dublin: Gill and Macmillan 1992.
51 It is interesting to note, as Lord Davidson does in the paper already cited, that when the Scottish Parliament by an Act of 1567 abrogated all laws which were not in accord with the Reformed Faith, based as that faith claimed to be on the Bible alone, the 'hardness of your heart' clause was invoked in order to allow for divorce on grounds of adultery and desertion.
52 'Propositiones de quibusdam quaestionibus doctrinalibus ad matrimonium christianum pertinentibus', *Gregorianum* (1978), 453–64.
53 The incidence of the dissolution of marriages of the unbaptised seems to have increased if anything in modern times; see V. Navarrete, 'Indissolubilitas matrimonii rati et consummati: opiniones recentiores et observationes', *Periodica* (1969), 415–89.
54 For more general information on divorce in Roman Catholic teaching see John T. Noonan, *Power to Dissolve: Lawyers and Mar-*

riages in the Courts of the Roman Curia, Cambridge (Mass.) 1972, and W. Bassett, *The Bond of Marriage*, University of Notre Dame Press 1968.

55 See R. L. McCartney, *Liberty and Authority in Ireland*, Field Day Pamphlet 9, Derry 1985, pp. 16ff.

56 For general background information see J. H. Whyte, *Church and State in Modern Ireland*, Dublin: Gill and Macmillan 1980.

57 See Brown, 'The Ten Years Conflict'.

58 Quoted by S. J. Brown in '"A Victory for God": The Scottish Presbyterian Churches and the General Strike of 1926', *The Journal of Ecclesiastical History*, 42 (1991), 599; the information on this issue used here is taken from this article.

59 Brown, '"A Victory for God"', pp. 615–16.

60 For those who know the history of the Scottish people and their culture, or even know that up to the twelfth century at least the very word *Scottus* meant an Irish person, a delicious irony appears in the use of such racist theories as is here in evidence by modern Scots.

61 Quoted in S. J. Brown, '"Outside the Covenant": The Scottish Presbyterian Churches and Irish Immigration, 1922–1938', *The Innes Review* 42 (1991), 28; to whom, once more, gratitude for information on this issue is owed.

62 Quoted in *ibid.*, p. 26.

4 THE CHRISTIAN EXPERIENCE OF POWER

1 See Jaeger, *The Theology of the Early Greek Philosophers*.

2 See references given in note 25, chapter I above; also John Shea, *Stories of God*, Chicago: Thomas More Press 1978, esp. pp. 171ff.

3 See, for example, Walter Wink, *Naming the Powers*, Philadelphia: Fortress Press 1984; Hans-Rudi Weber, *Power*, Geneva: WCC Publications 1989.

4 See The Holy Bible, RSV, ad loc.

5 The question as to whether the empirical world was created a finite length of time ago is a separate question, and in itself quite independent of the issue of 'creation out of nothing'.

6 The real philosophical question – and the point at which philosophy always becomes theology – is not: does God exist? but rather a question of discernment of powers, of those which are palpably matters of life or death for us, and of those that then appear most ultimate in our best estimation.

7 See John Gibson, *Genesis I*, Edinburgh: St Andrew's Press 1981, pp. 74ff.

8 See Norman W. Porteous, 'Royal wisdom', in *Living the Mystery*, Oxford: Blackwell 1967; note his reference to Rylaarsdam's thesis on p. 113, to the effect that *The Wisdom of Solomon* transfers to Wisdom the rule formerly played by the Spirit in judges, leaders, kings.

9 For more detail on Philo, and the general background of Greek theology shared at the time by Jews and emerging Christians, see Mackey, *The Christian Experience of God as Trinity*, chapter 9.

10 In this view of the matter the Genesis story of eating the forbidden fruit is simply, in story form, the point of Proverbs 8: 35, and of Ezekiel's castigation of the King of Tyre (both mentioned above): those who seek to adopt the wisdom (life) that comes from God, create and live; those who place their own wisdom on the divine level, destroy and die. (Eating the fruit of the tree of knowledge of good and evil is the story-telling equivalent of treating what you have so far digested as absolute or divine wisdom.) It is therefore a tale of perpetual human temptation, and of the never-learned lessons of yielding to it.

11 Russell, 'A Free Man's Worship', p. 59.

12 Here is what is called the economic Trinity: God the Father, the human person of Jesus in which the word–spirit of God is incarnate, and the corporate persona of the community in which the incarnation of Jesus as word–spirit continues in history. Space does not allow any consideration of the possibility of knowing an immanent Trinity in any way additional to knowledge of this economic Trinity. For such consideration see Mackey, *The Christian Experience of God as Trinity*; and 'Image and Metaphor in the Christian Understanding of God as Trinity' forthcoming in the Proceedings of the 400th Anniversary Colloquium on 'The Doctrine of the Trinity', Trinity College, Dublin, March 1992.

13 For a slightly fuller treatment of this controversial issue, and one in line with the development of thought in this context, see Mackey, *Modern Theology*, chapter 3, and *Jesus, the Man and the Myth*, London: SCM Press 1979, chapter on the resurrection of Jesus.

14 Johan Huizinga, *Homo Ludens, A Study of the Play Element in Culture*, Paladin Books 1970; the points and quotes from Stewart Parker are taken from his lecture 'Dramatis Personae' given at The Queen's University, Belfast, 5 June 1986, and published in Belfast by the John Malone Memorial Committee.

15 The detailed evidence for much that is claimed here on subjects such as resurrection, Eucharist, divinity of Jesus, can be found in Mackey, *Modern Theology*, chapter 3. It would be tedious for both writer and reader to repeat it here.

5 THE ANATOMY OF CHURCH

1 For historical details on development of Christian church structures and the cultic priesthood see, for example, Hans Küng, *The Structures of Church*, London: Search Press 1965; E. Schillebeeckx, *The Church With A Human Face*, London: SCM Press 1985; J. D. G. Dunn and J. P. Mackey, *New Testament Theology in Dialogue*, London: SPCK 1987, chapters on Ministry.

2 See *William of Ockham: A Short Treatise on Tyrranical Government*, ed. A. S. McGrade, Cambridge University Press 1992.

3 For key texts such as Luther's *On Secular Authority*, and Calvin's *On Civil Government*, see Harro Hoepfl, ed., *Luther and Calvin on Secular Authority*, Cambridge University Press 1991. It must not be forgotten that during the Peasant Revolt Luther gave his answer to the peasants' claim for social justice through his support of their Christian lordships, the princes.

4 Even in some other, perhaps older, models of soteriology, where Christ's death is regarded as a victory over Satan, the idea of penalty is present. Satan, not knowing that Jesus was divine and so innocent of all sin, brought about his death, due penalty only for sinful man, and so was duped and defeated, losing his power over humans!

5 A conference on the doctrine of the Trinity, held at Trinity College Dublin on the 400th anniversary of its foundation, was remarkable for the repeated warnings about the ideological consequences of the new social models of the Trinity.

6 Much fuller detail on these suggestions are available in Mackey, *Jesus, the Man and the Myth*, and *Modern Theology*, chapters 4–5.

Select bibliography

It is almost impossible to compose a comprehensive bibliography for a book which, like this one, deals in an interdisciplinary topic. So much depends on the author, and in particular on the author's choice of the points at which the disciplines – in this case mainly philosophy and theology – may best be thought to meet. The following is therefore a very selective bibliography indeed. It is really designed for those who might want to read themselves more fully into some of the major themes from which the argument of the book is in fact constructed. The order is not alphabetical; it represents in each case the order in which those who might want to study one of the themes might best proceed. It is inevitable that there is some overlap of relevance between the sections.

THE ANATOMY OF POWER

Hobbes, *Leviathan* (with introduction by C. B. MacPherson) Harmondsworth: Penguin 1968.

Locke, *Two Treatises on Government*, London: Routledge 1887.

Lukes, Steven, *Power*, Oxford: Blackwell 1986.

Jouvenel, B. de, *Power: The Natural History of Its Growth*, London: Hutchinson 1948.

Barry, B., *Democracy, Power and Justice*, Oxford University Press 1989.

Bottomore, T., *Elites and Society*, Harmondsworth: Penguin 1966.

Foucault, Michel, *Discipline and Punish*, Harmondsworth: Penguin 1979.

D'Entrèves, A. P., *The Notion of the State*, Oxford: Clarendon 1967.

Milbank, John, *Theology and Social Theory*, Oxford: Blackwell 1990.

Hart, H. L. A., *Law, Liberty and Morality*, Oxford University Press, 1963.

234

Devlin, Patrick, *The Enforcement of Morals*, Oxford University Press 1965.

Hannon, P., *Church, State, Morality and Law*, Dublin: Gill and Macmillan 1992.

THE ANATOMY OF MORALS

MacIntyre, A., *A Short History of Ethics*, London: Routledge and Kegan Paul 1968.

Kant, I., *Critique of Practical Reason*, London: Longmans 1959.
  Fundamental Principles of the Metaphysic of Ethics, London: Longmans and Green 1945.

Moore, G. E., *Principia Ethica*, Cambridge University Press 1903.

Murdoch, Iris, *The Sovereignty of Good*, London: Routledge and Kegan Paul 1970.

Williams, B., *Ethics and the Limits of Philosophy*, Harvard University Press 1985.

Taylor, Charles, *The Ethics of Authenticity*, Harvard University Press 1992.

MacIntyre, A., *After Virtue*, London: Duckworth 1981.
  Whose Justice? Which Rationality? London: Duckworth 1988.
  Three Rival Versions of Moral Enquiry, University of Notre Dame Press 1990.

Maclagan, W. G., *The Theological Frontier of Ethics*, London: Allen and Unwin 1961.

Gill, Robin, *A Textbook of Christian Ethics*, Edinburgh: T. and T. Clark 1985.

Lehmann, P. L., *Ethics in a Christian Context*, New York: Harper and Row 1976.

Mahoney, J., *The Making of Moral Theology*, Oxford: Clarendon 1987.

Hauerwas, S., *Character and the Christian Life*, San Antonio University Press 1985.

Bonhoeffer, D., *Ethics*, London: SCM Press 1978.

Wold, A. H., ed., *The Dialogical Alternative*, Oxford University Press 1992.

POWER SECULAR AND SACRED

McLellan, D., *Karl Marx: Selected Writings*, Oxford University Press 1977.

Bloch, Ernst, *On Karl Marx*, New York: Herder and Herder 1971.
  Man On His Own, New York: Herder and Herder 1971.
  A Philosophy of the Future, New York: Herder and Herder 1970.

Kolakowski, L., *Towards a Marxist Humanism*, New York: Grove Press 1968.

Religion, Oxford University Press 1982.

Sartre, J. P., *Existentialism and Humanism*, London: Methuen 1966.

Hawton, Hector, *The Humanist Revolution*, London: British Humanist Association Press 1963 (also from that Press: Margaret Knight, *Humanist Anthropology*).

Gill, Robin, ed., *Sociology and Theology: A Reader*, London: Chapman 1987.

Nicholls, D., *Deity and Domination*, London: Routledge 1989.

Clarke, S., *Civil Peace and Sacred Order*, Oxford University Press 1980.

Habgood, J., *Church and Nation in a Secular Age*, London: Darton, Longman and Todd 1983.

Gill, Robin, *Prophecy and Praxis*, London: Marshall, Morgan and Scott 1981.

Moltmann, J., *The Trinity and the Kingdom of God*, London: SCM Press 1981.

The Church in the Power of the Spirit, London: SCM Press 1977.

CHRISTIAN EXPERIENCE OF POWER

Wink, Walter, *Naming the Powers*, Philadelphia: Fortress Press 1984.

Weber, H.-R., *Power*, Geneva: WCC Publications 1980.

Holmberg, B., *Paul and Power*, Philadelphia: Fortress Press 1980.

Perrin, N., *The Kingdom of God in the Teaching of Jesus*, London: SCM Press 1963.

Rediscovering the Teaching of Jesus, London: SCM Press 1967.

Chilton, B., and McDonald, J. I. H., *Jesus and the Ethics of the Kingdom*, London: SPCK Press 1987.

Yoder, J. H., *The Politics of Jesus*, Grand Rapids: Eerdmans 1972.

Congar, Y. M.-J., *I Believe in the Holy Spirit* (3 vols.), New York: The Seabury Press 1983.

Lampe, G. W. H., *God as Spirit*, Oxford: Clarendon 1977.

Taylor, J. V., *The Go-Between God*, Oxford University Press 1972.

Dunn, J. D. G., *Jesus and the Spirit*, London: SCM Press 1975

McKenna, J. H., *Eucharist and Holy Spirit*, Great Wakering: Mayhew-McCrimmon 1975.

THE ANATOMY OF CHURCH

Schweizer, E., *Church Order in the New Testament*, London: SCM Press 1961.

Küng, H., *The Structures of Church*, London: Search Press 1965.

Dulles, A., *Models of the Church*, Dublin: Gill and Macmillan 1976.

Williams, *The Church*, London: Lutterworth Press 1969.

Küng, H., *The Church*, New York: Sheed and Ward 1967.

Schillebeeckx, E., *The Church with a Human Face*, London: SCM Press 1985.

Congar, Y. M.-J., *Lay People in the Church*, Westminster Md.: Newman Press 1967.

    Power and Poverty in the Church, London: Chapman 1964.

Index of names

Subject index